CARMEL-BY-THE-SEA, THE EARLY YEARS (1903-1913)

An Overview of the History of the Carmel Mission, the Monterey Peninsula, and the First Decade of the Bohemian Artists' and Writers' Colony

ALISSANDRA DRAMOV

authorHOUSE®

AuthorHouse™
1663 Liberty Drive
Bloomington, IN 47403
www.authorhouse.com
Phone: 1-800-839-8640

Published by AuthorHouse 12/17/13

ISBN: 978-1-4918-2414-6 (sc)
ISBN: 978-1-4918-2413-9 (e)

OTHER BOOKS BY AUTHOR

The Bohemian Biographical Guide for
Northern California (1865-1915)

<u>Coming soon:</u>

Carmel-by-the-Sea, The Growth Years
(1913-1943)

DEDICATION

In memory of Ginger, whose happiest moments were at Carmel Beach, where she chased after tennis balls, frolicked in the surf, and dug in the sand.

ACKNOWLEDGEMENTS

A special thank you to photo archivist and local historian Pat Hathaway, whose vast knowledge and extensive photograph collection are a treasure!

I owe tremendous gratitude to California historian Kevin Starr, Monterey Peninsula architectural historian Kent Seavey, and California art historian Scott Shields, not only for their works which proved to be so valuable in the research for this book, but for the inspiration their scholarship provided.

To B.D., thank you for all the time spent reviewing this material and for repeatedly encouraging me to "hang in there".

Lastly, to everyone who asked me through the years, "How's that Carmel book coming along?"... well, here it (finally) is!

CONTENTS

Photo Section III

1

The Early History of the Monterey Peninsula Area and the Establishment of Mission San Carlos Borroméo

THE NATIVE AMERICANS OF THE CENTRAL COAST

Well over a thousand years before Spanish explorers discovered the Monterey Peninsula, Native Americans inhabited the area. The main group along the coastline stretching from Monterey Bay down to Point Sur and up to San Francisco Bay, as well as the inland area to the coastal mountain range, was the Costanoan or Ohlone tribe. They were known as Costanoans, based on the name the Spanish gave them, "Costanos", which meant "coast people". The Rumsen, (also spelled Rumsien, Runsien, or Runsen) were part of the Costanoan tribe, who lived in what is now Carmel Valley, along the region around the south bank of the Carmel River. Other Native American groups in the area were the Esselen, (also spelled Escelen, Eslen, or Ensen), who lived to the south in what is now Big Sur and the Santa Lucia Mountains, and the Salinan, who lived inland, in the southern part of what is now Monterey County. The Costanoan language was in the Penutian linguistic family, while the Esselen and Salinan languages were in the Hokan linguistic family. The Costanoans (Ohlone) spoke several different dialects.

The Native Americans lived in villages, with tribal groups of several hundred members, bound by family ties. (Later, the Spanish called the clusters of villages "Rancherias".) These villages were headed by a male chief; the chieftainship was hereditary, passed on from father to son. The Native Americans relied on the plentiful natural resources around them for food, shelter, and clothing. The Costanoan men hunted sea lions and seals, as well as fowl and game (deer and elk), fished for salmon in rivers and streams, and collected shellfish, such as mussels. They ate whales that swept ashore, but they did not hunt whales. They made rafts out of tule, with paddles that had double-blades. They used bows and arrows, spears, and fish traps and nets. Their tools were made out of sharpened stone, shells, and bones. The women gathered and prepared food such as roots, berries, acorns, pine nuts, seeds, greens, and shellfish. However, there were more seeds than acorns along the coast. The Costanoans used fire for cooking and clearing vegetation. The women also made baskets, in different colors, from woven willow twigs. The baskets were made in various sizes, for different uses, such as to cook, carry food, hold water, serve food, and store goods.

The Costanoans lived in handmade huts made out of a pole frame of tule reeds covered by grass or brush to keep the water out. The 10-to-12 foot tall reeds were curved toward the center, to form a cone-shaped hut. These dwellings were between six and up to twenty feet in diameter. About ten to twelve of these huts made up a village. There was also a sweat house (or "temescal" in Spanish) in each village, which was usually near a river or water source. It was used by the men only, who gathered there for hours, built up a sweat, and then finished the process with a plunge into some cold water. The sweat house was used for health purposes. After giving birth to a child, the women used a birthing pit for several days. It was made of stones warmed by fire, which were covered with grasses. The women rested on it for several hours, and then afterwards immersed themselves into cold water.

During the warmer months, the Costanoan women usually wore two deerskin aprons, or short aprons woven out of grass or bark fiber, from the waist to the knees, while the men and children were naked. When it was colder, animal capes made of rabbit or otter skin were worn by all of the members of the village, and were also used as blankets or bedding. The Costanoans wore shell necklaces. Men covered themselves with mud. Women had tattoos. For rituals and ceremonies, the men wore feather headdresses. Tobacco was smoked. Native American tribes in California traded shells, jewelry, tools, baskets, hides, pelts, and sea salt with each other. They mostly traded through barter; but shells were also used as currency. However, the Native Americans sometimes had tribal or even familial clashes, which could be violent. The Salinans and Coastanoans fought and were considered enemies.

The Native Americans had their own culture, customs, rituals, ceremonies, and spirituality; these were expressed through music, song, dance, games, and story-telling. The medicine man (or shaman) was thought to have the power to cure the sick of their illness. The Costanoans believed in the myth that when the earth was created, it was covered with water, and the first animals on a mountaintop were the coyote, eagle, and humming bird. The Costanoans worshiped the sun, moon, and redwood trees as sacred, and they gave offerings and prayers to them. They participated in family life and practiced monogamy in marriage, except for the chief. The Costanoans mostly cremated their dead, however, those who were too poor or didn't have family were buried. Shells, beads, and seeds were placed over the body as part of the funeral. The belongings of the dead were burned and their names were not spoken. The Costanoans believed that those who passed away traveled to an island at the edge of the sea.

Overall, when the Spanish arrived, it is estimated there were between seven and ten thousand Native Americans who lived locally in the general Monterey region, while there were around 350,000 Native Americans in the state of California. The Native Americans lived their lives generation after generation among nature, until the Spanish arrived and colonized their land.

§

SPANISH EXPLORERS AND THE ESTABLISHMENT OF NEW SPAIN (1521-1821)

The era of European exploration began in 1492, when Christopher Columbus sailed west across the Atlantic Ocean for King Ferdinand and Queen Isabella of Spain and discovered the New World when he landed in the West Indies. Spanish explorer Vasco Núñez de Balboa arrived on the Eastern part of Panama in 1513 and made his way westward across the Isthmus of Panama and discovered the Pacific Ocean in September of 1513. Spaniard Hernán Cortés landed in Mexico in 1519 and conquered the Aztec region for the Spanish crown by 1521. This territory was designated as New Spain.

On June 27, 1542, navigator Juan Rodríguez Cabrillo, commissioned by New Spain, left from the Western coast of Mexico with two ships and discovered the Alta (or Upper) California Coast. His ships sailed into what would be the San Diego harbor on September 28, 1542. Cabrillo and his crew continued northward up the Pacific coast, yet he died along the way from gangrene, from what is believed to have probably been an infected broken arm. However prior to his death in January 1543, Cabrillo had instructed his pilot and crew to continue the voyage up the Pacific coast, which they did, about as far north as the California-Oregon border on March 1, 1543. Then they returned south to La Navidad, on Mexico's Pacific coast, where they had begun the voyage.

Sixty years later, on May 5, 1602, Spanish explorer, Sebastián Vizcaíno left from Acapulco, Mexico and traveled northward with three ships that carried two hundred men along with three Carmelite friars. They first landed at a harbor in Southern California on November 10, 1602, which Vizcaíno named the Bay of San Diego. Mass was celebrated there and then the crew sailed northward up the coast, and he named Santa Catalina Island, San Pedro, Santa Barbara, and Point Conception. As they approached what would become the Monterey Peninsula, Vizcaíno also gave the names to the coastal Santa Lucia mountain range and Point Piños (the headland at the entrance of Monterey Bay, near Pacific Grove) for the many pine trees there. On December 16, 1602, Vizcaíno sailed into the bay, which he designated Monterey Bay. (Monterey Bay is nearly 30 miles from point-to-point.) It was named after the Viceroy Gaspar de Zúñiga y Acevedo, Count of Monterey (Conde de Monterey), the Viceroy of New Spain, who had commissioned the voyage. The Viceroy was the governor or administrator who ruled as the King's representative in New Spain (Mexico). Mass was celebrated near a large oak tree on a hill above Monterey Bay and the land was claimed for God and King Phillip III of Spain, and marked by a large cross.

Before he left Monterey in early January 1603, Vizcaíno and eleven crewmembers explored the area over the hill to the south and discovered another "good" port (what would be Carmel Bay) and the river that winds into the Pacific Ocean, which he named El Río Carmelo (the Carmel River) in honor of the Carmelite friars who sailed with him. Carmel Bay is about two miles wide and four miles long. During the three weeks he stayed in the Monterey area, Vizcaíno wrote a highly favorable report, which was sent back to Spain, in which he described the abundance of pine and oak trees, the ample water supply, mild climate, and Monterey Bay's port, which he called a "noble harbor." He also incorrectly believed that Monterey Bay was "sheltered" from the wind. Consequently, his overly positive description led to confusion later on when subsequent explorers failed to recognize the location based on his recount.

Vizcaíno and his crew further traveled the Pacific coast as far up to Cape Mendocino and the Oregon border, but were forced to turn back. The weather was severe and treacherous and there was an outbreak of scurvy on board. Nearly a quarter of the crew (45 members) had died along the way home, by the time they returned to Acapulco, Mexico. It was not known at the time, but this would be the last expedition to Alta California by New Spain for 167 years.

THE MISSION ERA IN CALIFORNIA (1769-1834)

Spain largely relied on Jesuit missionaries to colonize the Northern Mexico and Baja California region of New Spain, as the European country lacked the manpower and finances to settle the region. Two Italian-born Jesuit missionaries, Fathers Eusebio Francesco Kino and

Juan Maria de Salvatierra(s), founded the missions in Baja (or Lower) California, along with some as far north as Sonora (the present southern Arizona border) and west to the Gila and Colorado Rivers (the present California border). The first Jesuit mission in Baja California was established in 1697. Eventually the Jesuits established a total of 18 missions in Baja California and they were in charge of those missions for 70 years.

King Charles III (Carlos III) of Spain came to power in 1759. He wanted to colonize Alta California as a way to permanently strengthen Spain's claim in the New World, and to prevent other powers such as England and Russia from settling on the Pacific Coast. Meanwhile, the Spanish king viewed the Jesuits as having become too powerful politically, since they did not report to the viceroy of Spain. King Charles III appointed José de Gálvez as Inspector-General (Visitador-General) to New Spain, in 1765. Gálvez made Captain Don Gaspar de Portolá the governor of Baja and Alta California in 1767. [Portolá was born in Catalonia, in the northeastern region of Spain in 1723 and was of noble birth. In the military he served the King of Spain as a dragoon captain in Italy, Portugal, and New Spain.] Following the king's orders, Gálvez assigned Portolá to expel the Jesuits in 1767 through 1768 in New Spain (Baja California and Mexico) and replace them with Franciscan friars. Gálvez also appointed Franciscan Father Junípero Serra as the Father-President (Padre Presidente) in charge of the missions in 1768.

Father Junípero Serra

Father Junípero Serra (1713-1784) was born as Miguel José Serra on November 24, 1713 in the village of Petra, on the western Mediterranean island of Majorca, Spain. He entered the Franciscan order in 1730 at age 16 and took the Franciscan order name, Junípero in 1731, at which time he began his six years of study to enter the priesthood, at the Convent of San Francisco in Palma. In 1737 at age 24, he was ordained a priest. As Father Serra studied for his Doctorate in Sacred Theology, which he received in 1742 at Lullian University in Palma, in Majorca, he also taught undergraduates in philosophy and theology, at the Convent of San Francisco from 1740 to 1743. Two of his students were Father Juan Crespí

(1721-1782) and Father Francisco Palóu (1723-1789), both Franciscan friars of the Carmelite order and natives of Palma. Crespí and Palóu became lifelong friends and accompanied Serra to the New World as missionaries. In 1749, Father Serra requested and was sent to Mexico to be a missionary, at the College of San Fernando in Mexico City, which was the Franciscan headquarters in Mexico, along with Fathers Palóu and Crespí. It is where the European friars who arrived for missionary work trained before their assignments in California and also where they retired after the completion of a lifetime of missionary work.

The friars landed in Vera Cruz, on the eastern side of Mexico, along the Gulf of Mexico, on New Year's Day in 1750 and Serra walked to Mexico City, a distance of 270 miles. Along the way he was reportedly most likely bitten by an insect, possibly a mosquito, and was subsequently troubled by an "ulcerated foot" or recurrent leg infection for the rest of his life. Father Serra, who was a little over five feet tall, was known for his austere life and his acceptance of suffering and self-denial. Serra would serve as a Franciscan missionary in Mexico for 18 years, many of which were spent in some of the most difficult regions of Mexico, such as the Sierra Gorda area, a mountainous region north of Mexico City, where the converts were resistant. He was in Sierra Gorda from 1750 to 1758, and then other parts of Mexico for a decade until 1768.

The Pious Fund

A Pious Fund had been set up in Mexico City, which accepted donations from wealthy individuals to sponsor the missionary activities. The money went to the establishment of each mission and to the missionaries as a stipend for goods, tools, bells, and other items such as seeds. There were usually two missionaries assigned per mission, along with about half a dozen soldiers, who were paid by the government.

The Sacred Expedition

To fulfill King Charles III's desire to claim Alta California for Spain, and to prevent England and Russia from gaining a foothold there, in 1768 Inspector-General José de Gálvez chose Captain Don Gaspar de Portolá and Father Junípero Serra to organize soldiers and missionaries respectively, with plans to settle and colonize Alta California. The three-prong plan was to set up the missions and presidios first, and then the pueblos, or towns. The Franciscan missionaries would establish the missions and convert the Native Americans to Christianity and thus extend Spain's hold over Alta California. These converts would also provide labor at the missions. Portolá would lead the soldiers who would establish the military presidios to maintain order and protect the settlements. Father Serra would be the head of the missions. He was 55 years old when he was selected to undertake this endeavor in Alta California, which was called the "Sacred Expedition".

Inspector-General José de Gálvez held a meeting in San Blas on May 16, 1768 to formulate the plans for the expedition. The Port of San Blas, located on the Western Coast of Mexico, along the Pacific Ocean, became a supply port, with warehouses, a shipyard, and a garrison. The excursions would depart from Mexico's Pacific Coast with the goal to set up headquarters in San Diego first and Monterey second, and then to found five missions, as a start, along the coast of Alta California. The new sites for missions would be spread outwards to fill in the spaces from the two central hubs of San Diego and Monterey, where the ports were located. Most of the Alta California missions would be situated along the Pacific Coast, rather than far inland, so that the missionaries could get supplies easily by ship. Monterey was chosen because of Vizcaíno's positive report from nearly two centuries earlier. The missions were located in areas with plentiful water and rich soil; often there was a river nearby and fields for crops and animals.

As part of the plan to travel to Alta California, Gálvez, Portolá, and Serra planned to have four separate parties, two would go by land and two by sea, with an additional supply ship, the *San José*, all to meet and establish a base camp in San Diego, from which to proceed northward. The Sacred Expedition consisted of 300 men (members of the military, Franciscans, and Christianized converts) and a total of three ships: the *San Carlos*, the *San Antonio*, and the *San José*. The first ship, the *San Carlos* left on January 9, 1769, from the Port of La Paz in Baja California, northward, and the second ship, the *San Antonio* left from there on February 15, 1769. The supply ship, the *San José*, which was filled with provisions, was delayed by several months and it never came; it was lost at sea with all the crew on the way to San Diego. On March 22, 1769 the first of the land parties with Captain Don Fernando Rivera y Moncada, along with Father Juan Crespí, took off from northern Baja California. For the trip to San Diego they took hundreds of domestic animals, such as cattle, horses and mules with them, however may of the animals did not make it. The second land party left Baja California for San Diego about two months later, on May 15, 1769, with Captain Don Gaspar de Portolá and Father Junípero Serra. Serra chose to make the journey by land, on part of the way he rode a mule, and on another part he walked, in spite of his health problems with his foot. The *San Antonio* was the first ship to reach San Diego on April 11, 1769. The second ship, the *San Carlos*, came in on April 29, 1769. Many of its crewmembers suffered from scurvy and had died or were near death. The first land party with Captain Fernando Rivera y Moncada, along with Father Juan Crespí, was the first to reach Alta California (San Diego) on May 14, 1769. At the end of June 1769, the second land party with Captain Gaspar de Portolá and Father Junípero Serra arrived. By July 1, 1769, after much physical suffering, hunger, and illness, all the land and sea parties joined together in San Diego, yet more than a third of the members of the entire Sacred Expedition, 100 had died. Most of the 200 or so who survived were sick and weak, and many of them didn't recover. The *San Antonio* ship was sent back to Mexico (San Blas) to pick up supplies and people and bring them back to Alta California.

From this base in San Diego, Father Serra stayed behind with a group that began to construct the settlement, which included building the mission and presidio. Serra also cared for the sick. On July 16, 1769, Father Junípero Serra founded and dedicated the Mission San Diego de Alcalá, the first California mission. Two weeks after the parties had first reunited, Gaspar de Portolá's land party left San Diego on July 14, 1769 northward by foot to find Monterey with plans to set up a settlement there. The overland group led by Portolá had 64 men; he also went north with Father Juan Crespí, who was the diarist for the party and kept a journal of the trek to later inform Father Serra of the details of their journey. By October 1769, as the Portolá group went along the coast northward, they passed the Carmel River and Monterey Bay but did not recognize Monterey from Vizcaíno's overly generous description of the harbor and continued northward. Their food supply was low, despite some food given to them by the Native Americans along the way, and sickness continued; even their mules had become frail from the shortage of food. However, Portolá's expedition party pressed on northward and reached San Francisco Bay in early November 1769. Portolá then decided to go back south, and his group arrived at Monterey Bay again on November 11, 1769, but still didn't know it. In search of food, they ate sea gulls and pelicans. The Native Americans who lived in what would be Carmel Valley gave the hungry members of Portolá's party seeds and pinole (ground corn flour) as food to eat. Along the way, Portolá's group had traded gifts such as glass beads, for seeds and fish with the Native Americans they encountered on their trip north. On December 10, 1769 Portolá's party put up a large cross at Carmel Bay and buried a letter in a bottle at its base, which announced that they had been there. Portolá's men also left a cross at Monterey Bay on December 9, 1769 on which they carved a message that stated the party was short of food and supplies and was going south to San Diego. The crosses were large enough so that they could be seen from the ships at sea. Finally, in spite of much hardship over six weeks, the party continued to travel southward along the coast and completed the 500 miles back to San Diego, when they arrived there on January 24, 1770. During the last twelve days of their return trip, the members of Portolá's group were starving, and they had to eat their mules. They had journeyed a total of 1,000 miles in six months, by the time they reached the Port of San Diego.

The establishment of the Monterey mission and presidio

At the San Diego settlement, food was low, so Captain Portolá urgently sent a ship, the *San Antonio*, to get more supplies from San Blas. Later, on February 10, 1770, he also sent a land party led by Captain Rivera, to bring back supplies from the Baja California missions. After waiting for two months, the San Diego group was hungry, desperate, and ready to give up the settlement and return back to Mexico, but their prayers were answered on March 23, 1770, when the *San Antonio*, filled with supplies from Mexico, arrived in San Diego. With their good fortune, Portolá then decided to try again to go north in Alta California to complete the expedition to locate Monterey and set up a settlement there. On Easter Sunday, April 16, 1770, Father Serra left by ship, the *San Antonio*, northward for Monterey Bay. On the next day, April 17, 1770, Captain Gaspar de Portolá's land party, which included Father Juan Crespí, trekked northward, and followed the same path as they had taken up the coast the previous year. Portolá also traveled with Lieutenant Don Pedro Fages and about 20 soldiers. Once again, the Native Americans they encountered on the trip gave them food along the way.

Portolá's party was the first to reach Monterey Bay on May 24, 1770, and this time when they reencountered it, they realized it was the one Vizcaíno had described. At the site of the cross they had left in December 1769, they found the Native Americans had placed meat, sardines, clams, and feather-topped arrows that had been broken and stuck in the ground; these were interpreted as a friendly sign. The group set up a camp nearby and lit three fires on the hilltop above Carmel Bay as signal for the *San Antonio*. Within one week Father Junípero Serra's expedition arrived by ship at Monterey Bay on May 31, 1770. The *San Antonio* fired its cannon as a signal when it approached. Portolá and Crespí rode over Carmel Hill to Monterey to meet the ship and the parties reunited on June 1, 1770. Then on Sunday, June 3, 1770 the Monterey mission and presidio were established. Father Junípero Serra dedicated Mission San Carlos Borroméo de Monterey, the second California mission. *[Mission San Carlos Borroméo was named in honor of Italian born Saint Charles Borroméo (1538-1584), a member of the Medici family, whose feast day is November 4th. San Carlos (Feast) Day is a yearly celebration at the mission, which marked the death of San Carlos on November 4, 1584.]* Father Serra blessed another cross, which was put in the ground; he sprinkled holy water on the beach and held mass near the oak tree where Vizcaíno had landed at Monterey Bay, before Portolá claimed the land for the King of Spain, Charles III. As part of a traditional Spanish custom when taking possession of new land, the royal flag was saluted. Captain Gaspar de Portolá grabbed a handful of grass, broke some twigs from the oak, and threw some soil and stones at the direction of the four points of the compass. Bells, which had been hung on the oak tree limbs, rang again and there was more gunfire. These sounds were said to have scared the Native Americans.

For about the next month, Fathers Serra and Crespí lived aboard the *San Antonio*, while construction, which was very basic and simple, began on a stockade and the presidio and mission in Monterey, so that Serra and Crespí could move in. Father Serra stayed in Monterey as the presidio and mission continued to be built. The Monterey Presidio, a military post, was established at a site about a mile away from the oak tree where the ship had landed, near the Mission San Carlos Borroméo de Monterey. The presidio was a square plaza, which had a temporary chapel in a storeroom. These early buildings were single-story and made out of logs and tree branches, covered with mud and lime plaster, with sod roofs and dirt floors. Members of the military worked as masons and carpenters; Lieutenant Fages was known to drive them hard. At this time, the population of Monterey's settlement, which was all male, was around 40; about 30 were soldiers and the rest were converts from Baja California, along with the two Franciscan friars. On July 9, 1770, Captain Gaspar de Portolá turned over the governorship of California to Lieutenant Pedro Fages. (Portolá had served as governor of Baja and Alta California for three years, from 1767 to 1770. Fages served his first term as governor from 1770 to 1774.) There was a farewell mass and Portolá set sail back to Mexico on the *San Antonio* to share the news and celebrate the founding of Monterey. *From 1777 to 1784, Portolá was mayor of Puebla in New Spain; he eventually returned to Spain by the mid-1780's and he died in Madrid.*

Mission San Carlos Borroméo del Río Carmelo

For nearly a year, the Monterey settlement had no contact with New Spain. With the limited amount of settlers and resources, those at the mission and presidio in Monterey had to wait for supplies to arrive by ship from San Blas (Mexico). Early on, it became evident to Father Serra that there were problems with the chosen site for the Monterey mission, but he did not have the power to make the decision to change its location. He wanted to move the mission because it needed to have a more convenient source of wood and water, along with more fertile soil for agriculture and a workforce of Native Americans. The decision where to situate the California missions was made by a scouting party of padres along with a military escort for protection. Once a site was chosen, the padres blessed the land, the soldiers helped build simple structures for shelter, and later more formal, durable buildings were constructed.

Father Serra and Lieutenant Fages also had disagreements over religious and military authority. Serra wanted to distance himself and the friars from the presidio because he did not want the military to meddle with the missions. Furthermore, some of the soldiers and their conduct were seen as a negative influence on the Native American converts. In May 1771, the *San Antonio* returned to Monterey, carrying food and workers along with more friars to found more missions. There was also a letter for Father Serra from the Viceroy of New Spain, which gave Serra permission to move the mission. Father Serra found a new site near the Carmel River on July 8, 1771. He asked Father Palóu to join him, in a letter, in which Serra wrote that he was so pleased with the beautiful location, that he would be happy to spend the rest of his life there. Father Junípero Serra relocated Mission San Carlos Borroméo de Monterey over the hill, five miles away to the south, near the mouth of the Carmel River, overlooking Carmel Bay, in what would become present day Carmel. Construction began soon after the site was selected in July 1771, and it took about six months to build the Carmel Mission, which was known as Mission San Carlos Borroméo del Río Carmelo. It was rededicated and mass was held on Christmas Eve, December 24, 1771. *[The Carmel Mission, located on Rio Road, is a National Historic Landmark #66000214, added to the National Register of Historic Places in 1966, and it is California State Historical Landmark No. 135.]* After the mission was officially moved to Carmel, the former mission in Monterey became the Royal Presidio Chapel.

As Padre Presidente, Junípero Serra used Mission San Carlos Borroméo del Río Carmelo as his headquarters. Father Serra lived in a very small cell, about a hundred yards from church, which had a table, chair, candlestick, a bed made out of boards, and one blanket. Father Juan Crespi and Father Francisco Palóu also lived at the Carmel Mission and helped Father Junípero Serra establish and run the California missions. The early years at Mission San Carlos Borroméo were filled with difficulties and hardship. The missions were isolated and there was little and infrequent communication with New Spain. In addition to crop failure and food shortages the missionaries had to rely on the yearly arrival of a supply ship from San Blas to bring needed goods, as well as news, yet some times the ships were delayed, or didn't come at all. Additionally, not only was there was a language barrier between the missionaries and the Native Americans, which made the religious conversion difficult, there was also resistance altogether from the Native Americans, and the missionaries had to rely on the soldiers for order.

Neophytes

The Native Americans who were more than nine years old and who had been converted to Christianity and lived at the mission were known as "neophytes". As envisioned, the missions were supposed to be temporary, not permanent, with the goal in ten years time, to educate the Native Americans and turn them into citizens and run a pueblo under civil law. The land was held in trust for the Native Americans and would be turned over back to them and after their work was done, then the missionaries were supposed to move on. The padres kept records of the number of Native Americans who were baptized (or whose "souls were saved") as a way to measure the success of their efforts. However, the neophytes were mostly treated as children who needed discipline and guidance, and the padres acted as if they were their parents. The padres used rigid discipline and even force to keep the converts in line and prevent them from slipping back into what the missionaries viewed as pagan, sinful, and uncivilized behavior. The neophytes weren't permitted to leave the mission and there were presidio soldiers who served as guards at the missions, or could be brought in if a situation arose, to keep the neophytes in line and to stop them from running away. Often harsh punishment, including physical beatings, was employed for disobedience or attempted rebellion. Additionally, the padres kept the neophytes on strict daily schedules, with three meals a day, mandatory attendance at church services several times a day, and work duties assigned with quotas to be filled by the male and female converts to support the mission. The Native American converts were put to work and supported the mission through farming, caring for livestock, or building structures. In the beginning, the first mission buildings, like those at the presidios, were very basic and were built out of logs, mud, and sticks. These early structures consisted of walls made from poles closely put together and plastered with mud. The walls were sometimes coated with a mixture of lime plaster. The roofs were covered with sod or tule. To provide protection, these buildings were enclosed by a stockade made of logs, held together without nails, because there were none available. There was also usually a small garden.

The San Francisco and Santa Clara Missions

New Spain's Viceroy Antonio María Bucareli (who served from 1771 to 1779) wanted to find a land route from Sonora to Monterey. Not only was the sea voyage long and dangerous, but an overland path would allow supplies to be transported by pack train and would provide a way for more colonists to settle in Alta California. Bucareli authorized Captain (later Lieutenant) Colonel Don Juan Bautista de Anza (1735-1788) to make two overland trips from Sonora, in Northern Mexico, to Monterey. Also, as part of his mission, Anza had been requested to pick a site for the presidio and mission in San Francisco and the mission in Santa Clara. The first trip was in January 1774. Juan Bautista de Anza left with 34 men and arrived in Monterey in April 1774. On the second trip, Anza left in October 1775 from Sonora and the group arrived at the Monterey Presidio on March 10, 1776. The large overland party had 240 men (soldiers as well as civilians), women, and children, and also several hundred domestic animals, including horses, mules, and cattle, which were the basis of the cattle herds at the ranchos in California. Anza brought the first non-native women to settle in the area. The government paid $800 for each soldier and his family from Mexico to settle the new establishments in Monterey, San Francisco, and Santa Clara. Juan Bautista de Anza went on to San Francisco to choose the site of the San Francisco Presidio and Mission San Francisco de Asís, which were founded in September and October 1776, respectively. He also chose the site of Mission Santa Clara de Asís, and then went back to Monterey; Anza left by horse back to Mexico on April 14, 1776.

On July 17, 1781 the Yuma Massacre occurred near the Colorado River, in which Native Americans killed a traveling land party of friars and soldiers, including Captain Fernando Rivera y Moncada, and kidnapped the women and children with them, which forced Mexico to abandon the overland route that Anza had established.

Father Serra's death

Throughout his years as a missionary, Father Junípero Serra walked thousands of miles. He traveled up and down California to found and visit the other missions, so that he could baptize and confirm the Native Americans into the Christian faith. During his life, Father Serra established a total of nine California missions. These were Mission San Diego de Alcalá (#1), Mission San Carlos Borroméo (#2), Mission San Antonio de Padua (#3) in 1771, Mission San Gabriel Arcangel (#4) in 1771, Mission San Luis Obispo de Tolosa (#5) in 1772, Mission San Francisco de Asís (#6) in 1776, Mission San Juan Capistrano (#7) (in 1775 and re-founded in 1776), Mission Santa Clara de Asís (#8) in 1777, and Mission San Buenaventura (#9) in 1782. Around this time, there had been more than 5,000 baptisms performed at all of these missions since they had been founded. Near the end of his life, when the Padre Presidente turned 70 years old and was quite sick with chest pains and weakness, he undertook his last major, statewide journey from August 1783 to January 1784. He went south by sea on a supply ship, *La Favorita*, to San Diego and then returned overland and stopped at all the missions along the way to visit the neophytes and perform confirmations.

In April 1784, after he recuperated at Mission San Carlos Borroméo, Father Serra made his final trip. He went north by mule to the missions in San Francisco and Santa Clara to give his blessings and confirm more of the neophytes. The padre returned to Carmel from the Santa Clara visit on May 26, 1874. He was sick and near the end of his life. Father Francisco Palóu was by Father Serra's side during most of his final days and he administered the Last Rites. Father Junípero Serra died on August 28, 1784, at age 70, (almost age 71) at his cell in the Carmel Mission. Church bells were rung to announce his death. As mourners came by to view Father Serra's body, which was on a table in the church, some of them took tiny scraps of cloth and hair from it. At Father Serra's funeral, the next day, Sunday, August 29, 1784 at Mission San Carlos Borroméo, the mission bells rang and every half hour, cannons fired from the ship *San Carlos* docked at Monterey Bay, as well as from the Monterey Presidio. There were 600 Native American converts, along with priests from other missions, soldiers from the Monterey Presidio, and sailors and officers from the *San Carlos*, who all came to pay their respects to Father Serra. He was buried at the mission in the afternoon in a sanctuary near the altar, and beside Father Juan Crespí, who had died in 1782.

Father Fermín Francisco de Lasuén becomes Padre Presidente (1785-1803)

After Father Serra's death, Father Palóu briefly succeeded him in 1784 as Padre Presidente, before he decided to return to Mexico City to the College of San Fernando to write a biography of Father Junípero Serra. (Palóu's first book, a history of the California missions, *Noticias de la Nueva California* was the first historical account written in California.) The Serra biography, *Vida de Junípero Serra*, was also known by its full title as *Relación Histórica de la Vida y Apostólicas Tareas del Venerable Padre Fray Junípero Serra, Y de las Misiones que fundó en la California Septentrional, y nuevos establecimientos de Monterey.* This book, *Historical Account of the Life and Apostolic Labors of the Venerable Father Junípero Serra, and of the Missions which He Founded in Northern California, and the New Establishments of Monterey*, was published in 1787 in Mexico City. Palóu's book on Serra's life, *Relación Histórica*, was widely read at the time in Spain, Mexico and California and was considered one of the earliest and most influential history books of early California. Father Palóu remained at the College of San Fernando. He died in Mexico in 1789.

In 1785, Father Fermín Francisco de Lasuén (1736-1803) became Padre Presidente and was head of the California missions for 18 years, from 1785 until his death in 1803. Lasuén was born in 1736 in Victoria, Spain, of Basque heritage. Before adulthood, he joined the Franciscan order and like Father Junípero Serra had done, he asked to go to Mexico as a missionary. In 1759, Lasuén arrived in Mexico, where he spent eight years in the Sierra Gorda region, and then six years at the Baja California missions. Afterwards, in 1773, Father Lasuén served at the Alta California missions under Father Serra, until he became Padre Presidente. Father Fermín Lasuén also made Mission San Carlos Borroméo his headquarters, just as Father Serra had done. By the mid-1780's, there were around 700 neophytes at Mission San Carlos Borroméo; it produced enough food for its population and to supply the Monterey Presidio, as well. Eventually, the missions became relatively self-sufficient as far as food supply, although there were always certain goods they couldn't make on their own.

Prominent foreign visitors at the Carmel Mission

In the late 1780's and early 1790's, during the time Father Fermín Lasuén was Padre Presidente, several prominent foreign navigators arrived by ship in Monterey on scientific expeditions. They also visited Mission San Carlos Borroméo, met with Father Lasuén, and were treated to formal ceremonies and festivals for visiting dignitaries. Before they left, these visitors often traded provisions from the mission for foreign goods they carried on their ships. These explorers had their artists who traveled with them sketch the Native Americans, along with plants, animals and the surroundings of the area. The journals and sketches were published or distributed in Europe and beyond. These publications, along with Father Palóu's books, were the first recorded history and eyewitness accounts of California mission life during the Spanish Era, and served to spread knowledge about California to the rest of the world.

Captain Jean François Galaup Comte de La Pérouse

The first two foreign ships to land at Monterey Bay were the *Boussole* and the *Astrolabe* of the Royal French Navy, under French scientist and navigator Captain Jean François Galaup Comte de La Pérouse (1741-1788?). La Pérouse was on a four-year, global scientific voyage for King Louis XVI of France. He traveled with cartographers, geologists, botanists, physicians, and scientists who took samples. There were illustrators, too, who sketched the Native Americans and drew what they saw during their ten days in Monterey in September 1786. La Pérouse visited Mission San Carlos Borroméo and was well-received. He wrote a description of his experience, along with his detailed observations of the Native Americans and their routines and conditions at the mission in his journals. La Pérouse compared their lives at the Carmel Mission to a slave plantation in the West Indies. The drawings made in 1786 during his visit are the first pictures documented of Mission San Carlos Borroméo. After he left, La Pérouse continued the voyage, and sometime, about two years later, the entire expedition was lost at sea and most likely shipwrecked southeast of New Guinea. Remarkably, since he had the foresight and had passed along his journals to other ships prior, his writings and the sketches made it to France, and thus his work survived and was published in 1797.

Alessandro Malaspina

In September 1791, the next foreign explorer on a global, scientific voyage who arrived at Monterey Bay was Italian-born Spanish Royal Navy navigator, Alessandro (Alejandro) Malaspina (1754-1810). He also had scientists and artists with him, including José Cardero, who drew the Native Americans along with their settlements, the Carmel Mission buildings, and the Monterey Presidio. (Malaspina's arrival was also of note because he had a Boston sailor, John Green with him, who became the first American in California, but Green died soon thereafter and was buried in Monterey.)

Captain George Vancouver

British Royal Naval Captain George Vancouver (1758-1798) on the ship, *Discovery*, visited Monterey in 1792 and 1793. Vancouver made three trips on his global scientific expedition, with an emphasis on the North Pacific Coast, on an assignment to find out how much land the Spanish had colonized. He was the third foreign visitor to the Monterey area, and he also spent time in San Francisco and at the Santa Clara Mission. Captain George Vancouver traveled from the Monterey Presidio to Mission San Carlos Borroméo by horseback. He visited the Carmel Mission while construction of the new church was underway; it had begun in 1793. This was around the time when Mission San Carlos Borroméo had about 800 neophtytes, nearly its largest population. Vancouver noted that the Native American converts did the stonework, under the direction of Manuel Ruiz. Two of Captain Vancouver's midshipmen, John Sykes and Harry Humphreys drew pictures of the Carmel Mission, Monterey Presidio, and other scenery in the area. Overall, Vancouver was treated well during his first visit, but later the Spanish authorities became suspicious of the intent of his travels in Alta California. During his voyages, Vancouver kept a diary, which was the basis of his book, *A Voyage of Discovery to the North Pacific Ocean and Round the World, 1791-1795*. He described his observations of the presidios and missions; he was critical of the way the Spanish maintained the settlements in California, and noted that the presidios were vulnerable to a foreign invasion. Although Vancouver died shortly after his book was published in 1798, it was widely received and printed in several European languages. It helped to increase knowledge of, exposure to, and curiosity about California.

The *Otter*

The first American ship to land in California was the *Otter*, from Boston. It was a commercial vessel involved in the sea otter pelt trade with China. This trade between New England and China would bring many more American ships to California. Under the command of Captain Ebenezer Dorr, the *Otter* arrived in Monterey Bay in October 1796. The members supplied themselves with food and water from Mission San Carlos Borroméo before they departed. Captain Dorr also had a dozen English convicts onboard (who had escaped from Australia's Botany Bay Penal Colony) whom he released on the Carmel shore, in the middle of the night.

Mission architecture and skilled crafts

During Father Fermín Lasuén's time as Padre Presidente, the now familiar style of mission architecture was put in place. Buildings were constructed of more durable and permanent adobe and stone walls, along with clay tile roofs, which replaced the initial mud and straw or thatch structures. In the 1790's, Spain authorized money for Father Lasuén to bring in several dozen master artisans from Mexico City to California. They trained the Native Americans converts in craft skills. These craftsmen taught the neophytes how to do blacksmith work, stonework, brickwork, and carpentry. Spanish stonemason Manuel Estevan Ruiz led the construction of the new Royal Presidio Chapel of San Carlos Borroméo or Capilla Royal in Monterey. It was built out of stone and completed in 1794, after fire destroyed the earlier presidio buildings, which were made of wood logs and adobe. For both endeavors, Ruiz trained and directed the Native Americans to do the labor. *[The Royal Presidio Chapel is located at 550 Church Street in Monterey and is National Historic Landmark #66000216 and State Historical Landmark No. 105. In 2008, it underwent a massive seven million dollar restoration.]*

The construction of the new stone mission church at Carmel's Mission San Carlos Borroméo also occurred under Father Lasuén's watch. The work began when he laid the cornerstone of the new church on July 7, 1793, and it was completed in 1797. It, too, was done under the direction of Manuel Estevan Ruiz. As with the Royal Presidio Chapel in Monterey, Ruiz taught and supervised the Native Americans who did the masonry. The stone for the Mission San Carlos Borroméo church building came from Carmel Valley and crushed abalone shells were used to make the mortar. When the actual mission church structure was completed, a religious ceremony and fiesta was held to mark the dedication in September 1797. However, construction continued for more than a decade and a half on the rest of the buildings that would form the mission compound, such as dormitories, granaries, and a school. The mission quadrangle was finished in 1815 and the occasion was celebrated with services.

The newly constructed buildings at the California missions had traditional Spanish, Moorish, and Roman architectural influences; these were often based on the padres' memories of Mexico and Spain, combined with local modifications. For example, the Moorish influence can be recognized in the stained glass, star-shaped window and the two bell towers at the front (façade) of the chapel of Mission San Carlos Borroméo. Around the mission buildings there were patios, walkways, corridors, arches, open courtyards, and gardens. The building walls were made of adobe brick and stone, and red clay tiles were used for the roofs. At the Carmel Mission, there was a kiln in which the Spanish-style, roof tiles were baked. The California missions included a church, quarters for the friars, a kitchen, storerooms, workshops, and additional sleeping quarters. Typically the mission complex was built in the form of a square, or quadrangle, with the largest building, the mission church, often in the northeast corner. There was a fountain or well for water, stables and corrals for the animals, gardens, orchards, and a cemetery alongside the church.

The master artisans taught the neophytes other specific skills, which contributed to the operation of the missions. The male neophytes learned how to do woodworking, tanning and leatherwork, pottery, and wine making. The female neophytes learned to how to sew, spin, weave, and cook. The Native American men worked in the gardens, orchards, fields, and vineyards that surrounded the missions and they tended the livestock: cattle, sheep, and horses. Several types of grain and crops were grown, along with grapes, olives, figs, and dates. Citrus trees including oranges and lemons were originally imported from Spain. The crops consisted of wheat, lentils, barley, peas, corn, and beans. Hides, tallow, soap, candles, and some food products including wine, were made at the missions; any excess amounts were traded at the Presidio for items such as tools, paper, locks, keys, and chocolate. These goods and supplies came from abroad on ships, which landed at the ports, such as Monterey. Foreign trade was not legal at the time in Spanish California, though it occurred.

Father Lasuén's death

Father Fermín Lasuén died in 1803, at the age of 67. He was also buried at Mission San Carlos Borroméo, near Father Serra. Father Junípero Serra started and Father Fermín Lasuén nearly completed the line of missions up and down Alta California. Father Lasuén was responsible for the establishment of nine additional missions in the chain, which brought the total to 18 at the time of his death. He founded: Mission Santa Barbara (#10) in 1786, Mission La Purísima Concepción (#11) in 1787, Mission Santa Cruz (#12) in 1791, Mission Nuestra Señora de la Soledad (#13) in 1791, Mission San José de Guadalupe (#14) in 1797, Mission San Juan Bautista (#15) in 1797, Mission San Miguel Arcángel (#16) in 1797, Mission San Fernando Rey de España (#17) in 1797, and Mission San Luis Rey de Francia (#18) in 1798.

The missionaries viewed success based on the number of Native Americans who were baptized, and Father Lasuén had increased the number of neophytes twofold at the California missions. At Mission San Carlos Borroméo during the 1790's, the population of Native American Christian converts reached its highest number of nearly 900. While he was Padre Presidente, agricultural production increased, as did the livestock numbers at the missions. Father Junípero Serra began and Father Lasuén continued to expand the first library in California at Mission San Carlos Borroméo, with nearly 400 volumes by 1800 on various topics. (The books were brought up from San Blas. Later, by 1836, there were close to 600 volumes.)

Subsequently, after Father Lasuén's death, mission construction declined. Only three more California missions were built: Santa Inés (#19) in 1804, San Rafael Arcángel (#20) in 1817, and the last one, Mission San Francisco de Solano (#21) in Sonoma in 1823. The final two were the northernmost in the chain.

El Camino Real

The string of 21 missions built between 1769 through 1823, mostly along the California coast, covered a distance of approximately 600 miles. Upon completion, the long road which linked the missions from San Diego to San Francisco and later, Sonoma, became known as El Camino Real, literally, "The Royal Road", also known as the King's Highway. The padres who traveled the road by foot scattered mustard seeds along the way, so that the path's border was marked with bright yellow blossoms. The missions were located approximately every 30 miles, which was about how far one could travel a day by horseback. Through the 1830's, they served as rest stops for weary horseback riders, and were a place that provided a free meal and overnight lodging, albeit sparse, for those who made the journey up and down El Camino Real. [*Although it initially began as a foot trail and dirt road, El Camino Real eventually became a wider, highly-traveled, stagecoach road, and then ultimately U.S. Highway 101, which runs through Northern and Southern California. El Camino Real is California State Historical Landmark No. 784.*] Now, most parts of the entire route between the missions are marked by large (cast-iron originally—later metal) bells, on curved, 11-foot posts, anchored in concrete. There are over 500 of them in the state, located every one to two miles along the way, as part of the El Camino Real Mission Bell Marker System. (They are managed by Caltrans.)

2

Mexican California and California Statehood

THE END OF SPANISH CALIFORNIA

Monterey

The Spanish king made the decision to have Monterey the capital of Alta and Baja California in 1776; it was implemented in 1777 and Monterey remained the capital until 1849. (The current governor at the time the decision was made was Don Fernando Rivera y Moncada, who served from 1774 to 1777. The new governor who took over that year was Don Felipe de Neve, who served from 1777 to 1782. Don Pedro Fages became Governor again for a second term from 1782 to 1791.)

There were pueblos, or towns, which formed around the missions and presidios, and civic pueblos, which under Spanish law were granted "four square leagues of land" by the Governor. The civic pueblo had a council house and a jail. It was ruled by an alcalde, who was a civil administrator, the equivalent of a mayor and judge, along with regidores, officers or councilmen, who were members of the ayuntamiento, or town council. This type of local government began in California in 1779. Monterey became a civic pueblo in 1795.

In Spanish California, individual land ownership was very limited. During the Spanish period (1769-1821) there were fewer than three dozen land grants given. The first ones were granted under Governor Pedro Fages starting in 1784, by petition. The early land grants went to retired members of the military and their families. These settlers in the pueblos were given a lot to build a house, and they eventually would receive title to the land.

MEXICAN INDEPENDENCE (1821)

By the early 19th century, the Spanish Empire was losing its power and the great distance made it difficult for Spain to control New Spain (Mexico), where there was growing discontent. As a result, New Spain was not paying attention to the California settlements, and did not provide them with regular supplies by ship. Additionally, the ship voyages from Spain primarily, but also those from Mexico, were expensive and perilous. In 1810, New Spain (Mexico) began to fight for independence from Spain, which took eleven years to achieve. Spain cut off supply ships to Mexico. Thus the California presidios and missions stopped receiving needed goods and supplies. As a result, California began to increase trade with ships mainly from New England, as well as Britain along with other foreign countries.

Sea otter trade

From the late 1700's through the early 1800's, the sea otter trade was dominant on the Pacific Coast, until the population of the animals was greatly reduced in the 1820's. This was largely due to Russian, British, and American traders along the entire Pacific Coast, who killed thousands of the otters a year. In 1812 along the California coastline, the Russian-American Fur Company built Fort Ross, 100 miles north of San Francisco Bay, which was used as the headquarters for its sea otter and seal trade. Fort Ross is 18 miles north of Bodega Bay, where the Russians also had an outpost. *[Fort Ross is State Historical Landmark No. 5.] [Bodega Bay and Harbor is State Historical Landmark No. 833.]* Though foreign trade was not permitted in Spanish California, it still occurred. As it was illegal, there were many smugglers. In California sea otter pelts were bartered for manufactured goods made in New England as well as products such as iron, sugar, and tobacco. In the global trade, the animal pelts (worth about $40 each) were traded for luxury products from China, such as silks and ivory, which were brought back to East Coast ports.

Hippolyte de Bouchard

During this time, as Mexico fought for its independence, the California presidios were in decline and not properly staffed, and often the soldiers were not paid nor well equipped. Many of the buildings were in also in disrepair, along with the absence of effective security. In November of 1818, two pirate ships, the *Santa Rosa* and the *Argentina*, with several hundred men aboard, commanded by a French-born, privateer (who represented the Republic of Buenos Aires), Hippolyte de Bouchard, landed at Monterey Bay. For a week, he and his men proceeded to destroy and burn the Monterey Presidio and then moved down the coast and did the same destruction to Mission San Juan Capistrano. These attacks came as the Spanish Empire was coming apart and unable to adequately defend its colonies; the forces at the Monterey Presidio, along with the Governor, were greatly outnumbered and after a brief attempt at defense, retreated to the Salinas Valley.

Transfer of power from Spain to Mexico

In 1821 New Spain (Mexico) won its independence from Spain, which ended Spanish rule and political authority over the New World colonies. It took one year, until 1822, for news of Mexico's independence to make it to California, and for the formal transfer of power from Spanish to Mexican governorship to take place later, in September of that year. In a ceremony at the Monterey Presidio in April 1822, the Mexican Flag was raised and everyone, including the presidio officers and the mission padres, swore allegiance to the new Mexican government. Alta and Baja California were governed by Mexico as a territory.

MEXICAN CALIFORNIA (1822-1846)

William Hartnell

The original hide and tallow trade in California began with the missions. The prominent British trading company at the time, at the start of the 19th century, was John Begg and Company, based in Liverpool. The main traders who represented the firm in California as agents from 1822 to 1828 were William Hartnell and Hugh McCulloch. William Edward Petty Hartnell (1798-1854) was born in England. He began work for John Begg and Company in South America. Hartnell worked out of Lima, Peru before he came to California in 1822 at age 24, at the opportune time in which Mexico had become independent and had opened ports in California for trade. He partnered with a Scotsman, Hugh McCulloch, who also worked for John Begg and Company, and they obtained an exclusive three-year agreement with the California missions to buy all of the hides produced, at $1/hide. In exchange they provided the missionaries and other settlers many needed goods from Peru, such as thread, cloth, buttons, cooking utensils, cocoa, and musical instruments. Hartnell spoke several languages including Spanish and German. (When he began working at John Begg and Company, so his name would be easier to pronounce, he made it sound "Spanish", and thus he was known as (Don) Guillermo Eduardo Arnel.) The trading duo was known as "Macala y Arnel" in Mexican California, and they covered all of the missions, with their headquarters in Monterey. In 1825 Hartnell converted to Catholicism and married Teresa de la Guerra, of Santa Barbara. Her father was Don José de la Guerra y Noriega, the head of one of the wealthiest and most influential Spanish families in California, which owned 326,000 acres of land. Teresa de la Guerra was 16 years old when they married; he had met her when she was 13. Hartnell's father-in-law's prominence would be an asset.

Hartnell tutored two Monterey-born, future leaders who would go on to be prominent members of Mexican California society: (General) Mariano Guadalupe Vallejo (1808-1890) and (Governor) Juan Bautista Alvarado (1809-1882). As both Vallejo and Alvarado were native to California and of Spanish heritage, they were known as Californios, the group of Spanish-speaking people who were born and lived in California, in contrast to those who had settled there from elsewhere.

In 1828, after increased competition for the hide and tallow trade in California, along with business losses and debts, McCulloch and Hartnell dissolved their partnership. Hartnell began to farm and ranch on land near Salinas, Rancho El Alisal, owned by the Sobaranes brothers. (In 1823, Feliciano and Mariano Sobaranes had petitioned for a land grant for Rancho El Alisal, along the Salinas River in Monterey County. The grant was confirmed in 1834.) In the early 1830's, Hartnell became a naturalized Mexican citizen, so he could get a land grant for a rancho. Afterwards, Hartnell's father-in-law, Don José de la Guerra helped him buy a portion of Rancho El Alisal, where he opened a school and was the schoolmaster and teacher. (Hartnell obtained 2,971 acres, while the Sobaranes brothers kept 5,941 acres.) William Hartnell was a powerful, well-respected member of the community, and he held several different government jobs and diplomatic roles through the years.

Bryant, Sturgis & Company

During the 1820's, the British firm John Begg and Company, through their agents, Hartnell and McCulloch, initially dominated the hide and tallow trade with the missions. However, by the late 1820's, the Boston firm, Bryant, Sturgis & Company became the leader in the California hide and tallow trade. Alfred Robinson (1806-1895) was the longtime, West Coast agent for Bryant, Sturgis & Company. He also converted to Catholicism and married into the de la Guerra family of Santa Barbara. Robinson later wrote a memoir about his time in Mexican California, titled, *Life in California Before the Conquest (1846)*.

The Custom House

The Port of Monterey was opened to foreign trade, which was legalized in 1821. In 1827, the Custom House at Monterey, a single-story building was built. It was the chief port of entry for all of Mexican California, where ships' goods were tallied, registered, and customs duties were paid, which brought in government revenue. The Custom House is California's oldest government building. [*It is National Historical Landmark #66000217 and*

State Historical Landmark No. 1.] The building was also a social gathering site during the Mexican California era, where families got together for music and dancing, often to celebrate the arrival of cargo ships and visiting Mexican officials. A second story was added to the Custom House as part of an expansion, which began in 1841. Thomas O. Larkin was in charge of the addition to the structure.

Thomas Oliver Larkin

Thomas Oliver Larkin, (1802-1858) originally a Yankee trader from Boston, who worked nearly ten years in North Carolina, arrived in California in 1832, where he rapidly established himself as a wealthy Monterey store keeper and merchant, and also a builder. Later, he was a prosperous financier and land developer. Thomas O. Larkin was influenced to come to California by and initially worked as a clerk for his older half-brother, John Rogers Cooper, who was one of the first American settlers in Monterey. [Sea captain, John Bautista Rogers Cooper (1791-1872), who was British-born, but a resident of Massachusetts, was captain of the *Rover*, a New England trading schooner. As an early resident of Monterey in the 1820's, he opened a store and built a large home, which later was known as The Cooper-Molera Adobe on 508 Munras Avenue, in the heart of downtown Monterey. In 1827, Cooper converted to Catholicism and married General Mariano Guadalupe Vallejo's sister. He became a naturalized Mexican citizen, and thus was able to amass a large amount of land in California.]

Through the years, Larkin became one of the leading and most important American citizens in Mexican California, and was relied upon by the U.S. government in diplomatic roles. Unlike his half-brother, he kept his American citizenship and never became a Catholic, nor a naturalized Mexican citizen. (Thomas O. Larkin and his wife, Rachel Hobson Holmes Larkin had the first child born in California to American parents, Thomas Larkin Jr., in 1834.) By 1835, he built the Larkin House, the first two-story house in California, in what became known as the Monterey Colonial style, which combined Spanish and East Coast architectural styles. It was made of plastered adobe, with a second floor wood balcony, framed windows, and a low-hipped (or pitched) roof. *[The Larkin House is located on 464 Calle Principal and Jefferson Street in Monterey and is State Historical Landmark No. 106.]*

Mission secularization (1834-1836)

The original plan behind the founding of the missions was that the land was being held in trust for the Native American Christian converts until they became educated citizens and thus would be ready to get their land back. Once this was achieved (in theory), it was expected to take about a decade, and the land would be returned to the Native Americans, then the missions, having completed their function, would become parish churches. The mission buildings and land would be incorporated as part of the pueblos, and the mission priests would move on to the next place.

By the 1830's, there was growing pressure for the Mexican government to secularize the California missions and thus break up the mission lands, which would increase the number of private landholders and end the church's hold on the best acreage. In 1833 the Mexican government ordered the secularization of the missions and the distribution of half of their lands, as well as half of the livestock, to the Native Americans. Civil administrators were put in charge of the rest of the land. The Mexican Governor of Alta California, José Figueroa (term 1833-1835) was in charge of the secularization, and he decided to phase in the process over a few years, rather than all at once, so ten missions were secularized in 1834, six in 1835, and the final five in 1836.

In 1834, an inventory of the Mission San Carlos Borroméo properties valued them at $46,000 to $47,000, which would decrease significantly in the years following secularization. Thus by the end of the 1830's, after mission secularization (1833-1836) was completed, the Catholic Church had lost its dominant position in California. The missions were converted into parish churches. The mission priests were left only in charge of the church, library, and their own dwelling. (Many of the Franciscan friars went back to Mexico or Spain.) The neophytes dispersed and thus there was no longer a workforce needed to sustain the missions. Mission San Carlos Borroméo along with the rest of the California missions soon began to fall apart, and the mission buildings fell into greater disrepair and ruin in the decades that followed. Throughout California, there was deterioration and plundering of the mission properties, with building materials such as adobe, wood, and roof tiles stolen. At the Carmel Mission, there was also theft of some of the relics from the church, along with tiles from the roof. In 1839 William Hartnell inspected and compiled a report on the missions, at the request of Governor Alvarado. (Alvarado served as Governor of Alta California twice: 1836-1837 and 1838-1842.) Hartnell reported complaints such as abuses in the secularization process and in the treatment of the Native Americans. Often as the years went by throughout California, some mission buildings were leased or rented and used for secular purposes, such as saloons, stables, warehouses, or inns. Others were torn down, as they had been abandoned or unsafe, or no one was available to do the costly, necessary repairs. Although half of the mission lands as well as livestock were supposed to be distributed among the Native Americans, many of them were cheated out of the land that was to be theirs. This was especially due to the fact that the Native Americans were not able to read the documents, nor comprehend what they were required to do to obtain what was supposed to be theirs. Additionally, many of the Native Americans were not prepared to live on their own because life at the missions was the only existence they knew. As some of the former neophytes were not able to get by on their own, there was looting of livestock and crops for survival.

The number of Native Americans had gone down significantly by the end of the Spanish and Mexican eras, as many thousands died because of the introduction of Western (or European) diseases, such as smallpox, mumps, measles, syphilis, and influenza, for which they had no immunity. With the high mortality rates of the Native Americans, it is estimated their population was reduced by one-half to two-thirds of what it was before the Spanish missionaries arrived, and the first mission was founded in 1769 in Alta California. By 1820, at Mission San Carlos Borroméo, the neophyte population was half of its highest point of nearly 900, down to around 400. By the mid-1820's, there were between 200 and 300 neophytes who lived at the Carmel Mission. The final count of the number of neophytes at the Mission San Carlos Borroméo, at the end of 1832, had the population between 150 and 185.

The Rancho Era (1833-1848)

Another result of mission secularization was that much of the vast, former church land was purchased by individuals and ended up in private ownership. Much of this previously controlled mission land made up most of the ranchos granted during the 1830's and 1840's in Mexican California. After independence from Spain, California's Mexican governors began to give out large land grants, often to their friends and political allies, who petitioned for the land. Around 500 to 600 land grants were awarded during this era. These went mainly to Mexican citizens of good standing, however anyone who became a naturalized Mexican citizen and accepted Catholicism could obtain a land grant. The distribution of land grants was also used as a way to populate the mostly empty lands of California, especially as the Native American population had greatly decreased. The land grants were the basis of the Rancho Era, or as California Historian Kevin Starr described the period as the "Age of the Dons", a pastoral time in California history dominated by large, family-based cattle ranches. These ranchos could cover anywhere from four to thirty square miles, covering tens of thousands of acres of land. A small rancho was around 25,000 acres, while the extremely large ones could be 50,000 acres. (Approximately 50,000 acres equaled 11 square leagues, as measurements were done at the time.) At the ranchos, some of the former neophytes worked as laborers, or did domestic work, while others were cowboys, or vaqueros. There could be as many as a hundred of these cowboys under the command of a foreman or "majordomo" ("mayordomo" in Spanish). The vaqueros did all the work with the cattle, including the round ups, branding, and slaughter, or mantanza. The Native American workers were often treated harshly.

During the Mexican California era, the economy of the Californios was based on cattle. After 1835, following secularization, private ranches, rather than the missions, were the main source of the hides. In fact, the dried cowhides were known as "California banknotes" and were worth as much as two dollars each. Hides and tallow produced at the ranchos were traded or bartered for manufactured goods, such as shoes, boots, and finer clothing, along with household items (china, flatware, utensils, and hardware) and furniture brought on foreign ships. (Trading ships from the East Coast made the voyage around South America's Cape Horn.) Some of the other products that these ships carried were dry goods, guns and gunpowder, liquor, tea, coffee, sugar, spices, and other foods. For the women, there were items such as shawls, jewelry, and combs. The California hides were taken back to Boston, where they were tanned and turned into shoes and other leather products, while the tallow went to Europe and South America, where it was used to make soap and candles. The hide and tallow trade with Britain, New England, Asia, and South America (Peru and Chile), and the Sandwich Islands (now Hawaii) expanded greatly in the Mexican California period, from 1821 to 1846.

Richard Henry Dana, Jr.

The hide and tallow trade of the 1830's in Mexican California, was described by Richard Henry Dana, Jr., in his widely read classic book, *Two Years Before the Mast* (1840). Author Richard Henry Dana, Jr. (1815-1882) was born to a well-to-do New England family in Cambridge, Massachusetts. His grandfather, Francis Dana was a jurist and Massachusetts Chief Justice; his father Richard Henry Dana, Sr. was a lawyer, poet, and essayist. Richard Henry Dana, Jr. studied with poet and philosopher Ralph Waldo Emerson. After two years of study, he left Harvard for medical reasons to become a sailor on the *Pilgrim*, a Bryant, Sturgis & Company ship. In August 1834, at age 19, Richard Henry Dana, Jr. departed from Boston on a voyage aboard the *Pilgrim* to Mexican California, via Cape Horn. He chose to work at sea as a way to regain his health, and was away during all of 1835 and part of 1836, including sixteen months he spent along California's coast, on the merchant ship involved in the hide and tallow trade. Dana kept a journal filled with his observations, which he used for his book. Early in 1835, the ship reached the California coast, and entered Monterey Bay in mid-January. During the time he spent in Monterey, he observed its importance as a port. Dana described how cargo was inspected and how trading aboard a ship occurred. He took note of the way the society in Mexican California was organized by hierarchy based on the amount of Spanish blood a person had. Dana liked the sound of the Spanish language and the way the Californios dressed. Yet he was critical of the character of the Californios, whom he generalized as, "...idle, thriftless people and can make nothing for themselves".[1] Richard Henry Dana, Jr. made observations about the California coastline, weather, and topography. He also visited the Carmel Mission in 1835. As he praised the vast size and potential of California, he predicted it would become part of the United States. Dana wrote, "In the hands of an enterprising people, what a country this might be!"[2]

In 1836, at the age of 21, Richard Henry Dana, Jr. returned to Boston. There he continued his studies at Harvard and graduated in 1837. He wrote *Two Years Before the Mast: A Personal Narrative of Life at Sea*, while he studied law and became a lawyer who specialized in admiralty law. The book was published in 1840 and has been in print ever since. It spread interest and information about California to a large audience. *Richard Henry Dana, Jr. visited California again in 1859. Late in his life, he and his wife traveled in Europe for a decade; they moved to Paris and afterwards to Rome, where he died in 1882.*

THE END OF MEXICAN CALIFORNIA (1846) AND CALIFORNIA STATEHOOD (1850)

Many of the problems that Spain experienced with the settlements in Spanish California also plagued Mexico during the 1820's through the 1840's. The Mexican government did not pay enough attention to the California territory just as had happened under Spanish rule earlier. This was due in part to the distance, as well as to internal political matters in Mexico. The inattention became more pronounced after the secularization of the missions in the mid-1830's. Additionally, the local political systems in California were ineffective because of rivalries, jealousies, and power struggles. It was costly and burdensome for Mexico to support the presidios and the pueblos. The viceroy in Mexico City sent little money for upkeep in California, thus many structures were in disrepair. The soldiers who manned the presidios were often outcasts,

---

1   Richard Henry Dana, Jr., *Two Years Before the Mast, A Personal Narrative*, (1840), 3rd Edition, 1985, p. 59

2   *ibid.*, p. 134

such as former convicts, who frequently had bad attitudes and were poorly paid, or at times were not paid for months.

The increased trade with New England, Europe, and South America during the Mexican era provided needed supplies of essential goods, as well as luxury items. However this trade and contact with the outside world and the new progressive ideas it brought, in turn, decreased Mexico's grip on the region. As more Americans and other foreigners arrived and settled down in Mexican California and married into local Californio families, the population grew. There was an increased resentment of Mexican control and a desire for local rule. So many new and heavy duties on imports were added on the cargo that arrived at the Custom House in Monterey, that trade fell off and smuggling increased, as did corruption. (The duty on a ship's goods was as high as 42%, in addition to other fees on the cargo.) Mexico also imposed increasingly higher tariffs on the California rancho products, hides, which were also expensive to transport from the inland ranchos. Additionally, there were political squabbles over who would control the Custom House, as the governor made the appointments. Inevitably, all of these factors would lead towards calls for California's independence.

Manifest Destiny

During this time in the 1840's, the United States expanded its territory, and lawmakers had a strong interest in acquiring California, whether by diplomacy, purchase, or through force, and thus war with Mexico appeared inevitable. Senators such as Thomas Hart Benton were proponents of what was called "Manifest Destiny", which was the belief that God wanted Americans to settle across the entire continent, stretching from the Atlantic Coast to the Pacific Coast. There were several challenges to Mexico's authority over California. For example, in October 1842, U.S. Navy Commodore Thomas ap Catesby Jones, who was in charge of the forces in the Pacific, the Pacific Squadron, sailed the *United States* into Monterey Bay. He raised the American flag at the Custom House, claimed Monterey for the United States, and then subsequently apologized for the mistake, which was attributed to a false assumption that the United States and Mexico were at war. Monterey merchant Thomas O. Larkin mediated between Jones and the ex-Mexican Governor, Juan Bautista Alvarado and convinced Jones that he was mistaken. (At the time of the incident, Manuel Micheltorena (term 1842-1845), the newly appointed Mexican Governor, was on his way to Monterey.)

John Augustus Sutter

John Augustus Sutter (birth name: Johann August Suter) (1803-1880) was born in Germany, but grew up in Switzerland, and his parents were Swiss. He was a "self-proclaimed" Captain in the Royal Swiss (army) Guard. Sutter left his family, wife and children in Switzerland and came to the United States in 1834. He was a trapper in the Rocky Mountains and Pacific Northwest for a while and was an adventurer, trader, and pioneer. In 1839 Sutter arrived in Monterey and became a naturalized Mexican citizen. He spoke Spanish and English. By the early 1840's, Governor Alvarado gave him a large land grant of nearly 50,000 acres, or 11 square leagues, in the Sacramento Valley area, near the Sacramento and American Rivers. Sutter called this area "New Helvetia" (New Switzerland). He built a large fort there, Sutter's Fort, with thick adobe walls as fortification. In 1841 Sutter bought the cannons, horses, and cattle from Fort Ross, the Russian fort along the Northern California coast, which the Russians had deserted. [Sutter's Fort in Sacramento is State Historical Landmark No. 525.] General Mariano Guadalupe Vallejo and John Sutter were two of the largest land owners in the northern area of Mexican California, with Vallejo in the Northwestern region, and Sutter in the Northeastern region. They protected the territory; both men had much power, status, and influence. Vallejo founded the Pueblo of Sonoma in 1835. Sutter employed many American immigrants who had recently arrived to the area, some of whom were Mormons. At times up to 500 people were at his compound. In addition to Sutter's Fort, he used his vast land for agriculture, ranching, and other trades. He had hunters and trappers, tanners, blacksmiths, carpenters, millwrights, and brandy distillers. Sutter also had a store, which sold needed supplies to overland travelers who had just crossed over the Sierra Nevada Mountains into the California foothills.

The discovery of gold 1848

James Wilson Marshall (1810-1885) was a blacksmith, carpenter, and millwright from New Jersey, who came to California in the mid-1840's, and worked for John Sutter. Marshall was building a sawmill for Sutter, to be used to cut lumber for construction. On January 24, 1848, in Coloma, in El Dorado County, Marshall discovered gold in the south fork of the American River, near Sacramento. *[The site is State Historical Landmark No. 143.]*

The Gold Rush of 1849

Samuel Brannan (1819-1889), an influential Mormon entrepreneur, became a merchant at Sutter's Fort. Shortly after gold was discovered in late January 1848, Brannan went to San Francisco in March of that year to spread the news. He staked a claim to the area where gold was discovered and he received royalties (of one third) from the Mormon miners, which made him one of the richest men in California. He also soon began selling mining equipment, which brought him much profit, as well. After President James K. Polk addressed Congress in December 1848 about the California gold discovery, the national and international gold frenzy went into full force. As word of gold spread, tens of thousands of Americans and many foreigners from around the globe, including Asia, South America, Europe, and Australia, flocked to California by land and by sea. Thus James Marshall's discovery on John Sutter's land in early 1848 triggered the California Gold Rush of 1849. As many made fortunes, however, others were not as lucky. In the aftermath of the Gold Rush, John Sutter lost many of his workers, who abandoned him to prospect. Along with the loss of his livestock, Sutter also had thousands of squatters on his land. Sacramento was the site of the worst squatters violence, including several deaths.

By 1852, after years of legal battles over the title to his land, which was confirmed, John Sutter had lost all of his money. During part of the 1860's and 1870's, the State of California had given him a pension of $250 a month. Sutter left California in the 1870's and moved to Pennsylvania. He spent much of his time trying to petition Congress. John Sutter died in a Washington D.C. hotel in 1880. James W. Marshall also received a state pension for a short while, in the 1870's *and he too died poor, in 1885, near Coloma, in El Dorado County, close to the location where he discovered gold.*

The Mexican-American War (1846-1848)

From 1844 to 1848 Thomas O. Larkin served as the first and only U.S. Consul at Monterey, and his home was used as the American Consulate at Monterey. Beginning in 1845, Larkin also served under President James K. Polk's administration (term 1845-1849) as a confidential State Department agent who received communication from the Secretary of State, James Buchanan. Thomas O. Larkin was told to diplomatically urge the Californios to become independent from Mexico and to join the United States as Americans. However, a dispute over the Texas border led President Polk, after he received congressional approval, to declare war with Mexico on May 13, 1846.

Bear Flag Revolt

As the calls for independence increased among Californios, small insurrections occurred more frequently, such as the Bear Flag Revolt. A group of about three dozen American settlers led by William B. Ide (1796-1852) captured General Mariano Guadalupe Vallejo, who was in charge of the Mexico's Northern California frontier. Though Vallejo was sympathetic to the Americans and even supported U.S. annexation of California, he was arrested along with other men and they were imprisoned at Sutter's Fort. The members of the Bear Flag Revolt declared a "California Republic", free of Mexican rule, in Sonoma on June 14, 1846. They raised a white flag with a grizzly bear and a star. The flag was designed by William L. Todd, whose aunt Mary Todd Lincoln was the wife of Abraham Lincoln. (In 1911 the official state flag of California was adopted and it is similar to the one used in the Bear Flag Revolt. It has a white background with a red stripe along the bottom, a brown grizzly bear in the center walking towards the left on grass, a red star in the upper left corner, and the words "California Republic" along the bottom beneath the bear, above the red stripe.) Robert Semple (1806-1854) who came from Kentucky originally, and was a dentist and a printer, was also a leader of the Bear Flag Revolt. James Marshall took part in it, as well. However the Bear Flag Republic did not last long, it remained just under a month. *[There is a Bear Flag Monument at the Sonoma Plaza where the events occurred; it is State Historical Landmark No. 7.]*

Sloat raises the U.S. flag at Monterey Bay, 1846

On July 7, 1846, the Pacific Squadron Commander, U.S. Navy Commodore John Drake Sloat (1781-1867), with three U.S. ships and over 200 sailors and marines, landed at the beach at Monterey Bay and raised the American flag at the Custom House at the Port of Monterey. After a 21-gun salute from the three U.S. ships, he read a proclamation of war that annexed Monterey and Alta California for the United States. Thus Mexican rule of California ended and U.S. annexation of California began without bloodshed or impediment. Sloat's proclamation was read in San Francisco a few days later and also in Sonoma, and thus those areas, as well as others, were annexed by the United States. General Vallejo and the other prisoners who were held at Sutter's Fort were released. Later in July 1846, Commodore Robert Field Stockton (1795-1866) replaced Commodore Sloat, who was in poor health and retired as head of the Pacific Squadron.

Reverend Walter Colton

During the period between 1846, after Commodore Sloat's landing and 1850, when California was admitted into the United States, there was a mixture of military rule and civilian administration in California. Under Mexican California's alcalde system, which remained in place, the alcalde was a powerful position, which combined the duties of mayor and judge, as well as sheriff, prosecutor, tax collector, and administrator. Reverend Walter Colton (1797-1851) came to Monterey in 1846, as the U.S. was at war with Mexico. He was appointed the first American alcalde of Monterey by Commodore Robert F. Stockton. Colton served in the post for three years, from 1846 to 1849. Colton had been a Protestant minister from Vermont. He graduated from Yale and Andover Theological Seminary. Colton had been a U.S. Navy Chaplain since 1831, and was the Navy Chaplain on the *Congress*, which was Commodore Stockton's ship.

Reverend Walter Colton was also a writer, journalist, and newspaper editor. One of his books was titled, *Ship and Shore* (1835). In Monterey, on August 15, 1846, Reverend Walter Colton along with Robert Semple founded and co-edited the first American newspaper in California, *The Californian*. It had separate columns in Spanish and English. The actual printing press was set up at the Custom House and the newspaper was printed on whatever paper could be found, including tissue paper and cigarette-wrapping paper. Samuel Brannan had founded a newspaper in San Francisco, *The California Star*, soon after *The Californian* was established, with its first issue on January 9, 1847. In January 1849, *The Californian* and *The California Star* joined and became the *Alta California* newspaper, published in English in San Francisco, from 1849 to 1891.

Colton Hall

Starting in 1847, Reverend Walter Colton built the two-story building known as Colton Hall in Monterey, located on Pacific Street between Jefferson and Madison Streets. As alcalde, Reverend Colton put convicts he arrested to work on the building. He also brought in money for the construction from the sale of town lots, fines on gamblers, and taxes on liquor. Colton Hall was finished in March 1849. It was built in the Federalist style, similar to other such buildings on the East Coast. Colton Hall was the first public building for secular use and unlike anything built at the time on the West Coast. It was made from white stone (Monterey shale), which was quarried nearby. Colton Hall featured a main, two-story wood portico with stairways on both sides, two-story columns, and a balcony. The lower floor was used as a schoolhouse, while the upper floor was a public town hall, which measured 70 feet long by 30 feet wide. *[Today the upper floor of Colton Hall is a museum, while there are city offices on the lower floor. It is State Historical Landmark No. 126.]* In 1849, Reverend Colton left California, and as he was still in the Navy, he was relocated to the Navy Yard in Philadelphia. He wrote a book about his time in California, *Three Years in California* (1850), which he dedicated to General Mariano Guadalupe Vallejo, his friend. *Reverend Walter Colton died in 1851, in Philadelphia shortly after the book was published.*

Treaty of Guadalupe Hidalgo

The Treaty of Guadalupe Hidalgo on February 2, 1848 ended the Mexican-American War. The United States government paid $15 million dollars for the Mexican land north of the Rio Grande River that the U.S. annexed. Mexico lost forty percent of its territory, one million square miles of land, including what became the states of California, Arizona, New Mexico, Nevada, Utah, along with parts of Idaho, Wyoming, and Colorado. The Rio Grande River was established as the southwestern border of the United States. The U.S. also paid $3.25 million dollars in compensation for claims that American citizens were owed by Mexico.

California Statehood

California's last military governor before statehood, General Bennet Riley (1787-1853), who was appointed April 12, 1849, called for a constitutional convention. California's first Constitutional Convention was held in Monterey and began on September 3, 1849. There were forty-eight delegates from throughout California and they met for six weeks on the entire upper floor of Colton Hall, from early September 1849 through mid-October 1849. Many prominent members of Mexican California society played a role. Robert Semple was a delegate and president of the Constitutional Convention. Other delegates who drafted California's first constitution were Thomas O. Larkin, Pablo de la Guerra (the son of Don José de la Guerra and William Hartnell's brother-in-law), John Sutter, and General Mariano Guadalupe Vallejo. William Hartnell did translation between Spanish and English. (In California, both Spanish and English were the legal languages until the second Constitutional Convention, in 1879, which resulted in the second state constitution. One change that came about was that English became the official language of the state.)

The Great Seal of the State of California with the goddess Minerva, the Roman goddess of wisdom, war, and commerce, was created and adopted during the convention. The seal also depicted a grizzly bear, agricultural products (wheat and grapes), a miner, sailing ships, and the Sierra Nevada Mountains in the background. There were thirty-one stars, which represented the number of states at the time, and the motto, "Eureka", which means, "I have found it!" at the top.

The convention delegates completed the document on October 12, 1849, and then held a ball that evening at Colton Hall to celebrate. They signed the constitution the next day, October 13, 1849. Cannons boomed in a

31-gun salute. On November 13, 1849 there was a general election, and the state constitution was ratified by a large margin, though the state had not been admitted into union yet, because there was the issue of whether California would be a free or slave state. Under the Compromise of 1850, California entered the union as the 31st state, a free state, on September 9, 1850. *[The divide over slavery in the United States led to the Civil War, which was fought from 1861 to 1865, and the Thirteenth Amendment in 1865 freed the slaves.]* On December 15, 1849, California's capital was moved from Monterey to San Jose, where the legislature met. In 1851, the state capital was transferred to Vallejo, and in 1853 it was relocated to Benicia. (In the late 1840's Robert Semple with General Mariano Vallejo and Thomas O. Larkin, developed the San Francisco Bay Area city of Benicia, which was a part of Vallejo's rancho land, along the Carquinez Strait.) In 1854, the state capital was moved to Sacramento, where it remains.

3

The Decline of Monterey and David Jacks

THE LAND ACT OF 1851

Once California was part of the United States, there was the question of how to confirm the validity of the land grants made during the Spanish and Mexican eras. The Land Act of 1851, passed by Congress, set up the Land Commission with a three member Board of Land Commissioners based in San Francisco, whose function was to decide the validity of these claims. The burden of proof of ownership was on those who held the title. The process of issuing land grant patents affected individual land-holders, along with towns and cities, as well as the missions. If the claims were determined to be valid, based on evidence presented, a patent was given by the United States government. However, many of the original Mexican land grant boundaries were not well defined and their documentation was questionable. This process to prove valid land ownership went on for years and years; it took an average of 17 years for patents to be given. It was expensive, due to the cost of hiring lawyers and the drawn out litigation; as a result many people went bankrupt because of these expenses. If the land grant claims were rejected, they could be reviewed by a district court or even appealed to the United States Supreme Court. The Land Commission existed for five years, until March 1856, and it went over 800 claims; 600 of them were accepted. The land claims that were ultimately rejected or deemed invalid became part of the public domain or public land. In the process, many people, as well as former pueblos, even the missions, lost their land.

Carmel Mission land

Mission San Carlos Borroméo del Río Carmelo, along with the other California missions, fell into disrepair in the years after they were secularized in the 1830's. In 1852, the tile roof of the Carmel Mission fell in; the neglected roof beams had rotted and had given way under the weight of the roof tiles. Once the roof collapsed, the mission's adobe walls followed, as they were no longer protected. The mission remained roofless for the next three decades. By the 1860's, according to a geological survey report by botanist William H. Brewer in 1861, the Carmel Mission was in such ruin that the walls were crumbling, birds made their nests inside the structures, and squirrels could be seen running around all over. Scientist William Henry Brewer (1827-1910) who was educated at Yale and in Europe, took part in a four-year geological survey of the entire state of California from 1860 to 1864. The results of the California Geological Survey were published in 1865. Later, letters he wrote to his brother were edited in a book, *Up and Down California in 1860-1864: The Journal of William H. Brewer* (1930).

On February 19, 1853 Archbishop Joseph Sadoc Alemany (1814-1888) filed petitions with the Board of Land Commissioners, which presented the land claims for the Catholic Church to receive title to the 21 California missions. (Catalonian-born Alemany began as a Dominican missionary who came to the United States in 1840. He became Bishop of Monterey in 1850, when California was a state. A few years later, he was named the first Archbishop of San Francisco; he remained Archbishop from 1853 through 1884, when he retired and returned to Spain, where he died in 1888.)

The land confirmed in the patents for most of the missions was limited. It mainly consisted of the areas associated with religious purposes, such as church buildings and cemeteries, along with gardens. On October 19, 1859 the patent was granted for the Carmel Mission and signed by

President James Buchanan. The title was for about nine acres of land, which went back to the Catholic Church.

THE DECLINE OF MONTEREY (1850's THROUGH THE MID-1870's)

As people rushed to California's gold country and as the state became more populated, Monterey's population dramatically decreased, especially among men. On a visit to Monterey in 1860 to 1861, William H. Brewer noted that the population was 1,600. He also noticed that more than half of the businesses in Monterey were either liquor shops or billiard saloons. Author Robert Louis Stevenson (1850-1894), who spent several months in Monterey in the fall of 1879, also observed, "There was no activity but in and around the saloons, where people sat almost all day long playing cards."[3] He wrote his descriptions of Monterey in the essay, "The Old Pacific Capital". Stevenson continued,

> "The town, when I was there, was a place of two or three streets, economically paved with sea-sand...There were no street lights. Short sections of wooden sidewalk only added to the dangers of the night, for they were often high above the level of the roadway, and no one could tell where they would be likely to begin or end."[4]

During most of the 1850's until 1889, Monterey was not incorporated as a city. Its incorporation was repealed in 1850, 1851, and 1853, and the city charter was changed so that Monterey was run by a Board of Trustees, rather than a city council. The trustees met infrequently, and as a result, Monterey did not have a vigorous form of government. Furthermore, Monterey had lost its importance as the leading port in California to San Francisco, because of the Gold Rush activity in Northern California. There was little economic industry other than Portuguese whalers, who could be found around Monterey Bay and Point Lobos in the 1860's,

---

3   Robert Louis Stevenson, "The Old Pacific Capital", *Across the Plains, with other Memories and Essays*, p. 93

4   *ibid.*, p. 92

and Chinese fishermen along what became the Pebble Beach and Pacific Grove coasts. Furthermore, Monterey not only lost its status as the state capital in 1849, but as the result of the election in November 1872, by a popular vote, it lost the Monterey County seat, which was moved to Salinas. Robert Louis Stevenson described Monterey as "...a mere bankrupt village..."[5] due to the loss of the state capital and the county seat, as well as the weakened local government. With the decline of its population, prestige, and clout, Monterey remained stuck in a bygone time and was cut off from much of the rest of the state for the next quarter century—from 1850 through the mid-1870's.

David Jacks

Since the Gold Rush era, the prospect of making a fortune enticed many to come to California. Among them was a Scottish immigrant, David Jack(s) (1822-1909), who left Scotland in 1842, when he was 19 years old, for the East Coast of the United States. After working for several years as a clerk in New York, he arrived in California in 1848, as a civilian who worked for the U.S. Army, and went to San Francisco, where he became a naturalized citizen in 1849. He came to Monterey in 1850 with $4,000, which he made by selling $18 revolvers marked up to $50 each in San Francisco. David Jacks worked in the 1850's as a clerk for two general store proprietors in Monterey. With the money he saved, he bought a few acres of land in Carmel Valley, where he started a farm; he grew potatoes, beans, and barley, and raised hogs, but failed to make a profit. After a yearlong trip back to Scotland, David Jacks returned to Monterey, in short order only to become Monterey County's largest and most powerful landowner, and along with that, the wealthiest, most notorious, and some would say most despised man in all of Monterey.

Delos Rodeyn Ashley

Delos Rodeyn Ashley (1828-1873) was an attorney who was hired in 1853 by Monterey to obtain the patent for the land, which had been granted to the pueblo of Monterey. The Monterey land grant was a total of 29,698 acres; the pueblo of Monterey had received it in 1826 from the

---

5   *ibid.*, p. 92

Mexican Governor José Echeandía. Mr. Ashley presented the necessary requirements to secure the patent and obtain the legal title of the grant for Monterey when he appeared in San Francisco at the U.S. Board of Land Commissioners in March 1853. During the mid-to-late 1850's Delos Ashley was a California state legislator. He was elected to the California State Assembly (1854-1856) and the California State Senate (1856-1857), and in this position he was able to influence and pass legislation that had an impact on his and his associates' interests in Monterey. For example, in 1857, the state legislature passed an amendment to Monterey's city charter, which allowed the trustees to sell its land at a public auction to pay for debts incurred in obtaining the title to its land. In 1855, Delos Ashley co-founded the *Monterey Sentinel* newspaper with John McElroy. In 1856 the paper was moved to Santa Cruz, and became known as the *Pacific Sentinel*, and later the *Santa Cruz Sentinel*.

Monterey pueblo land title

In 1856, the U.S. Board of Land Commissioners confirmed Monterey's land title and the city acquired the patent to the 29,698 acres of former pueblo land. Delos Ashley submitted a fee of $991.50 to Monterey for his legal services in 1853. However in view of Monterey's continued financial difficulties, there were no funds to pay Ashley. Under the law, which Ashley had played a role in, the Monterey trustees had to sell off the city lands to pay him. The notice of sale, however, did not appear in any local newspapers, and was only written as a minor item in the *Santa Cruz Sentinel*. It stated that all Monterey city lands were to be auctioned for the total sum of $1002.50 at 5pm outside of Colton Hall, on February 9, 1859. At that time and place, the only bidders were Delos Ashley and David Jacks. They purchased the entire parcel of nearly 30,000 acres of land surrounding Monterey as well as portion of the city itself for $1,002.50, which amounted to three cents an acre. Furthermore, the $1,002.50 which Monterey received from the sale of the land was used to pay Ashley's legal fee of $991.50, and $11 for the sale's expense, which added up to $1,002.50, the exact cost of the purchase. Delos Ashley and David Jacks received the title to the land that same day, February 9, 1859.

Delos Ashley remained in politics; he was California State Treasurer from 1862 to 1863. He sold his interest in the Sentinel *newspaper in 1865. Ashley moved to Nevada, which became a state in 1864, where he was elected as a Republican U. S. Congressman, for two terms, from 1865 through 1869. By 1868, Delos Ashley had sold the last portion of his land to David Jacks for $500. Delos R. Ashley died on July 18, 1873.*

David Jacks becomes the Monterey Peninsula's largest landowner

In 1861, when he was nearly 40 years old, David Jacks married a woman from a wealthy Californio family, Maria Christina de la Soledad Romie. (Her German-born parents went to Mexico in 1835, where she was born, and the family came to Monterey in 1841.) David and Maria Jacks would have seven children who survived childhood. Through the years, David Jacks was involved in many frequent lawsuits, both as a defendant and a plaintiff. In 1866 and again in 1877, the citizens of Monterey came together to sue Jacks to get back the city's land, but in spite of those two lawsuits, one of which eventually was carried to the U.S. Supreme Court, the sale stood. David Jacks used his powerful political connections for his benefit. For example, he would find out information about sheriff's sales of ranchos that belonged to owners who had defaulted on their tax payments. Jacks then bought the properties, paid the taxes, and either kept the land or resold it for a profit back to its previous owners. Jacks also was able to influence lawmakers in various ways; for some time he persuaded the California legislature to keep Monterey's government as a board of trustees, rather than a city council, which would have made Monterey a stronger, incorporated city. Many people not only hated David Jacks, particularly those who felt cheated by him, but he was even physically threatened at times, and had to hire a bodyguard. Eventually through questionable and insider business tactics and predatory financial lending, in which he took over property that had been used as collateral, David Jacks continued to amass local land. Much of this land included a number of ranchos, which made his total land holdings in the Monterey area around 90,000 acres. His land from two of these ranchos, Rancho Punta de Piños (Point Piños), 2,667 acres, and Rancho El Pescadero (Pescadero), 4,426 acres, amounted to more than 7,000 acres of land on the Monterey Peninsula. They consisted of scenic coastland, which would become Pacific Grove, Pebble Beach, and Carmel-by-the-Sea. Jacks also owned Rancho Aguajito, east of Rancho El Pescadero, which was 3,323 acres. In addition to being the largest landowner in Monterey County, as a businessman, David Jacks was involved in numerous other enterprises in the region. These included dairies, the sale of sand to glass manufacturers, and the sale of pine and cypress trees and seedlings to nurseries. He also rented portions of his vast land holdings in the Salinas Valley to farmers and on the Monterey coast to fishermen.

Chinese fishing villages

Since the mid-1850's there was a Chinese fishing village at Point Cabrillo, in what became Pacific Grove (at the site of the current Hopkins Marine Station and near today's Monterey Bay Aquarium and Cannery Row). There was also a Chinese fishing village at Point Alones (part of the Punta de Piños Rancho, now near Cannery Row in New Monterey) and at Pescadero (in what became Pebble Beach's Stillwater Cove). This was all land owned by David Jacks, who rented portions of it to the Chinese fishermen on the Monterey Peninsula. (When the Italian fishermen arrived in Monterey in the 1870's, the Chinese fishermen, who already collected abalone, began to fish for squid, especially at night, which they dried and sold to China.)

The Monterey wharf (1870)

The first Pacific Mail Steamship landed in Monterey in 1847, and the United States Post Office was established in Monterey in 1848. From that time onwards, there were regular, weekly steamer and schooner arrivals at the Port of Monterey. By the 1860's the inland areas, such as the Salinas Valley, where David Jacks owned and leased land, expanded the production of grain, as well as other agricultural and dairy products. In the late 1860's at the urging of David Jacks, the state legislature granted Monterey the title to the waterfront, to be controlled by the Board of Trustees. The Board of Trustees of Monterey in turn leased the property to David Jacks and several other business partners (Charles M. Goodall, Christopher Nelson, and George Clement Perkins) for $1 a year with the understanding that they would pay for the construction of the wharf. The Monterey wharf was built in 1870.

Goodall & Nelson began in 1860 as a tugboat company, which expanded by the mid-1860's, with added steamers and schooners between San Francisco and Monterey. When George Perkins joined the company in 1872, it was known Goodall, Nelson & Perkins. Perkins, a Republican, would be California's Governor (1880-1883) and a longtime U.S. Senator from California (1893-1915). Goodall, Nelson & Perkins bought out the Pacific Mail Steamship Company in 1874, and with the addition of their fleet, had a total of fifteen steamers and three schooners. The company, then known as Goodall, Nelson & Perkins Steamship Company, dominated the Pacific coastal trade from Alaska to the north, to Central America to the south. In 1876 it was renamed the Pacific Coast Steamship Company.

The Monterey and Salinas Valley Railroad (M&SVRR)

In 1874, David Jacks and a Salinas businessman, Carlisle Abbott, along with 72 other mostly small investors, chartered and built a 19-mile long, narrow gauge railroad between Monterey and Salinas, the Monterey and Salinas Valley Railroad (M&SVRR), at a cost of $300,000 in capital stock in the company. Jacks was the treasurer of the railroad. The Monterey and Salinas Valley Railroad was built to offer a cheaper way to transport agricultural products from the area, and provide an alternative to the Southern Pacific Railroad, which since 1872 ran from San Jose south through Salinas and down to Soledad, and charged high rates. Many of those who invested in the M&SVRR also hoped it would increase their land values. It transported passengers, freight, and agricultural products from Salinas to the Monterey wharf, where the Pacific Coast Steamship Company coastal steamers arrived and on an average day transported about 300 tons of produce up to the San Francisco market and then across the country.

§

PACIFIC GROVE METHODIST RETREAT

At the invitation of David Jacks, in 1873, a Methodist minister, Reverend J. W. Ross, visited the area, which became Pacific Grove. The pine trees, ocean, fresh air, and climate were similar to other health resorts on the East Coast, yet Pacific Grove had the advantage of a temperate climate nearly year-round. Ross made the trip to improve his respiratory health, and after a few months outdoors, the minister recovered. In 1874, Reverend Ross returned with his brother and both of their wives, who all had respiratory problems as well, and their conditions also improved. Reverend Ross invited Bishop J. T. Peck from San Francisco, who was a member of the Methodist Retreat Association, to show him the area. The Bishop chose to start a spiritual retreat and health resort there along the coast. The Methodists established the Pacific Grove Retreat Association in June 1875 and David Jacks gave them 100 acres for the formation of the religious retreat in Pacific Grove, located along the shoreline east of Point Piños. It was known as the Pacific Grove Retreat, also "God's Kingdom By-the-Sea", and was advertised as a "Christian Sea-side Resort", modeled on the town of Ocean Grove, New Jersey. Jacks also loaned the group $30,000 for construction of the town streets, buildings, and other improvements to the site. The acreage was divided into lots, which Jacks sold, starting at $50 a lot. Tents were set up and cottages were built on these residential lots, the smallest of which were 30 by 50 feet for the tents, while the larger ones were 30 by 125 feet for the cottages.

The first religious camp meeting or summer encampment was held in August 1875 for three weeks. Around 400 people attended, and most camped in tents. There were indoor sessions at a tent set up where Jewell Park is today, and outdoor prayer sessions, held at the rocky promontory, referred to as "Lovers of Jesus Point", and now known as Lovers Point. The summer encampment became an annual event. Soon, in 1879 the Pacific Grove Retreat was a site for Chautauqua meetings, the first in the West, as well as a location for where some other religious groups met every year. (The Chautauqua movement was popular in the late 19th and early 20th centuries across the United States, and it featured adult education, entertainment, lectures, cultural activities, concerts, and family-oriented events, usually held outdoors.)

4

The Railroads and The Hotel Del Monte

THE RAILROADS AND THE BIG FOUR

The Transcontinental Railroad (1869)

During the 1850's and 1860's the number of railroads and amount of railroad track in the United States increased. The Central Pacific Railroad came about in 1861 in Sacramento, when four Northern California businessmen, Collis Potter Huntington (1821-1900), Amasa Leland Stanford (1824-1893), Charles Crocker (1822-1888), and Mark Hopkins (1813-1878), known as the "Big Four", though they were also referred to as "The Associates", partnered along with engineer Theodore Judah (1826-1863). Huntington and Hopkins operated a profitable business, Huntington & Hopkins Hardware Store, in Sacramento, while Crocker sold dry goods. Stanford, a grocer, was also a lawyer and Republican political candidate. [*The building where the Big Four had their offices and the Huntington & Hopkins Hardware Store was located in downtown Sacramento is National Historic Landmark #76000541.*] Congress passed and President Abraham Lincoln signed the first Pacific Railway Act of 1862, which gave the go ahead for two railroad companies, the Central Pacific and the Union Pacific, to lay track that would join both sides of the country and create the first transcontinental railroad in the United States. The Central

Pacific Railroad would build the western-most portion, which began in Sacramento in 1863 and would go eastward. *[The site where construction began in Sacramento on January 8, 1863 is State Historical Landmark No. 780.]* While the Union Pacific Railroad would begin in Omaha, Nebraska, and would go westward from the Missouri River. The Central Pacific and Union Pacific Railroads secured federal incentives such as land grants, loans, bonds, and financial bonuses (for each mile of track built, which varied based on the difficulty of the terrain) from Congress, along with state and local governmental subsidies. Under the Pacific Railway Act, the railroad companies had the right to take timber for construction use. These railroad companies obtained millions of acres of government land and thus became the largest landholders in the Western United States. To further encourage the rapid construction of the railroad tracks, as an incentive for each mile of completed track, the railroad companies also received title to an additional 6,400 acres of land from the government, which the railroads would, in turn, sell to settlers. Congress passed a second Pacific Railway Act of 1864, which extended the deadline date for completion and amended parts of the first act. For example, it gave the railroad companies mineral rights in the land grants. It provided even more financial subsidies and land; it doubled the land grants for each mile of completed track to 12,800 acres, an additional incentive for the two railroad companies to continue the construction.

The Big Four earned millions of dollars in profits. They gained tremendous power along with this wealth in the United States, especially in California. As a further illustration of their political clout, Leland Stanford was not only president of the Central Pacific, but also was the governor of California from 1862 to 1863, and later was a U.S. Senator from California, from 1885 to 1893. (He established the private Leland Stanford Junior University (Stanford University), in Palo Alto, in honor of his only child, his son, Leland Stanford, Jr. (1868-1884) who died as a teenager in 1884. The university was founded in 1885, but opened in 1891.) Charles Crocker oversaw construction of the Central Pacific Railroad. Much of the work, which was hard, unsafe, and compensated by low pay, was done by thousands of Chinese laborers. Many of these workers were new immigrants and referred to as "Crocker's Pets". (Irish immigrants did much of the work on the construction of the Union Pacific Railroad).

On May 10, 1869 the last spike, which was made of gold, was hammered into the final railroad tie by Central Pacific president Leland Stanford at a ceremony at Promontory Summit in northern Utah (Utah Territory). Thus the Union Pacific and Central Pacific railroad tracks were joined. It took six years, from 1863 to 1869, to construct the First Transcontinental Railroad. During the 1860's and 1870's other railroads were soon built, which crisscrossed the country. (*After the Civil War ended, the amount of railroad track across the United States nearly doubled, from 30,000 miles of track in 1860 to more than 52,000 miles of track in 1870. By 1880 there were 93,000 miles of railroad track, and by 1900 there were 193,000 miles of railroad track in the United States, a sixfold increase in four decades.*) The expansion of the railroads brought economic growth, reduced shipping costs, and expanded markets nationally to ship manufactured goods, as well as agricultural products from California. The growth of the railroads also fostered the settlement of the Western frontier. The decision as to where a route would run could make the difference in whether a town would flourish or wither.

Southern Pacific Railroad

The Big Four expanded their control in California in the 1860's and 1870's through the acquisition of other smaller, independent railroads, as well as shipping carriers. In 1868, the Big Four acquired a second railroad line, the Southern Pacific Railroad, which had been established in 1865. The actual railroad had not been constructed yet, although it had state and federal charters and land grants to build it from San Jose to the Colorado River, at the California-Arizona border. That route would form the western part of a southern transcontinental railroad. Eventually, by 1883, under the Big Four, the Southern Pacific Railroad constructed a line that went through Southern California, the Southwest (Arizona and New Mexico), and the South (Texas and Louisiana). This route from Los Angeles to New Orleans was known as the "Sunset Route" on the "Sunset Limited" train. (Through further acquisitions, in the mid-to-late 1880's, the Southern Pacific Railroad went into the Pacific Northwest, with a link from Portland, Oregon to the Sacramento Valley.)

In the 1870's the Central Pacific became part of the Southern Pacific. By 1885 the two railroads were consolidated and controlled by the Big Four. Under the newly set up holding company, the Southern Pacific Company was headquartered in San Francisco, though incorporated in Kentucky. (Leland Stanford who was a California Senator at the time, was also president of the Southern Pacific until 1890, when its vice president, Collis Huntington became its president.) The Big Four, through their control of the Southern Pacific Railroad, were known to use business practices such as lowering rates and having disputes over routes with rival carriers in order to take over or drive their competition out of business. Customers and farmers criticized the high rates they had to pay in areas where the Southern Pacific was the only carrier. The Big Four also had tremendous public and political influence. In California by 1882, the Southern Pacific Railroad had received eleven and a half million acres of land from the government. These factors inspired hatred toward the Southern Pacific Railroad and the members of the Big Four. The Big Four's empire went far beyond just railroads. By the 1870's and 1880's they had almost total control over nearly all forms of transportation throughout California, including railroads, steamships, riverboats, passenger and freight ferries, and street cars. Critics perceived the Southern Pacific as an octopus with tentacles which tightly grasped control of an extensive and monopolistic transportation empire, with a corrupting influence over politics, politicians, and the media. *In 1880, a violent and deadly incident at Mussel Slough, in California's San Joaquin Valley, between settlers and law enforcement officials who tried to evict them on behalf of the railroad was the subject of Frank Norris's novel,* The Octopus: A Story of California *(1901). [The location marking the site of the deadly incident, which was originally in Tulare County at the time, is in Kings County and is State Historical Landmark No. 245.]*

Pacific Improvement Company

In 1878 the Southern Pacific Railroad's Big Four set up, owned, and operated the Pacific Improvement Company as a holding company involved in land development, real estate, and construction. (During the 1870's, prior to the Pacific Improvement Company's formation, this business was handled by the Western Development Company and its predecessor, the Contract and Finance Company.) The Pacific Improvement Company bought, developed, and promoted land in towns and resorts and constructed water systems and roads for the communities. The land in these developments built along the Southern Pacific railroad lines, was sold to settlers and immigrants and thus the areas became populated. These real estate operations were the most lucrative part of the Pacific Improvement Company's business. The Pacific Improvement Company, a private company, became one of the biggest Western corporations, with ownership of subsidiary companies including hotels and resorts, public utilities, mining operations, and water systems, along with transportation: shipping, steamships, ferries, and electric streetcars, and also a publishing business.

Southern Pacific Railroad line extends to Monterey

The 19-mile, narrow gauge Monterey and Salinas Valley Railroad, which was established by David Jacks and others in 1874 to provide a transportation alternative to the Southern Pacific Railroad, continuously lost money since it began. When the Southern Pacific cut its rates the M&SVRR was not able to compete and stay in business any longer. By 1879, the Monterey and Salinas Valley Railroad was sold to the Southern Pacific Railroad at a bargain price in a foreclosure auction sale, in the Southern Pacific's pattern of buying competing railroads for a greatly reduced sum, after it had driven them out of business. Shortly after the Southern Pacific Railroad bought the Monterey and Salinas Valley Railroad in 1879, the Big Four decided to extend the standard gauge Southern Pacific Railroad, which ran from San Francisco and ended in Castroville, further south, down to Monterey. In January 1880 construction finished on the extension of the line from Castroville to Monterey and the Southern Pacific Railroad also built a terminal in Monterey. This line became known as the Del Monte Express, the Monterey Express, or the "Daisy" Train, which was said to be the fastest train that the Southern Pacific Railroad ran on the Pacific Coast. The 125-mile trip from San Francisco to Monterey took three and a half hours, and the trains made the round trip twice a day. As railroad service was established between Monterey and San Francisco, there was now a connection to the transcontinental railroad and this brought visitors from around the country to the Monterey Peninsula. The beauty of the Monterey Peninsula, along with the success and popularity of the Pacific Grove Retreat and the number of people it attracted to the area had spurred the Big Four to act. They saw tremendous potential and financial opportunity in the transformation of the Monterey Peninsula into a resort and tourist destination, as well as a real estate development.

THE HOTEL DEL MONTE

In 1880, the Pacific Improvement Company bought 7,000 acres of land on the Monterey Peninsula from David Jacks, which included Rancho El Pescadero and Rancho Punta de Piños, along with 148 acres in Monterey, all for $35,800. (The land that Jacks sold included the Pacific Grove Retreat.) This price for the total amount of land came to around $5 an acre. The purchase included coastal land in the area that would become the Del Monte Forest, Pebble Beach, and the Seventeen Mile Drive. The Pacific Improvement Company also bought 144 acres of land from the Toomes family in Monterey for $5,300. (Albert G. Toomes (1817-1873) was a settler from Missouri who arrived in California in 1841. He spent most of the 1840's in Monterey where he partnered in a carpentry business with another American settler, Robert Hasty Thomes, from Maine.)

Charles Crocker led the Big Four's effort to establish an immense, luxury, resort hotel in Monterey, the Hotel Del Monte, described as "the Queen of American Watering Places". It was located about a quarter mile from the newly built Southern Pacific Railroad Depot in Monterey. Southern Pacific Railroad workers constructed the hotel. By June of 1880, after 100 days of labor and several hundreds of thousands of dollars in costs, ranging from a quarter to a half million dollars, the Pacific Improvement Company opened the Hotel Del Monte. It became one of the most elegant and exclusive resorts on the West Coast, if not all of the United States. The Hotel Del Monte was designed by Arthur Brown, Sr., who worked as a civil engineer for the Central Pacific and Southern Pacific Railroads. He was the Superintendent of the Bridge and Buildings Department. *[In his career, Arthur Brown Sr. did much work for the Big Four, and also oversaw the construction of the Crocker, Hopkins, and Stanford mansions on San Francisco's Nob Hill. There is sometimes confusion between him and his son, Arthur Brown,*

Jr., (1874-1957), an École des Beaux-Arts, Paris, educated architect, who went on to great prominence through his works which included San Francisco's City Hall, War Memorial Opera House, Coit Tower, and Temple Emanu-El, to name a few. Prior to the turn of the 20th century, there was also a well-known, unrelated architect in the San Francisco Bay Area, Arthur Page Brown (1859-1896), originally from New York, who designed the San Francisco Ferry Building.] The two-story Hotel Del Monte hotel was 380 feet long and 110 feet wide with large verandas. It had an 80-foot high tower, 50-foot turrets, which provided a sweeping view of the area, and a steep roof. The Hotel Del Monte was made of wood, and originally built in the Stick Style, which has been described as an eclectic mixture of Swiss, Gothic, and Victorian styles. (The Stick Style was used in the United States in the period from 1860 to 1890 and was popular in resort architecture and in homes in such locations as Newport, Rhode Island, Cape Cod, Massachusetts, and other New England coastal areas. Some of the characteristics of the Stick Style included extensive use of wood, steep pitched roofs, diagonal stickwork on the exterior, broad turrets, and large porches.)

The name of the hotel came from the Spanish word, "El Monte", meaning a grove of trees, as the hotel and its surrounding property were situated among oak, pine, and cypress trees. The Hotel Del Monte grounds covered 126 acres that were lavishly landscaped with rare plants, shrubs, flower-lined pathways, flowerbeds, lawns, and Arizona Gardens with cactuses. The landscape gardener was European-trained, Rudolph Ulrich. One of the most unique attractions was a giant outdoor maze of cypress hedges, which were four-feet thick and seven-feet high, known as the Cypress Maze, where the guests would walk through for entertainment. The gardens and pathways had benches, as well as swings and sand boxes for the children. There were lawn (and later surfaced) tennis courts, archery and croquet grounds, and a racetrack. A horse stable on the hotel grounds had telephone communication to the hotel. In the early years, the hotel guests were picked up at the train depot by horse-drawn carriages. There was a manmade, eleven-acre lake on the property, called Laguna del Rey, with rowboats; an attraction that was said to have been modeled on the Italian Riviera. About a half mile away from the Hotel Del Monte, along the Monterey Bay waterfront, there was a large bathing pavilion or bathhouse with a glass roof. It had four heated tanks of salt water, each with different temperatures. Each tank was 150 feet by 50 feet and held 275,000 gallons of water in total, which was all steam-heated. There were 200 dressing rooms for the guests.

The rates at the Hotel Del Monte began at $3 a day and $17.50 for a week's stay. The hotel was very large and designed to accommodate several hundred guests. There was a main lobby with ornate chandeliers and a large wooden staircase, a huge ballroom where Saturday night dances were held, a reading-room, a ladies' billiard room, a gentlemen's reading room, and a dining room, which could seat 500 people. The interior had elegant furniture. Near the hotel, there was a men's clubhouse with a billiard room, a bowling alley, a smoking room, and a bar. The Hotel Del Monte had an extensive staff of hundreds of workers to care for the grounds and the guests. These included many Chinese workers who were gardeners, housekeepers, laundrymen, and kitchen staffers. The Hotel Del Monte had gas lighting and there was hot and cold water. Initially, the water came from an artesian well on the property, but it proved to be insufficient for the impressive hotel and grounds.

Water pipeline

Shortly after the Hotel Del Monte opened, the Pacific Improvement Company had applied for water appropriation rights through Monterey County. The Pacific Improvement Company needed large amounts of water for its properties and thus built substantial water projects for its various land developments. In the early 1880's the company bought a vast amount of land in Carmel Valley, including Rancho Los Laureles (6,625 acres), part of the huge Rancho Los Tularcitos (26,581 acres), along with thousands of additional acres in Carmel Valley. Along with the purchase of the land, the Pacific Improvement Company obtained water rights and decided to use the Carmel River, which went through Carmel Valley, as its water source for the Hotel Del Monte and its surrounding land on the Monterey Peninsula.

In 1883, the Pacific Improvement Company spent several hundreds of thousands of dollars and used 700 Chinese laborers to build the original, Old Carmel River Dam on the Carmel River, where it was joined by San Clemente Creek, about 18-miles upstream from the Pacific Ocean. They constructed a 25-mile pipeline, 12-inches wide and made of iron, which carried the Carmel River water the distance to the Monterey Peninsula. (In 1921, the San Clemente Dam was built upstream from the original dam that the Pacific Improvement Company built on the Carmel River in the 1880's. Demolition work to tear down the San Clemente Dam for environmental and seismic safety reasons began in 2013. In 1949, an additional dam, the Los Padres Dam was built on the Carmel River, 25-miles upstream from the Pacific Ocean.) There were two reservoirs to store the water from the Carmel River on the Monterey Peninsula. The first one was built in Pacific Grove in 1883, and the other, the Clay Pit Reservoir was built in the Del Monte Forest in 1888. The first reservoir held 16,000,000 gallons of water, and the second, a much larger reservoir, held 140,000,000 gallons of water. The Pacific Improvement Company employed hundreds of Chinese workers to build the massive reservoirs. The water was distributed through pipes to the Hotel Del Monte and other parts of Monterey and Pacific Grove. The company advertised, "An Inexhaustible Supply of Pure Mountain Water is piped to every Lot and Street" from the Santa Lucia Mountains for its property developments. As an indication of the Pacific Improvement Company's powerful influence, the Hotel Del Monte was excluded from the city limits of Monterey when the city was incorporated in 1889, and therefore didn't have to pay property taxes to the city, in exchange and in gratitude for the water the Pacific Improvement Company brought to the area. (The Pacific Improvement Company's water system eventually became the Monterey County Water Works.)

The Seventeen Mile Drive and the Del Monte Forest

The Pacific Improvement Company built a scenic road or drive around the Monterey Peninsula, starting at the Hotel Del Monte and going along the shoreline, past the Chinese fishing villages through Pacific Grove, the Del Monte Forest, and the areas that would become Pebble Beach and Carmel-by-the-Sea. The Carmel Mission was one stop along the route. Construction of the route began in the early 1880's and the work to grade and macadamize the road was done by Chinese workers. (This 18-to-25-mile road was later known as the Seventeen Mile Drive and it is now a private, gated, toll road in Pebble Beach.) The Hotel Del Monte offered its guests a horse and carriage ride, known as a tally-ho, along the

Seventeen Mile Drive. (In 1884, Joseph O. Johnson, the Superintendent of the Pacific Grove Retreat for the Pacific Improvement Company, built a livery stable on Lighthouse Avenue in Pacific Grove. In 1886 he expanded it into the Mammoth Livery Stable, one of the largest on the West Coast. The stable provided horses and carriages for the Hotel Del Monte guests, and was a place where the guests could leave their personal horses and carriages, which they had brought with them. The Mammoth Livery Stable covered two blocks between Forest Avenue and Fountain Avenue to Laurel Avenue. It had an 80-foot high tower and stalls for nearly 100 horses. The stable burned down in 1909 in an arson fire.) These horse and carriage rides (tally-hos) were popular, entertaining, and gave visitors the opportunity to view the beauty of the area. Later the Pacific Improvement Company used the tour to show the Hotel Del Monte's wealthy guests real estate lots they could buy from the company.

Hotel Del Monte guests

The Hotel Del Monte promoted Monterey's year-round, comfortable and healthful climate, which appealed to East Coast visitors. The establishment attracted many elite and well-to-do guests who were part of national and international society. For example, some of the visitors included members of the Vanderbilt family, Joseph Pulitzer, and Andrew Carnegie. Additionally, three United States presidents stayed at the Hotel. President Benjamin Harrison visited in 1891, President William McKinley came in 1901, and President Theodore Roosevelt arrived in 1903. President Roosevelt rode horseback on a tour of the Seventeen Mile Drive. Since 1889, the local, weekly paper, the *Monterey Cypress*, wrote of the arrival of prominent guests and their social activities, along with sporting events at the Hotel Del Monte.

The Wave

The Southern Pacific Railroad company used and manipulated the media to get positive coverage and shape public opinion in its favor. Along with advertising, the Southern Pacific Railroad spent money on promotional publications, which appeared in newspapers and were authored by writers who were paid by the railroad. The Southern Pacific also published books and had its own literary publications such as magazines, brochures, and maps. These came through the railroad's literary bureau, which was a part of the Passenger Department. Its staff wrote articles to promote passengers to travel on the railroads, visitors to stay at its resorts, and new residents to buy its real estate properties. In the mid-to-late 1880's the Hotel Del Monte even published its own promotional publication, *The Wave*, which was founded and edited by Major Benjamin Cummings Truman (1835-1919) who was the head of the railroad's literary bureau for eleven years from 1879 to 1890. (Ben Truman was a Civil War Union officer, President Andrew Johnson's secretary, and a newspaper correspondent for the *New York Times* and other papers, including those he owned. He was the author of several books. One of his books was *Tourists' Illustrated Guide to the Celebrated Summer and Winter Resorts of California Adjacent to and Upon the Lines of the Central and Southern Pacific Railroads*.) Initially, the Del Monte *Wave*, which appeared as a weekly periodical in Monterey, was pure advertisement or "boosterism" for the hotel, and was used to publicize the Hotel Del Monte's grandeur and its society guests, in an attempt to bring in tourists and real estate buyers.

Sunset magazine

In 1898 the Southern Pacific Railroad founded *Sunset* magazine to promote tourism and settlement, and thus further its real estate interests and railroad lines in the West. The monthly magazine was named for the Southern Pacific Railroad route, the Sunset Route, from Los Angeles to New Orleans, on the Sunset Limited train. (The Southern Pacific Railroad owned *Sunset* magazine until 1914, when it was sold to a company that consisted of the magazines' employees. They ran it until 1928 when it was sold to Laurence W. Lane.)

The first Hotel Del Monte fire (1887)

The Hotel Del Monte experienced several devastating fires in its history. The first fire on April 1, 1887 destroyed the entire building. It was suspected to have been deliberately set, but the former hotel manager, E. T. Simmons, who was charged with arson was acquitted at trial. The Hotel Del Monte was rebuilt in less than a year and reopened in 1888. It was built in an even more luxurious fashion than it had been previously done. The hotel was expanded to three stories with a main building, 185 feet by 115 feet, and two new larger annexes or wings, where the guest rooms were located. The two wings connected to the main building by what were designed to be fireproof arcades made of curved glass and iron. The new hotel could accommodate 750 guests and had an enormous dining room. The Hotel Del Monte was designed in a Swiss Chalet style, with glass-enclosed verandas, lavish landscaping, and exotic gardens. In the 1890's, the Hotel Del Monte offered additional outdoor activities for the guests to partake in, such as golf, polo, hunting in Del Monte Forest, and fishing in Monterey Bay. These sporting offerings were in addition to the already existing recreational activities, such as tennis, boating, and swimming. In 1897 the Del Monte Golf Course was built, which was one of the oldest on the West Coast. It began as a nine-hole course, and in 1903 another nine-holes were added, to make it an 18-hole golf course.

St. John's Episcopal Church (Chapel of St. John the Evangelist)

St. John's Episcopal Church, (also called Chapel of St. John the Evangelist) was initially situated alongside the Hotel Del Monte grounds. The one-acre of land for the church was given by Charles Crocker's estate, and guests raised money for its construction. It was designed and built around 1890 to 1891 by English-born and trained architect Ernest Albert Coxhead (1863-1933). It resembled an English country church. It was made with a stone and wood-shingle exterior, in the Shingle Style, and looked similar to a children's storybook cottage. The chapel was often used for weddings. (The church was moved to its current location, on the southwest corner of Mark Thomas Drive and Josselyn Canyon Road in Monterey in the 1950's. Additions such as a new entrance were made.)

THE PACIFIC IMPROVEMENT COMPANY AND PACIFIC GROVE

The Pacific Improvement Company expanded the acreage of Pacific Grove, from the original 100 acres of the Pacific Grove Retreat purchased from David Jacks, to 470 acres. Through the end of the 1800's and into the 1900's, the Pacific Improvement Company began to sell town lots, promote, and develop the town of Pacific Grove. It was advertised as a healthful summer resort with a year-round, temperate climate. In 1883, an agreement was announced that the Pacific Improvement Company would handle the financial matters for the Pacific Grove Retreat. However all of the morality issues and strict rules about personal conduct ("blue laws") would remain and be controlled by the Pacific Grove Retreat Association. The property deeds had restrictive covenants, which forbid alcohol and gambling, including cards, dice and billiards. Dancing was not allowed. In homes, window shades had to be up all day, until 10pm, when they were lowered and the lights were turned off. Beach clothing had to be made from an opaque material, and there were specifications on how much a bathing suit had cover. The Pacific Grove Retreat was entirely surrounded by a fence except for the side that faced the bay, and the gate was locked at 9 pm. There was a strict curfew for those under 18 years old.

El Carmelo Hotel

The Pacific Improvement Company built a hotel in Pacific Grove, El Carmelo Hotel, in 1887. The three-story El Carmelo Hotel was on Lighthouse Avenue between Grand and Fountain Avenues. It had more than 100 rooms, and even featured a hydraulic elevator. The hotel had an ocean view in the back and a Victorian-style garden in the front. The Hotel Del Monte's landscape gardener, Rudolph Ulrich also landscaped the El Carmelo Hotel. Room and board cost two dollars a day, and thus was less expensive than a stay at the Hotel Del Monte. The El Carmelo Hotel's clientele was more middle class, while the Hotel Del Monte attracted wealthier guests. In 1910, the El Carmelo Hotel was renamed The Pacific Grove Hotel, to avoid confusion with the town of Carmel.

St. Mary's-by-the-Sea Episcopal Church

The first church in Pacific Grove was St. Mary's-by-the-Sea Episcopal Church, which was organized in 1887. It was constructed in 1888 on land given by the Pacific Improvement Company. The church was located on 12th Street and Central Avenue. Its style resembled an old English Gothic chapel. Bay area architect Ernest Coxhead built the Parish Hall in 1893. In the mid-1890's San Francisco artist and designer Bruce Porter

(1865-1953) created some of the stained glass windows, including the glass over the altar.

Southern Pacific Railroad extended to Pacific Grove

In 1889 the town of Pacific Grove incorporated and became a city. Later that year the Southern Pacific Railroad extended its railroad line to Pacific Grove, once again using Chinese laborers for the construction. There were special lower railroad rates for the thousands of summer visitors who attended the Chautauqua.

Painting of Father Junípero Serra. Photo by R. J. Arnold, c. 1880.
(Courtesy of Pat Hathaway, California Views Photo Collection.)

Royal Presidio Chapel, (San Carlos Presidio Church), 550
Church Street, Monterey. Photo taken 1930. (Historic American
Buildings Survey; courtesy of Library of Congress.)

"The Mission of San Carlos Near Monterey", drawing by John Sykes, part of British Captain George Vancouver's expedition, c. 1790. (Historic American Buildings Survey from California Pioneers Original; courtesy of Library of Congress.)

Mission San Carlos Borroméo, view from hill to rear of mission grounds, with the Santa Lucia Mountains shown. Drawing by La Pérouse, c. 1839. (Historic American Buildings Survey; courtesy of Library of Congress.)

Mission San Carlos Borroméo, view from the east, prior to 1835. Painting by Oriana Weatherbee Day, c. 1880, de Young Museum, San Francisco. (Historic American Buildings Survey; courtesy of Library of Congress.)

Mission San Carlos Borroméo, star window. No date given. (Historic American Buildings Survey; courtesy of Library of Congress.)

Interior of Father Junípero Serra's (restored) cell at Mission San Carlos Borroméo. Photo taken 1937. (Historic American Buildings Survey; courtesy of Library of Congress.)

General Mariano Guadalupe Vallejo was born in Monterey. He was in charge of the Northern frontier region of Mexican California. General Vallejo was involved in the founding of Sonoma, Vallejo, and Benicia, California, which was named for his wife. Photo by Isaiah West Taber, c. 1880 to 1885. (Courtesy of Wikipedia; U.S. public domain.)

Governor Juan Bautista Alvarado served two terms as the Mexican governor of Alta California, (1836 to 1837 and 1838 to 1842). Also born in Monterey, Alvarado was the nephew of General Vallejo, and grew up with him. Date of image unknown. (Courtesy of Wikipedia; U.S. public domain.)

Custom House, Custom House Plaza, Monterey. No date given. (Historic American Buildings Survey; courtesy of Library of Congress.)

Larkin House, 464 Calle Principal, Monterey, view from northeast. Photo taken before 1900. (Historic American Buildings Survey; courtesy of Library of Congress.)

Gold miners, El Dorado, California. Photo c. 1848 and 1853.
(Courtesy of Library of Congress.)

Colton Hall, Pacific Street between Madison and Jefferson Streets,
Monterey, east elevation. Photo c. 1890. (Historic American
Buildings Survey; courtesy of Library of Congress.)

Mission San Carlos Borroméo, roofless, view from the north,
with Carmel River in the distance which flows into Carmel Bay.
Photo c. 1860. (Historic American Buildings Survey from Golden
Gate Park, San Francisco; courtesy of Library of Congress.)

David Jacks, Monterey. Photo c. 1888. (Courtesy of Pat
Hathaway, California Views Photo Collection.)

Chinese fishing village along the Monterey Coast. Photo c. 1907.
(Copyright N. H. Gere, Los Angeles; courtesy of Library of Congress.)

Monterey wharf, now Fisherman's Wharf, Monterey. Pacific Coast
Steamship Company schooner. Photo by C.W.J. Johnson, c. 1880.
(Courtesy of Pat Hathaway, California Views Photo Collection.)

Monterey and Salinas Valley Railroad Depot, Monterey.
Photo by C.W.J. Johnson, c. 1879. (Courtesy of Pat
Hathaway, California Views Photo Collection.)

Pacific Grove Retreat, view looking up Forest Avenue. Sketch c. 1877.
(Courtesy of Pat Hathaway, California Views Photo Collection.)

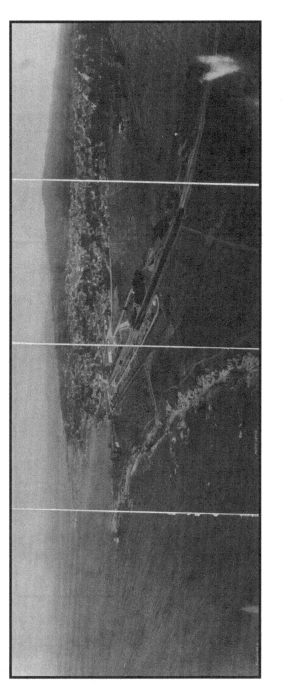

Pacific Grove coastline, panoramic view, with Point Piños Lighthouse in forefront. Photo c. 1906. (Copyright deposit George R. Lawrence; courtesy of Library of Congress.)

The Huntington & Hopkins Hardware Store, (1861-1877), The "Big Four Building", 220-226 K Street, Sacramento, California. (Historic American Buildings Survey, California State Library Collection Photo from Cerinda W. Evans, *Collis Potter Huntington, Volume I*; courtesy of Library of Congress.)

Celebration at Promontory Summit, Utah (Territory) to mark the completion of the construction of the First Transcontinental Railroad, which joined the Central Pacific and Union Pacific Railroads. Photo by Andrew J. Russell, May 10, 1869. (National Park Service; courtesy of Wikipedia; U.S. public domain.)

Hotel Del Monte, Monterey, California. Photo by William Henry Jackson, c. 1906, Detroit Publishing Co., Copyright deposit. (State Historical Society of Colorado, 1949; courtesy of Library of Congress.)

Among the many prominent visitors to the Hotel Del Monte was Sir
Henry Morton Stanley (1841-1904), Welsh-American journalist, explorer
and author, (shown second from the right) with his party standing on the
back of the Southern Pacific train in Monterey, March 19, 1891. Stanley
was remembered by the greeting, "Dr. Livingstone, I presume?", which he
spoke upon his discovery of the missing Scottish missionary and explorer,
David Livingstone in Africa in 1871. (Courtesy of Library of Congress.)

The Southern Pacific Del Monte Express train near Lovers Point in
Pacific Grove, at the foot of Grand and Forest Avenues. Photo c. 1910.
(Courtesy of Pat Hathaway, California Views Photo Collection.)

Mission San Carlos Borroméo, roofless, view of interior ruins.
Photo c. 1860. (Historic American Buildings Survey from California
State Library, Sacramento; courtesy of Library of Congress.)

Mission San Carlos Borromeo, front view of ruins.
Photo by Eadweard Muybridge, 1876. (Historic American
Buildings Survey; courtesy of Library of Congress.)

Father Angelo Casanova presiding over the opening of Father
Junípero Serra's grave at Mission San Carlos Borroméo, interior
view of church. Photo taken July 3, 1882. (Historic American
Buildings Survey; courtesy of Library of Congress.)

Gathering for the dedication of the new roof at Mission San Carlos
Borroméo, on the 100th anniversary of Father Junípero Serra's
death. Photo by C.W.J. Johnson, August 28, 1884. (Courtesy
of Pat Hathaway, California Views Photo Collection.)

Mission San Carlos Borroméo, with its new roof, view from the
west. Photo c. early 1900's. (Historic American Buildings Survey, *San
Francisco Chronicle* Collection; courtesy of Library of Congress.)

Captain John Cooper House and the Cooper-Molera Building, in the distance, where businessman Honoré Escolle had his store, on the corner of Munras Avenue and Polk Streets, Monterey. The Hartnell Creek Bridge is seen in the foreground. Photo by C.W.J. Johnson, c. 1880. (Courtesy of Pat Hathaway, California Views Photo Collection.)

5

The Duckworth Brothers and Carmel City

LANDOWNERS NEAR THE CARMEL MISSION

William Martin

The William Martin family, originally from Scotland, arrived in Monterey in 1856. They had been on their way to the California Gold Rush country, but instead decided to settle along the coast, near the mouth of the Carmel River. The Martin family first leased then bought land around the Carmel River in 1859, as well as land along the Pajaro and Salinas Rivers. They built the Martin Ranch on their two hundred acres north and west of Mission San Carlos Borroméo del Río Carmelo. Their ranch was also known as the Mission Ranch because it was so close by to the Carmel Mission. They farmed potatoes and barley and had a dairy; they became the leading ranchers in the area. (The present-day boundaries of their land are Santa Lucia Avenue, the Hatton Fields area, and the Carmel River.) (*In the late 1980's, Clint Eastwood purchased twenty-two acres of the Mission Ranch, with existing structures, which he renovated. They became part of Clint Eastwood's Mission Ranch Hotel and Restaurant.*)

William Hatton and the Del Monte Dairy

William Hatton (1849-1894), an Irish immigrant, came to California in 1870. He arrived after a seven-year experience as a merchant seaman, which he began at age 13. When Hatton first settled in the area, he apprenticed to become a dairyman. He began to work near Salinas, at the St. John Dairy. He eventually bought the 640-acre dairy property in the Salinas Valley. William Hatton married his wife, Kate Harney in 1875 and they would have seven children. In the 1880's William Hatton was hired by the Pacific Improvement Company to manage its dairy, ranch, and cattle in Carmel Valley. (Carmel Valley with its plentiful green pastures was ideally suited for dairies.) The Del Monte Dairy was headquartered at the old Boronda adobe at the former Rancho Los Laureles. William Hatton expanded and updated the operation, which supplied all of the dairy products (butter, cheese, and milk) for the Hotel Del Monte and were delivered to the hotel daily by horse-drawn wagons.

The origin of Monterey Jack cheese

There is an ongoing question as to the origin of the popular Monterey Jack cheese. Many agree that the cheese was first produced in California by the Franciscan missionaries. Afterwards the cheese ("Queso del País") was made in Carmel Valley by Dona Juana Cóta de Boronda at the Boronda adobe dairy and sold to support her family. It was said to have been named for the heavy jack, which held a board in place over the cheese as it was made. However, others claim that businessman David Jacks, who was involved in various enterprises including dairies, marketed Monterey Jack cheese, and as such, it was named after him.

William Hatton's other dairies

In 1888, William Hatton also managed and leased the dairy at Rancho Cañada de la Segunda (4,367 acres). It was situated north of the Carmel River, near the mouth of Carmel Valley, east of what is now Highway One. (Dominga de Goñi Atherton, who was the widow of Faxon Dean Atherton, had owned the former rancho since 1869. Faxon, a large landowner and financier in California, who died in 1877, was the father-in-law of California author Gertrude Atherton.) By 1892, Hatton bought

Rancho Cañada de la Segunda, and it became his Lower Dairy. (It is the current location of the Barnyard Shopping Village.) The Hattons began to build their house on part of this land. (In the area where Carmel Knolls is now located.) The large, Victorian home, with eighteen-rooms, was partially finished in 1894. William Hatton died at the age of 45, that same year. His wife, her brother, John Harney, and later their sons continued to live on the property and manage his businesses after his death.

Honoré Escolle

By 1870, a French businessman in his mid-thirties, Honoré Escolle (1834-1895) had become a significant landholder in the area. Escolle left France as a teenager and lived in New Orleans for several years, until 1852, when he moved to Monterey. He established himself in Monterey, where he owned a general store, bakery, and pottery kiln. With time, he bought vast amounts of land across three California counties, including Monterey and San Luis Obispo Counties. Escolle had land in Carmel Valley and the Salinas Valley; he had orchards and a dairy. (The warm, fertile Carmel Valley was an ideal site for fruit and nut orchards. Ranchers grew fruits such as apples, pears, apricots, nectarines, and cherries, along with nuts such as almonds and walnuts.) Among Escolle's landholdings were thousands of acres over the steep slopes above Carmel Bay, the woody area north of the Mission Ranch, north of the Carmel River, and west of Hatton's Lower Dairy. The tract of land, Rancho Las Manzanitas was not good for cattle grazing or planting fruit trees because of its steep slope and the extensive growth of manzanitas. Escolle did not put much value on the land and considered it "useless". (The manzanita plant is an evergreen, native shrub, with thick leaves and light colored flowers in the spring. It produces a fruit that resembles small apples; the Spanish name literally means, "little apples".) Through the years, Honoré Escolle became powerful politically in Monterey; he was the treasurer and a member of the Board of Trustees, which ran the local government. In 1883, he sold water rights from his land on the Carmel River to the Pacific Improvement Company for the pipeline that carried water to the Hotel Del Monte.

§

THE SPANISH MISSION REVIVAL ERA (1890-1920)

From the 1880's onward, works from many artists and writers, most of them Californians, began to focus attention on the state's history, and particularly the deterioration of the missions at that time. Books by authors Helen Hunt Jackson, Gertrude Atherton, and Mary Austin; articles by writers Robert Louis Stevenson, Charles Fletcher Lummis, George Wharton James, and Charles S. Aiken; and paintings by artists William Keith, Henry Chapman Ford, Edwin Deakin, Chris Jorgensen, and William Sparks raised public awareness of the poor, rundown condition of California's mission buildings, as well as the mistreatment of the Native Americans. These literary and artistic pieces often advocated the importance of the missions and the Native Americans to California's cultural heritage, along with the imperative to protect both. As more of the public became knowledgeable about the state's history, the number of visitors and tourists to the state's missions and other historic landmarks increased. Furthermore, as a result, contributions came in from the public for repair of the sites, along with larger donations from wealthy individuals for the restoration and preservation of structures, such as the missions. These efforts contributed to the Spanish Mission Revival era, which started in the late 19th century and continued through the 1920's. During this period, California's Spanish and Mexican eras were romanticized and viewed nostalgically. These sentiments appeared in art, architecture, literature, and other forms of cultural expression.

Helen Hunt Jackson

Through the 1880's, author Helen Hunt Jackson (1830-1885) made several trips to California and became an expert on the state's history: the missions, the ranchos, and the Southern California Native American reservations. Jackson wrote articles about the California missions for *Century* magazine, and some of her articles were published in the book,

Glimpses of California and the Missions (1883). She had visited Mission San Carlos Borroméo in the early 1880's and wrote about its sorry state.

> "It is a disgrace to both the Catholic Church and the State of California that this grand old ruin, with its sacred sepulchers, should be left to crumble away. If nothing is done to protect and save it, one short hundred years more will see it a shapeless, wind-swept mound of sand. It is not in our power to confer honor or bring dishonor on the illustrious dead. We ourselves, alone, are dishonored when we fail in reverence to them. The grave of Junípero Serra may be buried centuries deep, and its very place forgotten; yet his name will not perish, nor his fame suffer. But for the men of the country whose civilization he founded, and of the Church whose faith he so glorified, to permit his burial-place to sink into oblivion, is a shame indeed!"[6]

Helen Hunt Jackson also did research, conducted investigations, and wrote a government report on the Native Americans, all the while she actively tried to improve their living conditions. Jackson wrote a best-selling novel set in Southern California titled, *Ramona* (1884).

Father Angelo Casanova and the Carmel Mission restoration

Father Junípero Serra had been buried at the Mission San Carlos Borroméo del Río Carmelo after his death in 1784. His grave was opened in 1856 to check on his remains and to quell the rumors that they had been taken. In 1863, Father Angelo Delfino Casanova, who was originally from Italy, came to the Monterey Parish. Saddened by the Carmel Mission's condition, from 1875 to 1880, he began an effort to restore the mission and to return it to a more dignified state. The mission had reached its worst condition in the 1870's, which included vandalism of the ruins. By 1877, a roof was replaced on one of the rooms, and Father Casanova began to hold mass at the Carmel Mission again, including on the annual San Carlos (Feast) Day on November 4th. He continued repair work and clearing of debris of the church in 1882. Once again, there were

---

6   Helen Hunt Jackson, *Glimpses of California and the Missions*, 1914, p. 47

rumors about the remains of Father Serra and the other missionaries who founded Mission San Carlos Borroméo. Juan Crespí, Francisco Lasuén, and Julian López (a 35-year old missionary who died in 1797) were all buried at the mission. On July 3, 1882, many hundreds of invited spectators gathered to witness the event, as Father Angelo Casanova opened the padres' tombs, located under the floor by the main altar, to show that the remains were present in the coffins. Then the tombs were closed up again and covered with stone slabs.

Starting in 1879, Father Casanova sought donations for the restoration of Mission San Carlos Borroméo del Rio Carmelo. In the fall of 1879, while he stayed on the Monterey Peninsula, author Robert Louis Stevenson visited Mission San Carlos Borroméo several times including on San Carlos (Feast) Day. He noted its rundown condition and its urgent need of repair.

> "...I am moved, by sentiment, to pray for restitution or at least repair. And when I think how, as time goes on, visitors will flock to such a curiosity, as they flock to similar curiosities in Europe by the hundred and the thousand, and how the managers of our hotels, or their successors, may have cause to bless the man who put a roof on Carmel Church..."[7]

By 1880, when the Hotel Del Monte opened, there were more visitors to the Monterey Peninsula and a greater interest in the region's history. When hotel guests frequently took horse and carriage rides along the Seventeen Mile Drive to sightsee the area, the crumbling Carmel Mission was one stop along the scenic route. At first, Father Angelo Casanova had the guests pay ten cents to see the ruins; later, he increased the amount to fifteen cents. Many of these well-to-do visitors donated additional money to the mission repair fund. The opening of Father Junípero Serra's tomb in 1882 brought publicity to the cause and led to further fundraising by Mrs. Leland Stanford and other prominent, civic-minded Californian philanthropists to restore the state's missions. (Later, Mrs. Stanford also

---

7   George R. Stewart, Jr., Introduction to "San Carlos Day, An Article in a California Newspaper by Robert Louis Stevenson," *Scribner's Magazine*, Volume LXVIII, August 1920, p. 209-211

gave $5000 to build a monument to honor Father Serra, located at the Monterey Presidio. It was dedicated on June 3, 1891.)

The Carmel Mission's new roof in 1884

In 1884, the repair work started at the Carmel Mission. Father Angelo Casanova's fundraising was successful and paid for the reconstruction of the Carmel Mission roof. However the style that was chosen: a peaked, steep, Gothic, wood-shingled roof, which was a commonly used at the time, was not the correct one for the structure, nor was it in proportion to the building. Even though the new roof protected the mission from further damage, the style that was selected did not fit in with the original design, which had a "low-pitched tile roof". [The wood roof would stay in place for half a century, until the 1930's, when a more thorough and skillful restoration of the Carmel Mission was done by craftsman Harry Downie.] To celebrate the completion of the new church roof, there was a re-dedication ceremony at the Carmel Mission on August 28, 1884. The date marked the one hundredth anniversary of the death of Father Junípero Serra. Between four to five hundred people attended the event, including brothers Santiago J. Duckworth and Belisario E. Duckworth, two real estate agents from Monterey.

THE DUCKWORTH BROTHERS & CARMEL CITY

Brothers Santiago (or "S. J.") and Belisario (or "B. E.") Duckworth wanted to establish a Catholic Summer Resort near Mission San Carlos Borroméo, similar to the Methodist retreat recently set up in Pacific Grove. In February 1888 Santiago and Belisario Duckworth acquired the rights to develop some of the Rancho Las Manzanitas land from French businessman, Honoré Escolle. The 324 acres covered what would be northeastern Carmel, north of the Carmel River. (The area borders Monte Verde Street to the west, Twelfth Avenue to the south, Carpenter Street to the east, and what is now Valley Way to the north.) The Duckworths paid for the property to be surveyed, plotted, and recorded, while Escolle was to get half of the future profits from sales of the land. They signed the deal in February 1888. In May 1888 the first official map was filed with the Monterey County Recorder's Office in Salinas for what was called Carmel City. The town was laid out in a grid pattern, with one hundred thirteen blocks total in the commercial and residential areas. Santiago Duckworth, who worked on his own from that point onwards, without his brother, began to subdivide the land into home sites. He used Hispanic and Chinese laborers to clear shrubs and mark off the lots. There were 700 parcels. The residential lots were 40 by 100 feet in size, with corner lots for sale at $25, while "inside" lots cost $10. The business lots were 25 by 100 feet, and sold for around $50. The main street, Ocean Avenue was 100 feet wide and was restricted to businesses. The intersection of Ocean Avenue and Broadway Street (later renamed Junipero Street) was the heart of Carmel City and the business district. The sale of land in Carmel City began in July 1888, and was part of the real estate boom in California during the late 1880's. The first advertisements for Carmel City appeared in April 1889, which read as follows:

> "CARMEL CITY
> MONTEREY CO. CAL.
> CATHOLIC SUMMER RESORT.
> S. J. DUCKWORTH,
> REAL ESTATE AGENT
> ALVARADO ST.
> MONTEREY CAL."[8] [9]

Seven lots were sold the first day the ad appeared. By the end of the month, 38 lots had been purchased; by the end of 1889, 200 lots had been sold. Half of those were purchased by people from San Francisco, such as Mrs. Abbie Jane Hunter, who bought seven lots in 1889. She started the Women's Real Estate Investment Company in Carmel in 1892, and worked with S. J. Duckworth to get people to buy land in Carmel City. Mrs. Hunter bought 164 acres in Carmel City and sold 300 lots, half of those were to teachers, writers, and professors, mostly from San Francisco. She was joined by a relative of hers, Delos E. Goldsmith,

---

8   Sydney Temple, *Carmel by-the-Sea*, p. 56-58

9   Kent Seavey, *Images of America, Carmel A History in Architecture*, p. 26

a carpenter, who built two Queen Anne style cottages in 1888 on the northeast corner of Guadalupe Street and Fourth Avenue. His carpenter shop, located on the southwest corner of San Carlos Street and Ocean Avenue, was Carmel City's first business establishment. He went on to construct several additional houses on Carpenter Street as well as other board-and-batten houses in Carmel City.

The Bathhouse

Mrs. Abbie Jane Hunter was responsible for getting the Carmel Bathhouse built. Delos Goldsmith constructed the Bathhouse on Carmel Beach, at the foot of Ocean Avenue in 1889. The Bathhouse building had a wall of windows that faced the Pacific Ocean. It would be one of the main places where Carmelites would gather for the next forty years to enjoy the beach and to observe the Pacific Ocean, especially during storms. It was also the site of wedding receptions and other social gatherings. A tank on the roof held water heated by the sun, which was used for the showers. Bathing suits and towels rented for twenty-five cents. Sandwiches, popcorn, candy, and lemonade were also sold.

Hotel Carmelo

In 1889, Delos Goldsmith also built the Hotel Carmelo for S. J. Duckworth. It was in the heart of the downtown area and at the entrance to the town, on the northeast corner of Ocean Avenue and Broadway Street. However, at that location, it was also ten blocks away from the beach. Visitors, especially those who came to Carmel City to buy lots, stayed at the eighteen room, two-story structure which could accommodate forty guests. A dance party was the first community event held at the hotel on July 4, 1891. [In 1898, another hotel was built in Carmel City. The Hotel Carmel was a two-story, wood shingle building, with a sun porch, located on the northeast corner of San Carlos Street and Ocean Avenue. It was built in the Arts and Crafts or the Bay Area Regional Style.]

The "Carmel Bus"

Visitors to the Del Monte Hotel as well as the Hotel Carmelo would take the Southern Pacific Railroad train, the Del Monte Express, to Monterey.

The Monterey railroad station was around three miles north of Carmel City. Those going to the Hotel Carmelo would then take a four horse-drawn carriage, the "Carmel Bus", from the Monterey railroad terminal to the town. When they reached Carmel Hill, a dirt road, about a mile from Carmel City, all of the male passengers would walk up the hill to lighten the load. Once they reached Carpenter Street they would get back on the carriage for the remainder of the trip to the Hotel Carmelo. The entire stage trip took well-over one hour. (This form of transportation was used until the first motorized buses, which held sixteen passengers, were introduced in 1912. Automobiles also began to be a more common sight around that time, too.) The Hotel Carmelo was nowhere near as lavish as the Hotel Del Monte, therefore it was harder to attract visitors and potential buyers to Carmel City. The Southern Pacific Railroad line did not get any closer to Carmel City, so visitors had to continue to endure the Carmel Bus stage ride over Carmel Hill. (After the Southern Pacific Railroad extended its line from Monterey to Pacific Grove in 1889, there were plans to bring the railroad tracks all the way to Carmel, but this never happened.)

Carmel City's difficulties in the mid-1890's

Carmel City had grown from 1889 to 1892. The real estate boom in California in the 1880's ended with the nationwide economic downturn in the mid-1890's. This financial slump not only made it difficult for real estate promoters to sell land, but it also hurt tourism in Carmel City. In 1893 when the real estate market had collapsed, Santiago Duckworth bought an additional 27 lots in Carmel City from Honoré Escolle for ten dollars. (The land included the city block that would one day be the location of the Carmel Plaza shopping center, between Broadway (now Junípero) Street, Mission Street, Ocean Avenue, and Seventh Avenue.) Mrs. Abbie Jane Hunter was one of those in Carmel City affected by the economic depression of the 1890's. Despite her efforts, on Valentine's Day, February 14, 1895, she was forced into foreclosure and lost her house. By the late 1890's she had to sell all of her interests in Carmel City. Santiago Duckworth also had a hard time selling lots and sales decreased. The development was losing money and was near bankruptcy, so by 1894 he gave up on his plans for the town. S. J. Duckworth put the remaining unsold lots in Carmel City in his mother-in-law's name, as a way to rid himself of the properties. In April 1895, a San Francisco physician, Dr. W. Saunders, saw an opportunity in the hundreds of unsold lots in Carmel City, which he bought at a reduced price from Honoré Escolle. A few days later, he also purchased land from the San Francisco (and Pacific) Glass Works, located west of Monte Verde Street, the western limits of Carmel City, for a total of 89 acres of beach and sand dunes.

6

Carmel-by-the-Sea Becomes a Town: Frank Devendorf, Frank Powers, and the Carmel Development Company

CARMEL-BY-THE-SEA

Crescent-shaped Carmel Bay has bright, blue water on clear, sunny days; its waves crash against the white sandy beach. As the glowing sun sets above the horizon, beautiful sunsets turn the sky shades of red, orange, and pink. The fog often appears in the early mornings or late afternoons and keeps the temperature cooler. On foggy days, the greyish color of the water matches the grey skies. Pine and cypress trees grow along the coast, with cypress tree branches often shaped and twisted by the wind. The sloping and shifting sand dunes of Carmel Beach are shaped by the wind, the powerful surf, and winter storms. Since its first days, many creative and artistic people have been drawn to the beauty of Carmel-by-the-Sea's natural scenery. Then and now, these surroundings serve as an ever-present inspiration for the work of poets, artists, writers, and photographers. George Sterling was one of the earliest poets to be in awe of Carmel's beauty. His poem, "The Islands of the Blest", from A *Wine of Wizardry*, captures the images of Carmel-by-the-Sea's landscape.

"In Carmel pines the summer wind
    Sings like a distant sea.
O harps of green, your murmurs find
    An echoing chord in me!

On Carmel shore the breakers moan
    Like pines that breast a gale.
O whence, ye winds and billows, flown
    To cry your wordless tale?

Perchance the crimson sunsets drown
    In waters whence ye sped;
Perchance the sinking stars go down
    To seek the Isles ye fled.

Sometimes from ocean dusks I seem
    To glimpse their crystal walls,
Dim jewels of mirage that gleam
    In twilight's western halls..."[10]

Frank Devendorf

At the turn of the 20th century, the future of Carmel-by-the-Sea's growth and development would come through the efforts of two men: one a prominent California land developer and the other a notable San Francisco attorney. James Franklin Devendorf, (1856-1934) who was originally from Michigan, where he grew up on his family's farm, came to San Jose as a young adult in 1874. He worked as a department store clerk. At the age of 21, Frank Devendorf married a music student, Lillian ("Lillie"), in 1877. (They would remain married for 57 years, and had four daughters: Edwina, Marion, Myrtle, and Lillian, three of whom pursued artistic careers. Their eldest, Edwina, was born deaf and couldn't speak.) Soon after he married, Devendorf had a health scare of tuberculosis, while in his early twenties, which led him to take up real estate. It was

---

10   George Sterling, "The Islands of the Blest", A *Wine of Wizardry*, p. 21-23

at the time of California's real estate boom during the 1880's. He was a real estate developer for 25 years in California's Santa Clara and Central Valleys. Devendorf developed and sold land in subdivisions in San Jose, Gilroy, Morgan Hill, and Stockton. In the 1890's, he had taken his family on a vacation to Carmel, which included a picnic at Carmel Bay. Frank Devendorf was impressed by the area's beauty, and could visualize Carmel becoming a town.

Frank Powers

Frank Hubbard Powers, (1864-1920) whose family became wealthy during the Gold Rush, was born in Calaveras County, California. He grew up on a ranch near Fresno. Powers graduated from the University of California at Berkeley with a law degree and began his career practicing law in the Central Valley. He was a member of the California state legislature in 1895. In 1891, he married artist Jane Gallatin (1868-1944), the daughter of a prosperous Sacramento financier, Albert Gallatin. *[The Victorian house where she grew up in Sacramento was later owned by the father of journalist Lincoln Steffens, and it eventually became the Governor's Residence for six decades. The Governor's Mansion in Sacramento, on 1524 H Street, on the southwest corner of 16th and H Streets is State Historical Landmark, No. 823.]* (Frank and Jane Gallatin Powers would have four children: a son, Gallatin and three daughters, Grace, Marion, and Dorcas.) Frank Powers eventually practiced law in San Francisco. As a law partner at several San Francisco firms through the years, as well as a member of many prominent clubs, such as the San Francisco Bohemian Club, Powers built up considerable social connections among San Francisco's elite society members.

The Carmel Development Company

As a result of the economic depression of the mid-1890's, Powers and Devendorf, each on his own began to acquire land in Carmel City at bargain prices. Frank Powers purchased the largest portion of the land in Carmel, including the beachfront. In November 1900, he bought the seven hundred lots and the eighty-nine acres of beach and sand dunes property from Dr. W. Saunders, who had never developed the land in the more than five years he owned it. In 1901, Santiago Duckworth came to Frank Devendorf eager to make a deal: he wanted to exchange all of his unsold Carmel City lots for whatever Devendorf had to offer in return. Devendorf proposed to trade him some land in Stockton for the Carmel lots and the two men agreed. Thus Devendorf acquired the rest of the unsold lots in Carmel City. He also bought more of Honoré Escolle's land. It in unknown exactly how Frank Powers and Frank Devendorf met, but they soon joined forces with their like-minded vision, appreciation of nature, and complimentary talents to create a new community. On November 25, 1902, Devendorf and Powers formed the Carmel Development Company, with Powers as the financial man, while Devendorf was the manager, with his people and promotional skills. They reorganized, refinanced, and renamed Duckworth's Carmel City development. In early 1903 the first map of Carmel-by-the-Sea was filed with the Monterey County recorder, and it was again mostly in a traditional grid pattern. Frank Powers also named some of the streets, such as Casanova, San Antonio, and later Scenic. Devendorf had a cottage on Lincoln Street and Sixth Avenue, yet he and his family resided some of the time at their home in Oakland. Powers continued to conduct business in San Francisco.

Water

Since Carmel-by-the-Sea's first days, there were questions about where the water would come from to support the population. In those early years, Carmel-by-the-Sea's water supply was undependable. Initially water came from the Carmel River through the 25-mile, iron pipeline from Carmel Valley that the Pacific Improvement Company had built to deliver water to the Hotel Del Monte and surrounding areas. Later, the Carmel Development Company installed a pump from the Carmel River and a new water pipe was built so that water was piped in to the town and stored in a large tank at the corner of Ocean Avenue and Mountain View Avenue. Frank Devendorf personally delivered water in a barrel, by horse-drawn carriage, for the homes up the hill from that location.

"The Father of Carmel"

Through his many years as a real estate developer, Frank Devendorf earned the reputation as an honest, kind-hearted man who treated people well, not as someone out to make a fast buck at the expense of others. Devendorf (or "Devy" as he was affectionately called) was friendly. He helped buyers select lots that would be right for their needs; he was not a high-pressure salesman. Devendorf would take prospective buyers around town in his horse and buggy carriage to choose their site. Most residential lots cost about fifty dollars; they were sold for five to ten dollars down with five dollars a month as payment on the balance. Frank Devendorf was known for his leniency when mortgage payments were due. He also provided purchasers of land help with building their cottages. Carmel-by-the-Sea's residents turned to him when they needed someone to solve a problem, great or small. He felt everyone had the right to be a property owner, so he consciously made sure Carmel-by-the-Sea would welcome and be centered around middle class American families, in a populist, Jeffersonian ideal. Frank Devendorf earned the nickname, "Father of Carmel".

Professors' Row

In a brochure distributed in 1903 to attract new residents, Devendorf advertised that the town had one mile of beach. He wrote that he was looking for those he affectionately called, "brain workers" to settle in the town, such as college professors, schoolteachers, and others who earned a living through creative, artistic, or intellectual work. Stanford University president Dr. David Starr Jordan (1851-1931) was one of the first educators to build a home in Carmel in 1904. (Jordan was an ichthyologist, instructor, author, and later global peace activist.) He had first visited the area in 1880, as a young scientist employed by the U.S. government to conduct a census of the Monterey Peninsula; even early on he was captivated by Carmel Bay's scenery. In late 1904, David Starr Jordan bought lots on the corner of Camino Real Street and Seventh Avenue, where he built a Shingle-style home. Several blocks of Camino Real, south of Ocean Avenue and just three streets up from the beach, became known as "Professors' Row". Many professors mostly from Stanford University, though some were from the University of California at Berkeley, had homes and lived there during the summer. Another one of the Stanford professors who resided in Carmel was zoologist and author, Dr. Vernon Lyman Kellogg (1867-1937). He wrote many science textbooks, including some with Dr. Jordan, who was a good friend. In the years to come, various other educators, artists, and writers were drawn to the town for its creative atmosphere and natural scenery.

Coastal Laboratory in Carmel

In 1909, the Carnegie Institution of Washington, D.C. founded a Coastal Laboratory in Carmel, as part of its Department of Botanical Research. The long-time director of the Carmel laboratory was scientist, botanist, and tree expert, Dr. Daniel Trembly MacDougal (1865-1958). He was specifically knowledgeable on Monterey pines. The Coastal Laboratory was located on Twelfth Avenue. (It remained in Carmel for nearly thirty years, until the institute closed in 1940.) Dr. MacDougal also was director of the Desert Plant Laboratory in Tucson, Arizona, and he divided his time between Carmel and Tucson.

Carmel's first medical facility

Around 1906, a San Francisco doctor who moved to Carmel, Dr. William Himmelsbach, began the town's earliest hospital, known as "The Pine(s)" Sanitarium. He opened it at the home he lived in on the northeast corner of Dolores Street and Ninth Avenue. The house was built by his parents in 1902, and it had been designed by renowned Bay Area architect Willis Polk (1867-1924).

The Pine Inn

The Carmel Development Company bought the Hotel Carmelo in 1903, and that year the entire structure was moved to a new location, which was viewed as more desirable as it was closer to the beach. The entire hotel was transported five blocks away, from Ocean Avenue and Broadway Street, to the corner of Ocean Avenue and Monte Verde Street. Moving the hotel was no small feat; a team of mules was used to pull the building down Ocean Avenue on rollers made of pine logs. The newly relocated hotel reopened with a celebration on July 4, 1903. The Carmel Development Company used the hotel as a place to house prospective clients who were interested in buying lots, and thus the hotel rates were kept very affordable. The Hotel Carmelo itself made up the annex and formed the basis of the newly renamed, Pine Inn. When there were too many guests at the Pine Inn, tents were set up at an adjacent lot. These tents rented for one to three dollars a week. The Pine Inn served meals for around forty cents. The first restaurant, which opened on the corner of Ocean Avenue and Dolores Street, was run out of a tent by a couple from Pacific Grove, Mr. and Mrs. Melvin Norton, who charged twenty cents for meals. A livery stable was established at the site of the old Hotel Carmelo, at Ocean Avenue and Mountain View Avenue. In the early 1900's, the Coffey brothers ran the stable and they also operated sightseeing tours on horse and buggy. The horse drawn stage, or "Carmel Bus" as it was called, continued to transport guests from the Southern Pacific Railroad Depot in Monterey to the Carmel hotels, such as the Pine Inn. The livery stable was also one place where the stages to and from Monterey stopped.

M. J. Murphy, Carmel's builder

A major reconstruction and expansion of the Pine Inn Hotel, including the addition of a sun-room which faced the ocean, was done in 1904 by M. J. Murphy. One of the first and longest-practicing builders in Carmel-by-the-Sea was Michael J. ("M. J.") Murphy (1884 or 1885-1954). (His nickname was "Rock".) Murphy was from Utah and arrived in Carmel when he was in his teens, around 1900. He built his first cottage in Carmel-by-the-Sea by 1902, at the age of seventeen, for his mother, Emma. The small white cottage had clapboard siding and Queen Anne style windows with decorative sashes, in the Victorian fashion. *(This house, "the first Murphy", was saved from demolition in 1990, by the Carmel Heritage Society, a non-profit organization that preserves Carmel-by-the-Sea's culture and history. The group held a public campaign called, "Save-the-First-Murphy", which resulted in the city of Carmel's purchase of the house. It was lifted by crane and moved to Lincoln Street and Sixth Avenue, near the Harrison Memorial Library, where it is now open to the public and maintained by The Carmel Heritage Society.)* Shortly after constructing a home for his mother, Murphy married Edna Owens, and they permanently made Carmel-by-the-Sea their home. He worked for the Carmel Development Company and began building small, board-and-batten cottages. Murphy's work served to set the pattern of Carmel-by-the-Sea's architectural style and distinctive character for well over three decades. M. J. Murphy was known for his use of natural, local, good-quality building materials, such as redwood, along with Carmel stone for retaining walls, walkways, and chimneys. Many of the homes he constructed were built in the Craftsman or Arts and Crafts style, also described in Northern California as the Bay Area Regional Style, which combined the natural setting and environment in the design.

The Craftsman or Arts and Crafts Style

The Craftsman style, which had become popular in California between 1901 through 1930, was part of the Arts and Crafts movement, which began in England around the 1870's, and spread to North America and Europe. It came about as a criticism, response, and rejection of the Industrial Age and its mechanization and the Victorian Era, with its excessive decoration and clutter. The Arts and Crafts movement brought back simplicity, harmony with nature, and placed a value on craftsmanship in architecture, furniture design, and the decorative arts. (The style was featured in the *Craftsman Magazine*, published from 1901 to 1916.) The Craftsman style houses were generally made of wood. They typically included an overhanging roof, exposed rafters, a large porch, and a simple interior, often with built-in wood bookshelves. [*Perhaps the most famous Craftsman house built during that time was the Gamble House in Pasadena, California done by Southern California architects, brothers Charles Sumner Greene and Henry Mather Greene in 1908. Years later, Charles Sumner Greene became a resident of Carmel-by-the-Sea.*]

Carmel's early architectural style

In the early 1900's, as Carmel-by-the-Sea grew, most of the homes which were built were simple cottages or bungalows, though some were so basic, they were described as being more like shacks. Frequently the bungalows were in the Craftsman style, typically made from plentiful local building materials, such as wood, with stone, which fit in with the natural surroundings around them. On average it cost five hundred dollars to build a small house or cottage in Carmel. Frank Devendorf had arranged for building supplies to be brought in, mostly from dismantled houses from San Francisco. These supplies were sent by ship from San Francisco down to the Monterey wharf, where they were transported to Carmel by a horse-drawn stage, or surrey, over Carmel Hill. The building supplies were proportionally divided in the coach so that the load would be balanced and thus could be hauled over the steep hill. Once the parts reached Carmel, they were reassembled as cottages. One time, after the 1906 San Francisco Earthquake, due to a shortage of building and lumber materials in Carmel, one of the shipments from San Francisco contained only doors, which had come from Victorian houses that had been destroyed by the quake. This led to the construction of the Door House in 1906 on Lincoln Street between Ninth and Tenth Avenues. The entire house was built with eight-foot tall, four-paneled Victorian doors set vertically. (*The home was spared demolition in the 1990's by the Carmel Preservation Foundation.*)

Many of the cottages in Carmel were surrounded by stone footpaths, colorful gardens, and wooden picket fences. Local history authors Daisy Bostick and Dorothea Castelhun describe the common sight in Carmel's early days,

> "Little low redwood cottages, snuggle in among the silver green trunks of oaks, they hide back of masses of wild lilac, or peep out over the tops of quaint, moss-flecked wooden palings."[11]

Some of the homes had a small guesthouse as well, where visitors stayed. In addition to permanent residences, there was also an increasing demand for summer cottages in Carmel-by-the-Sea. A cottage or bungalow would rent for six dollars a month. There were no street numbers on the houses, a tradition that continues to this day in Carmel-by-the-Sea proper. (*This also means the United States Postal Service doesn't deliver mail directly to one's house, and thus all mail has to be picked up at the post office.*) Directions to find a home were given by compass coordinates (north, east, south, or west) of the intersection of any two given streets. In the early days, when visitors arrived, they usually would use a knocker or cowbell to announce their arrival, as doorbells were considered something from the "big city". If the homeowner was not there, the guest would write a note on a pad of paper and pencil that had been left outside. Another item frequently found outside of a home was a large dust brush used to clean one's shoes

---

11   Daisy Bostick and Dorothea Castelhun, *Carmel at Work and Play*, p. 29

prior to entering a home, as the streets were not paved and thus were dusty. There were also no curbs or sidewalks, and no streetlights in the residential areas, so locals devised what was known as the Carmel lantern (or "bug") to maneuver the streets at night in the darkness. It was an empty can with a candle stuck through the inside, so the person could hold the bottom end of the candle. The can protected the candle flame from being blown out by the wind. (There was no electricity in Carmel-by-the-Sea until 1914. Residents typically used wood-burning fireplaces for warmth, while kerosene lamps provided light. Brick or stone fireplaces were common in most of the homes. Natural gas was not available in Carmel until the 1930's.)

"A Village in the Forest"

In the summer, Carmel-by-the-Sea's roads were dusty and dry. The early sidewalks in the downtown business area were made of wood with gullies cut out for drainage. The street signs were carved out of wood, a style that remains to this day. Out of town visitors, especially those from the big cities, frequently complained about ruining their shoes after walking even a short distance on the bumpy, uneven, dust-filled streets. Furthermore, as part of the town sloped downward towards the bay, during the winter when the rains came, the roads were muddy and nearly washed away because of the flowing mud. To prevent mud and water from running downhill, pine trees were planted throughout the town to help stop erosion. As a result, Carmel's streets were often covered in a bed of brown pine needles.

A central tenet of Frank Devendorf's was that a community should fit into its surroundings and the natural environment. Thus he wanted many trees in Carmel-by-the-Sea. Devendorf always planted a few trees with each lot he sold, and encouraged new homeowners to grow trees with saplings he gave them. Soon, many of Carmel-by-the-Sea's homes were surrounded by trees. Devendorf was known to go around town in his horse-drawn buggy, to select locations for new trees; afterwards, Japanese workmen cleared the space and planted young pine trees. In 1904, a column of trees was established down Ocean Avenue. Devendorf also had cypress trees planted along Scenic Road and San Antonio Street, the two streets closest to the beach. These trees also provided privacy and served as a buffer against the ocean winds. In addition, Devendorf also chose other areas that were previously flat grassland, such as Carmel Point, to plant trees. By 1907, the Carmel Development Company had increased the amount of land it owned and the lots offered for sale, with the purchase of part of the Martin Ranch, near where the Carmel River meets Carmel Bay. The coastal area included Carmel Point, originally known as Point Loeb, which was south of Carmel Beach. (Carmel Point was also the site of Carmel-by-the-Sea's one and only golf course, which had been built by a Scotsman, Philip Wilson. The golf clubhouse was located around San Antonio Street and Fourteenth Avenue. The golf course remained open until World War One; afterwards the land was subdivided.)

A brochure from the Carmel Development Company in 1911 established the protection of trees, and gave them a near "sacred status" which would continue into the future.

> "All trees, shrubs, and personal property on the streets... are reserved and preserved by the [Carmel] Development Company and listed on the [Carmel] Development Company maps which are filed on record. In this way the cutting of trees...is prevented, and so far as possible the natural appearance of the streets is safeguarded."[12]

Trees seemed to have the right of way when it came to building roads; it was not uncommon to see streets in Carmel-by-the-Sea constructed so that they curved around an existing tree. In addition to pines, the trees commonly planted in Carmel-by-the-Sea included cypress, eucalyptus (which came from Australia), elm, oak, and redwood. It is estimated that Devendorf was responsible for the growth of thousands of trees in Carmel, which transformed the town's appearance. Carmel-by-the-Sea became "A town in a pine forest", as described in a 1913 promotional map by the Carmel Realty Company, or a village in the forest. For all of these reasons, Devendorf was regarded as a "latter-day Johnny Appleseed."

---

12   Sharron Lee Hale, *A Tribute to Yesterday*, p. 22

DOWNTOWN CARMEL:
EARLY BUSINESSES AND PUBLIC SERVICES

In November 1903, one year after Frank Powers and Frank Devendorf formed the Carmel Development Company, there were thirty families who lived in Carmel-by-the-Sea, and about half of them worked for the town in some way. A promotional brochure stated there were over seventy-five permanent residents. Carmel-by-the-Sea offered a hotel, which could house a hundred guests, several boarding houses, a general store, a dry goods store, two restaurants, and a livery stable. Two years after the Carmel Development Company came into existence, Powers and Devendorf had sold $60,000 worth of lots in Carmel-by-the-Sea. By 1908, the town's population was 300. With the increase in new residents, along with visitors, more small businesses were set up on Carmel's version of "Main Street", Ocean Avenue. These retail establishments provided essential goods and services for the growing population. Initially, the stores were located between San Carlos and Lincoln Streets on both sides of Ocean Avenue. Many of the structures were built out of wood in the popular, Western style with "false fronts". The Carmel Development Company ran a company store, located on the corner of Ocean Avenue and San Carlos Street, which provided groceries and other general merchandise. It was the first modern building in the town, made of concrete block, with a stone front and a flat roof. At first many of the stores in Carmel-by-the-Sea were open only during the summer, the busiest time of year. Later, as the number of permanent residents grew, the stores were open year round. Additional stores soon cropped up on Ocean Avenue to serve residents' various other needs. These included a butcher shop, a bakery, a hardware store, a drugstore, and a grocery store, along with a plumber, too. Fresh milk from William Hatton's dairy, located at the mouth of the Carmel Valley, was delivered daily by horseback to Carmel-by-the-Sea's residents. Carmel's first barber arrived in 1906 and worked out of a tent. That same year the Carmel Bowling Alley was opened on Ocean Avenue, which also advertised, "Pool, Cigars and Tobacco". The Carmel Drug Store, originally the Palace Drug Store, was established in 1910 on Ocean

Avenue near San Carlos Street. (It is one of the few remaining original businesses from Carmel-by-the-Sea's earliest days.)

In Carmel-by-the-Sea's first years, before automobiles became prevalent, one of the central gathering sites in town was the tile-roof covered, watering trough on Ocean Avenue and San Carlos Street. Horseback riders frequently met at the location. In 1908, an informal fire fighting force began in Carmel, which consisted of twenty volunteers. These Carmelites were equipped with twelve, one-gallon buckets along with twelve long-handled shovels. Their equipment was stored in a shed. The water to fight fires either came from the large water holding tank on Ocean Avenue and Mountain View Avenue or the horse-watering trough.

Louis Stanislas Slevin

By 1903, Louis Stanislas Slevin, a summer visitor who had moved to Carmel, bought a lot on Ocean Avenue for $325 dollars. It was located between San Carlos and Dolores Streets. Slevin established a stationery store and offered miscellaneous items for sale such as coins and stamps, fishing tackle, model ships, abalone jewelry, and postcards. Slevin, an avid photographer for four decades, from the early 1900's through 1940, also processed film and sold cameras. (Another well-known photographer of this time who chronicled the area, as well, along with the Forest Theater officially, was Lewis Josselyn.) Slevin's many photographs made up a thorough collection of countless local attractions, both everyday and special events in Carmel-by-the-Sea and on the Monterey Peninsula. He also wrote a local history book, *Guide Book to the Mission of San Carlos at Carmel and Monterey* (1912). The book's preface stated that it was written to answer the many questions that Slevin had been asked repeatedly over the past decade. As part of Louis Slevin's unofficial duties as a shopkeeper, he provided countless answers to the most common queries about the weather, the prices of the lots, and the location of the Mission. (Louis S. Slevin sold his store in 1934, and part of it became Spencers Stationery. He died in 1945.)

Post Office

In 1903, Frank Powers went to Washington D.C. to request a post office designation for Carmel-by-the-Sea from the federal government, which was granted. Prior to that time, the Carmel Development Company handled the mail, which was delivered by stagecoach, in leather pouches, then sorted at the Carmel Development Company's store. Louis Slevin became Carmel-by-the-Sea's first postmaster in 1904; he held the post for the next decade. All of the mail that arrived in town was sorted at Slevin's shop. (*The location of the town's post office has changed six times in Carmel-by-the-Sea's history. In the 1930's it was situated on the southwest corner of Ocean Avenue and Mission Street. In 1951, the post office was relocated to its current site at Dolores Street and Fifth Avenue. Carmel-by-the-Sea's zip code is 93921. There is still no home delivery of mail nor has there ever been because there are no street numbers on the homes in the incorporated area of Carmel-by-the-Sea.*)

Delos Curtis

Another well-known shopkeeper was Charles Delos Curtis. In 1908, he married business owner Catherine More. They ran a popular shop on Ocean Avenue, near Slevin's store, which sold ice cream, candy, and souvenirs. They had purchased the establishment from Thomas Burnight in 1912. Curtis was known for his generosity and civic mindedness, and was well-liked in town.

The Community Bulletin Board

Long before the days of mass communication, one of the ways Carmelites exchanged messages was through the community bulletin board. After Carmel-by-the-Sea was founded, the bulletin board was established at a prominently located fence on Ocean Avenue, between Slevin's store and the Carmel Bakery. Residents posted notes, checked notices about meetings or services offered, and learned of local news. The bulletin board also functioned as a lost and found of sorts for Carmelites. For example, it was not uncommon to see random, mismatched shoes, a pair of glasses, or hanging keys, all waiting for their owners to reclaim them. One announcement read, "Lost--two loaves of bread. Will the finder please return to *** at **. If eaten, please bring 25 cents." (The bulletin board was later located a little further down on Ocean Avenue on a fence near Lincoln Street. The bulletin board remained a mainstay in town on Ocean Avenue until 1925.)

Schools

Within a few years after it was founded, Carmel-by-the-Sea began to develop into a full-fledged town with a public school, public library, and churches. In 1904, the first school class met in Delos Goldsmith's carpenter shop. There were seven students and the teacher was Miss Mary Westphal. Frank Devendorf and the Carmel Development Company financed this first school and then donated a cottage for its use. By 1906, when there were enough children in Carmel-by-the-Sea to make it possible, the first "formal" public school with eight grades was established at the corner of San Carlos Street and Ninth Avenue. The Sunset School began as a two-room, Mission Revival style building, with an arched entry. There were forty-eight students and two teachers. The second teacher added was Mr. Saxe. As the number of school age children in the town increased, the Sunset School gradually expanded in size and enrollment through the years. (The Sunset School remained at this location for nearly six decades. In 1965, the building became the Sunset Community and Cultural Center.)

Library

In 1904, a library was started in the cottage of Mrs. Helen Jaquith, who would let Carmelites borrow a book as long as they would donate a book. Frank Powers organized the Carmel Free Library Association on October 5, 1905. The first year it had ten members, and by the end of the next year the membership went up sevenfold, to 70. Carmelites donated one dollar a year for library dues. As part of the newly formed Carmel Free Library Association, members collected books from residents to stock the library. Within the first two years, nearly five hundred books were given to the newly formed library. In 1908 the Carmel Development Company donated a wood-shingled cottage to serve as the library, located on Lincoln Street between Ocean and Sixth Avenues. The first librarian, Ms. Hoyt, was hired at a salary of fifteen dollars a month. By 1909, there were more than fifteen hundred books in the library. A promotional brochure from the Carmel Development Company in 1911 boasted that the town's library contained over two thousand books. The organization was renamed the Carmel Library Association that year. (The current library, The Harrison Memorial Library, designed by architect Bernard Maybeck (1862-1957) and built by M. J. Murphy, opened by 1928 at the corner of Ocean Avenue and Lincoln Street.)

Churches

In Carmel's earliest days, churches for several religious denominations were established. Catholic services continued to be held at Mission San Carlos Borroméo del Río Carmelo. The Christian Scientists held the first services within Carmel-by-the-Sea's city limits at the Hotel Carmelo. (The Christian Scientist Church is now located on Monte Verde Street between Fifth and Sixth Avenues.) By 1905, through the Carmel Development Company, Frank Devendorf donated two lots for the construction of a community church, the first Methodist Church, located on Lincoln Street and Seventh Avenue. (In 1940, local architect Robert Stanton designed a new building and the church was renamed the Church of the Wayfarer.) Members of the Episcopal Church met in several different buildings, including the Carmel Bathhouse and the basement of the Pine Inn, until 1913, when the All Saints' Church was constructed on Monte Verde Street between Ocean and Seventh Avenues. (In 1946, the church buildings and lots were purchased by the city and became Carmel City Hall. A new church was built and the All Saints' Episcopal Church is presently located on Dolores Street and Ninth Avenue.) The fifth denomination, Carmel's Presbyterian Church began in 1911, with a chapel on Dolores Street and Eighth Avenue. (In 1954, a new Presbyterian Church was built on Ocean Avenue and Junipero Street, near Mountain View Avenue, at the old livery stable site.)

Santiago Duckworth on a horse cart, overlooking Carmel City, with a
view of Carmel Bay in the distance. Photo by C.W.J. Johnson, c. 1890.
(Courtesy of Pat Hathaway, California Views Photo Collection.)

Looking east up Ocean Avenue, in Carmel City. The Hotel Carmelo,
which was built on the northeast corner of Ocean Avenue and Broadway
(later Junipero) Street, in 1889, is on the left. Photo by C.W.J. Johnson, c.
1890. (Courtesy of Pat Hathaway, California Views Photo Collection.)

The Carmel Bathhouse, located at the foot of Ocean Avenue on Carmel Beach, was built by Delos Goldsmith in 1890. Photo by E. A. Cohen, no date given. (Courtesy of Henry Meade Williams Local History Department at the Harrison Memorial Library, Carmel, California.)

A four-horse drawn carriage or "tally-ho" (known as the "Carmel Bus") with passengers in front of the Hotel Carmel on the northeast corner of Ocean Avenue and San Carlos Street. The hotel was constructed in 1898. (Courtesy of Henry Meade Williams Local History Department at the Harrison Memorial Library, Carmel, California.)

(Photo on upper left) View of Carmel Bay and Carmel-by-the-Sea taken from what is now Pebble Beach, with cypress trees in the foreground. Photo by Arnold Genthe, c. 1906 to 1911. (Courtesy of Arnold Genthe Collection, Library of Congress.)

(Photo in center) View of Carmel Beach looking south. "Cooke's Cove" is in the foreground, with Carmel Point in the distance, and Point Lobos in the far distance. Photo by Arnold Genthe, c. 1906 to 1911. (Courtesy of Arnold Genthe Collection, Library of Congress.)

(Photo on lower left) View of Carmel Bay from Carmel Point, near where the Carmel River runs into the Bay. Point Lobos is seen in the distance. Photo by Arnold Genthe, c. 1906 to 1911. (Courtesy of Arnold Genthe Collection, Library of Congress.)

Real estate developer James Franklin Devendorf became known as "The Father of Carmel". He established Carmel-by-the-Sea with business partner Frank Powers. (Courtesy of Henry Meade Williams Local History Department at the Harrison Memorial Library, Carmel, California.)

Attorney Frank H. Powers was the co-founder of the Carmel Development Company with Frank Devendorf. (Courtesy of Henry Meade Williams Local History Department at the Harrison Memorial Library, Carmel, California.)

Albert Gallatin House, where Jane Gallatin Powers grew up, view of north elevation, 1527 H Street, Sacramento, California. Photo by Jack E. Boucher, October 1960. (Historic American Buildings Survey; courtesy of Library of Congress.)

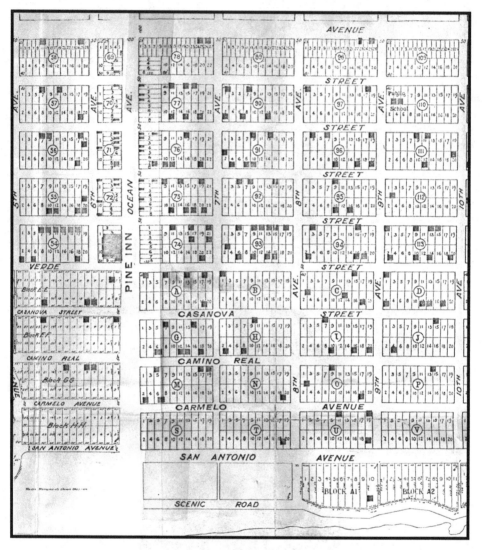

Carmel Realty Company promotional map of Carmel-by-the-Sea in
1913. The seaside village was described as, "A Town in a Pine Forest".
(Courtesy of Henry Meade Williams Local History Department
at the Harrison Memorial Library, Carmel, California.)

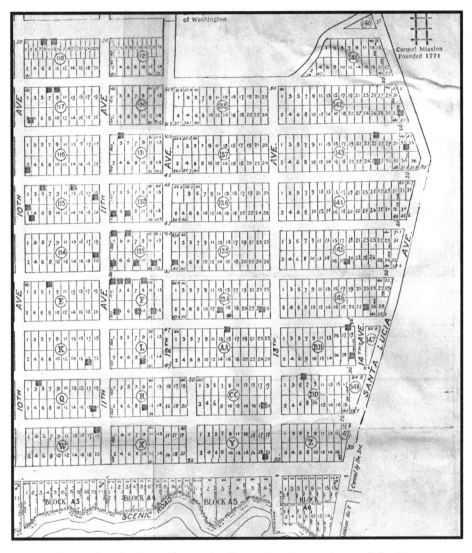

The area bordered to the west by Ocean Avenue, to the south by Scenic Road, to the east by Santa Lucia Avenue, and to the north by San Carlos Street is now sometimes referred to as the "Golden Rectangle", and is considered the prime real estate area of Carmel-by-the-Sea.

Two wood-shingled houses on "Professors' Row", Camino Real Street, off Ocean Avenue in Carmel-by-the-Sea. Photo c. 1908. (Courtesy of Henry Meade Williams Local History Department at the Harrison Memorial Library, Carmel, California.)

One of Carmel's main hotels, the Pine Inn on Ocean Avenue and Monte Verde Street, had tents set up nearby for extra guests. Photo by L. S. Slevin in 1904. (Courtesy of Henry Meade Williams Local History Department at the Harrison Memorial Library, Carmel, California.)

"The First Murphy House", built in 1902, by builder M. J. Murphy, on Lincoln Street and Sixth Avenue in Carmel. Murphy is pictured in the center, with his mother, Emma, on the left and wife, Edna, on the right. Photo c. 1906. (Courtesy of Henry Meade Williams Local History Department at the Harrison Memorial Library, Carmel, California.)

The John P. Cogle house on San Carlos Street between Fifth and Sixth Avenues is an example of one of the early homes built around 1905 to 1906 in Carmel-by-the-Sea. Cogle worked as a foreman in charge of clearing trees for the Carmel Development Company. (Courtesy of Henry Meade Williams Local History Department at the Harrison Memorial Library, Carmel, California.)

Early businesses on Ocean Avenue between San Carlos and Dolores Streets in downtown Carmel. Louis S. Slevin's Stationery Store and Post Office are on the right. Burnight's Ice Cream & Candies, Carmel Bakery are to the left. The community bulletin board is the fence located in between the two buildings. Photo by L. S. Slevin, c. 1910. (Courtesy of Henry Meade Williams Local History Department at the Harrison Memorial Library, Carmel, California.)

Journalist and author Perry Newberry at the community bulletin board in downtown Carmel. Photo by L. S. Slevin, 1924. (Courtesy of Henry Meade Williams Local History Department at the Harrison Memorial Library, Carmel, California.)

The horse watering trough at Ocean Avenue and San Carlos Street, in downtown Carmel. Photo c. 1908. (Courtesy of Henry Meade Williams Local History Department at the Harrison Memorial Library, Carmel, California.)

The First Carmel Library. The wood-shingled cottage was located on Lincoln Street, between Ocean Avenue and Sixth Avenue. Photo 1909. (Courtesy of Henry Meade Williams Local History Department at the Harrison Memorial Library, Carmel, California.)

7

Carmel-by-the-Sea Artists and the Arts and Crafts Club

EARLY BOHEMIAN MONTEREY, AN ARTISTS' MECCA

Bohemian artists, writers, and poets from the San Francisco Bay Area began to discover the Monterey Peninsula as early as the 1860's, and from the 1870's onward, they visited even more frequently. As an increasing number of artists spent time in Monterey, it became known as an "Artists' Mecca". With its attractive visual features such as the scenic landscape and coast, along with the crumbling old adobes and other buildings from an earlier era in the state's history, these Bohemian artists found the Monterey Peninsula's scenery provided them with much subject matter for their works. Through the mid-1870's and 1880's, the Bohemians encouraged other fellow artists to come to the area, to visit or to stay, so they could sketch and paint. One of these who discovered the beauty of the Monterey area was painter William Keith. Later, by 1900, well-known Bohemian artist, Charles Rollo Peters, who had lived in Europe, was among those who chose to make his home in Monterey.

William Keith

Scottish-born painter William Keith (1838-1911) was a respected artist, who also gave lectures and taught many young, up-and-coming artists in San Francisco. Keith was a naturalist; he had a deep love, respect, and appreciation for nature. He spent a lot of time outdoors and made numerous repeat visits to inspirational locations in California, such as Yosemite and the Monterey Peninsula. He painted many landscape scenes of these places, for example, he painted Carmel Bay, Cypress Point, and other outdoor scenes from his trips to the Monterey Peninsula in the 1890's and early 1900's. William Keith also made a complete set of paintings of all the California missions, including Mission San Carlos Borroméo del Río Carmelo. He was one of the earliest Bohemian artists to buy land in Carmel-by-the-Sea, where he planned to build a house and studio on the parcel he purchased.

Charles Rollo Peters

San Francisco native, artist Charles Rollo Peters II (1862-1928) studied art in San Francisco and in Paris. He became well-known for his nocturne paintings, and was referred to as the "Poet of the Night", for these haunting moonlight landscapes and seascapes, painted in dark, monochromatic colors, such as blue and green. Often set at nighttime, the only illumination in his works was a flickering candle in the window of a structure or the moonlight in the painting. Peters spent several years living in Europe. He had a studio in San Francisco, and took regular sketching and painting trips to the Monterey Peninsula, where nighttime scenes of the Carmel Mission, adobes, cypress trees, and coast became the subjects of his artwork. By the mid 1890's, Peters moved his family to Monterey. In 1900, he bought 30 acres of land, and over the next year he built a large home and studio with a sweeping view of Monterey Bay. Charles Rollo Peters entertained his many Bohemian friends from the San Francisco area at his estate. It was called "Peters Gate", so named for the two gates at the entrance, designed by prominent San Francisco architect and friend, Willis Polk.

CARMEL-BY-THE-SEA'S EARLY ARTISTS

Jane Gallatin Powers

Once Carmel-by-the-Sea was established in the early 1900's, a significant number of artists came to live in the town permanently. Frank Powers' wife, Jane Gallatin Powers (1868-1944) was a painter. As a child, Jane traveled with her family throughout Europe, including Paris, Rome, and Capri, where she developed her love of art. At the start of the 1900's, she studied art in San Francisco. Jane Gallatin Powers did portrait, landscape, and still life paintings. When Frank Powers co-founded Carmel-by-the-Sea in 1902, they moved to the town and bought an old Spanish property on nine acres of land along the Carmel Beach sand dunes. (It was near the current entrance to Pebble Beach.) They called it "The Dunes" and they restored it. By 1903, Jane Powers became the first artist to open a studio in Carmel, as she had converted a log barn on the property for that use. She was active in the local artists' community and is credited with bringing creative people to Carmel-by-the-Sea and in helping to develop it into an artists' colony.

Mary DeNeale Morgan

One of the first Bohemians to arrive in Carmel-by-the-Sea in 1903 was artist and landscape painter Mary DeNeale Morgan (1868-1948). She would become a lifelong resident. A native San Franciscan, her grandparents came from Scotland and were early settlers on the Monterey Peninsula in 1856. As a child, her family moved to Oakland. Mary DeNeale Morgan began her art education with William Keith, who was a neighbor and family friend. She continued her studies at the San Francisco Art Association's California School of Design starting in the mid-1880's, and many of her classmates also became future prominent artists. Mary DeNeale Morgan exhibited her work in San Francisco and Oakland, where she had a studio in 1896. (She also taught art at Oakland High School for a short while.) She first visited Carmel on a sketching and painting trip with the Pacific Coast Women's Press Association. At that time, in 1903, she managed the Pine Inn for about a month when it opened. (Frank Devendorf was a friend of her family.) Starting in 1904,

Morgan began to live in Carmel-by-the-Sea during the summers, in a cottage on Monte Verde Street, but she spent the winters in Oakland. From 1910 onwards, she made Carmel her permanent residence. Mary DeNeale Morgan's paintings were done outdoors ("en plein air") and she captured some of Carmel-by-the-Sea's most beautiful coastal sights: cypress trees, sand dunes, and seascapes in pastels, watercolor, oil, and tempera. On her artwork she used the name, "M. DeNeale Morgan". (At the time many female artists concealed their gender by using their initials when they signed their work.)

Sydney Jones Yard

Watercolorist Sydney Jones Yard (1855-1909) was one of the first well-known artists to make Carmel-by-the-Sea his home. He was born in Illinois and studied art in Chicago and London, where he learned watercolor techniques, which became his specialty. Yard came to California in 1882 and began his career as a photographer in San Jose and Palo Alto. (He and a partner ran a photography business.) In the 1890's, Sydney Yard exhibited his watercolor and oil paintings in San Francisco. He also taught watercolor painting. In 1904, he and his wife, Fannie, moved to Carmel-by-the-Sea. They lived in a shingled cottage he built in 1905 on Lincoln Street near Seventh Avenue. In 1907, he also built an adjoining studio. Sydney Yard's artwork included landscapes with oak trees, gardens, and coastal scenes, such as Carmel Bay and the sand dunes. He was known for having his door open to visitors. His daughter, Elizabeth "Besse" Genevieve Yard, married landscape and seascape painter, Charles Chapel Judson in 1904. *(Sydney Yard had a heart attack outside of the post office in Carmel (Slevin's store on Ocean Avenue) on January 1, 1909. He died at age 54. The next year, Mary DeNeale Morgan moved into his studio and home on Lincoln Street.)*

Charles Chapel Judson

Artist Charles Chapel Judson (1864-1946) was from Detroit, Michigan but spent his childhood in Kansas City. He studied art in Europe and in San Francisco. Since the late 1890's, Judson made many visits to the Monterey Peninsula, especially during the summer. From 1904 onwards, he frequently spent time in Carmel-by-the-Sea with his in-laws. Judson painted landscape scenes of the region, such as the coastline, sand dunes, rivers, hills, and trees. He signed his work, "C. Chapel Judson". Judson taught art at the University of California at Berkeley from the early 1900's until 1923.

Christian Jorgensen

Norwegian-born landscape painter Christian ("Chris") August Jorgensen (1860-1935) studied art and architecture in San Francisco and later in Italy. He became an art instructor in San Francisco. Jorgensen married one of his students, artist Angela Ghirardelli (1859-1936), who was the daughter of the founder of San Francisco's Ghirardelli Chocolate Company. (Chris and Angela had a son and a daughter.) In 1889 the couple made their first visit to the Monterey Peninsula, with many more to come. Around the turn of the century, they also began to reside in Yosemite, where they would spend part of the next two decades. Jorgensen built a home and a studio there. He loved nature and the outdoors and expressed it in his work. Chris Jorgensen's California landscape paintings portrayed the Sierras, Yosemite, and other scenic locations. He and his wife took five years to tour the state by horse and buggy and see the twenty-one California missions, all of which he painted in watercolor and oil. In 1905, Jorgensen and his family settled in Carmel-by-the-Sea on Camino Real Street and Eighth Avenue, just a few blocks up from Carmel Beach, an area of the town with an expansive view of the Pacific Ocean. He designed and built by hand a stone mansion for Angela, with a large fireplace and a two-story, 25-foot tall stone tower. The tower had a star-shaped window, made of stained glass, which was said to have been modeled on the one at Mission San Carlos Borroméo. His art studio was located in the tower. (Years later, the Jorgensens' studio and home eventually became part of the La Playa Hotel.)

Alida Ghirardelli

Chris Jorgensen and Angela Ghirardelli Jorgensen's niece, Alida Ghirardelli (1881-1909) also became an artist. She studied art with Jorgensen, and then furthered her studies in San Francisco and Paris. Following her time in Europe and after the 1906 San Francisco Earthquake, Alida moved to Carmel-by-the-Sea, where she resided with her aunt and uncle. While she lived in Carmel, she took a daily swim in Carmel Bay. On August 16, 1909, as she swam in Carmel Bay, 28-year old Alida Ghirardelli was pulled by the undertow and drowned. *(There has been an often repeated, but inaccurate story that Chris Jorgensen's wife, Angela, was the one who tragically drowned in Carmel Bay, but it was in fact his niece, not his wife, who died that year.)*

Arthur Honywood Vachell

Painter Arthur Honywood Vachell (1864-1933) was born in Kent, England. He and his older brother, Horace Annesley Vachell (1861-1955) were both educated at Harrow, a highly respected, public school in England. In the early 1880's, Arthur came to California with his sister and her husband. Along with Horace, Arthur bought and operated a cattle and horse ranch near San Luis Obispo. The Vachell brothers, later along with their younger brother, Guy, became real estate developers. Through most of the 1880's they successfully ran their 3,000-acre ranch, until they hit hard times because of a drought and the failure of their real estate office. The members of the Vachell family were sportsmen, and they are said to have introduced the sport of polo to the West Coast. In the late 1880's Arthur Vachell along with his brother, Horace first visited the Monterey Peninsula. In 1891, Arthur studied art in Italy. (Horace had also studied painting in Florence, but did not pursue an art career. Rather, after he left California in 1899 and returned to England, Horace Annesley Vachell became a well-known author. He wrote many books; some of his novels were based on his experience in California as a rancher.) Arthur Vachell moved to Carmel-by-the-Sea, and by 1905 he began to build his home on Thirteenth Avenue between Lincoln and Monte Verde Streets. As a watercolorist, he was known for his landscapes, garden scenes, and seascapes of Carmel Beach. Arthur Vachell was active in Carmel's artistic community and was a good friend of Carmel artists Sydney Yard, Mary DeNeale Morgan, and Ferdinand Burgdorff.

Laura Wasson Maxwell

Painter Laura Wasson Maxwell (1877- 1967) was born in Carson City, Nevada to a pioneer family. She grew up in San Francisco and expressed an interest in art as a child. Her first formal art training was with Sydney

Yard, initially in San Francisco and later in Carmel-by-the-Sea. She had moved to the area in 1906, but left for some time to study art in New York, Boston, and Europe. While she was away, she traveled extensively, with trips to Asia, Europe, and Mexico. Maxwell was known for her watercolor and oil paintings of Monterey Peninsula landscapes, marines, and particularly florals. She was a friend of Mary DeNeale Morgan.

Ferdinand Burgdorff

Artist Ferdinand Burgdorff (1881-1975) was born in Cleveland, Ohio and studied art at the Cleveland School of Art. He also studied in Paris. Burgdorff first came to California in 1907, on his way back from Santa Fe, after an extended stay in the Southwest. Burgdorff painted scenes of the desert landscape. Soon after he arrived in San Francisco, he established a studio in Carmel-by-the-Sea. He illustrated for *Sunset* magazine. Ferdinand Burgdorff was an etcher, printmaker, painter, and he used oils, pastels, and watercolors. He was known for his paintings with desert themes, such as Native American villages, old mining towns and canyons, along with landscape scenes from around the Monterey Peninsula area, such as Central Coast lighthouses and trees. Burgdorff was friends with artists Charles Rollo Peters, Sydney Yard, Mary DeNeale Morgan, Arthur Vachell, and sculptor Jo Mora.

The Arts & Crafts Club of Carmel

A few years after the town was founded, Carmel's artists formed an Arts and Crafts Club. A key member who started the group in 1905 was retired Wellesley teacher, Eliza ("Elsie") J. Allen, previously an editor of *Harper's Magazine*. The first meeting to set up the club was held at Elsie's home, and she was chosen as its president. Jane Gallatin Powers became vice president, while Louis Slevin was treasurer of the Arts and Crafts Club. The organization was formally incorporated later in 1906 as the Arts and Crafts Club of Carmel. In 1906, Mrs. Josephine Foster was chosen as president of the group. (In 1906 her home, the Stonehouse, was built. The large Craftsman house with a stone exterior was located on Eighth Avenue between Monte Verde and Casanova Streets. It is now a bed and breakfast inn.) Some of the other Carmel artists and community members who were involved in the Arts and Crafts club included Mary DeNeale Morgan, Arthur Vachell, Fannie and Sydney Yard, Chris Jorgensen, and Laura Maxwell. Also in 1906, a committee of artists selected two lots, raised money, and purchased land on Casanova Street between Eighth and Ninth Avenues to construct a clubhouse. They paid $600 for the land. The building was built in July 1907 at a cost of $2,000. Sydney Yard helped with fundraising and oversaw the construction of the gallery, which was 30 feet by 50 feet, along with the picture hanging for the first exhibit. The clubhouse formally opened on August 1, 1907 with the first annual Arts and Crafts Club art show. Every August there would be at least a month long exhibit of paintings and craft works. Through the years, the clubhouse also became a gathering center for the community, where other cultural activities were held. The club's mission was to promote a wide range of the arts—including crafts, drama, music, and literature. Artists and craftspeople, along with a diverse group of well-known speakers were invited to share their knowledge. The Arts and Crafts Club of Carmel was run as an artists' cooperative. The artists who exhibited were charged a thirty percent commission on the sale of their works to maintain the clubhouse. The organization also held popular fundraisers that involved nearly all of the residents of the town. One of the most notable was the yearly festival called, "the International Dutch Market", where participants wore traditional Dutch attire and made their way down Ocean Avenue accompanied by a noisy band, with musical instruments including an accordion, banjo, and drums.

The Arts and Crafts Club Summer School of Art

In 1910, the Arts and Crafts Club of Carmel began an annual Summer School of Art. Mrs. Fannie Yard was the first Arts and Crafts Club Summer School Director. The classes included drawing and painting, along with crafts such as jewelry and leatherwork, as well as music, dancing, and photography. During the 1910's, Mary DeNeale Morgan was an art instructor at the school, as were Arthur Vachell, Laura Maxwell, Bay Area painter Xavier Martinez, and sculptor Edwina Devendorf. Experts in their fields were invited to the Summer School as instructors. Highly influential and respected Impressionist artist and instructor William Merritt Chase (1849-1916) came to Carmel-by-the-Sea in the summer of

1914 to teach the art classes. Chase offered painting instruction both in the classroom and outdoors, and provided critiques, talks, and answers to the students' questions. At the end of the summer session, he gave his own paintings, which he had done while in the area, as prizes to his top pupils.

Mary DeNeale Morgan was the Director of the Arts and Crafts Club Summer School of Art in the late 1910's. The yearly summer classes continued into the mid 1920's. The Arts and Crafts Club sold its clubhouse building in 1922, which eventually lead to the establishment of the Carmel Art Association in 1927, as local artists needed a place to exhibit their work. The Carmel Art Association was formed by many of the same artists who had been active in the Arts and Crafts Club.

THE HOTEL DEL MONTE ART GALLERY, 1907

After the 1906 Great Earthquake and Fire in San Francisco, a large number of the artists who lived in the San Francisco Bay Area not only lost their homes, studios, and paintings, but also the places where they showed their work. One year later, at the luxurious Hotel Del Monte, a new art gallery was formed where California artists could exhibit and sell their artwork. (Previously the hotel had an informal art gallery.) In early 1907, a series of meetings with prominent Northern California artists and the General Manager of the Pacific Improvement Company, Mr. A. D. Shepard, led to the formation of the gallery. Artists such as Charles Rollo Peters, Xavier Martinez, and William Keith, as well as photographer Arnold Genthe, were among those who took part in the planning and development. The Pacific Improvement Company paid the $5,000 cost to build the new gallery, which was located in a converted, old ballroom. Genthe, Martinez, and Charles Chapel Judson were also among the group of seven jurors who selected the works for the Hotel Del Monte Art Gallery's opening show on April 20, 1907, in which 75 paintings were shown. More than 30 artists exhibited their work; about a third of the paintings displayed were by female artists, including Mary DeNeale Morgan and Alida Ghirardelli. Other artists whose work was in the first exhibit included Chris Jorgensen, Charles Chapel Judson, Xavier Martinez, William Keith, and Charles Rollo Peters, along with Arnold

Genthe, who had photographed the destruction from the San Francisco Earthquake.

The longest serving curator at the Hotel Del Monte Art Gallery was artist and writer Josephine Blanch, who held the job for thirty years, since the early 1910's. (Josephine Mildred Blanch (1864-1951) was a landscape and portrait painter. She also wrote newspaper and magazine articles about California artists. Blanch studied art in San Francisco and was a friend and classmate of Mary DeNeale Morgan.) The Hotel Del Monte Art Gallery became an important gallery on the West Coast, and a venue that specifically highlighted California artists. Around 40 artists per year were chosen to have their artwork on display, and many prominent artists served as jurors to select the work to be exhibited. Over the next three decades, many other artists with ties to Carmel and the Monterey Peninsula exhibited their paintings at the gallery.

8

The Coppa Crowd of Bohemians Comes to Carmel-by-the-Sea

"BOHEMIA OF THE SEA"

In the early twentieth century, Bohemians from San Francisco and the Bay Area were attracted to Carmel-by-the-Sea for its natural scenery, along with its mild climate and the simplicity of life it offered. The town drew free-spirited and sometimes eccentric people with artistic, literary, and other creative talents, and it became known as "Bohemia of the Sea." This was partially through the persuasive efforts of the town's founders and San Francisco Bohemian Club members, Frank Powers and Frank Devendorf. They spent time in the city with a goal to recruit the Bohemian artists and writers who lived there. Powers and Devendorf aimed to convince them to move down to the seaside town, buy a lot, and build a house. Carmel-by-the-Sea also gained its reputation and became widely known largely through the personality and presence of poet George Sterling, San Francisco's "King of Bohemia". For roughly the first decade of the town's existence, he was the center of nearly all of the social activity and he passionately encouraged others to move there. George Sterling is credited as being the leading person who made Carmel-by-the-Sea into a Bohemian artists' colony.

San Francisco's Bohemians

Founded in 1872, the San Francisco Bohemian Club was a place where journalists, artists, writers, poets, and musicians, along with businessmen and civic leaders met to socialize. It was an all-male group whose members included poets George Sterling and Joaquin Miller, writers Jack London and Ambrose Bierce, photographer Arnold Genthe, and artists William Keith, Xavier Martinez, and Charles Rollo Peters, among many others. At the beginning of the 20th century, another San Francisco gathering place for local Bohemians was Coppa's Italian restaurant, which opened in 1903. It was located at 628 Montgomery Street, at Washington Street, on the ground floor of the Montgomery Block Building, a four-story brick building built in 1853. The building, which originally had law and business offices, became an affordable workplace with studios for artists, musicians, actors, and writers. It earned the nickname, the "Monkey Block" because of its offbeat, Bohemian tenants. The Coppa crowd was mostly male, although by a secret vote, a few women were accepted in the group, usually based on their looks, as well as their talents. The legendary Bohemian get-togethers took place at a large table at the center of the restaurant and often lasted until the early morning hours. Coppa's was filled with smoking, drinking, eating, conversation, and laughter. The restaurant owner, Giuseppe "Papa" Coppa (1860-1948), who was said to have been an aspiring artist himself, often gave his Bohemian customers some leeway. He kept the food affordable, around 50 cents for a sizeable, five course meal with wine, and extended them credit, as he let them sign notes for their meals rather than pay upfront. Coppa was a Paris-trained chef from Italy, who served good food, such as fresh shrimp, sand dabs, abalone chowder, spaghetti, and "dago red" (wine), along with deserts of flaky pies and almond tarts with whipped cream. He also allowed the artists to draw and write quotations all throughout the restaurant's red wallpaper covered walls. Artwork by Xavier Martinez and Perry Newberry appeared on the walls of Coppa's restaurant, as did poetry from George Sterling, who was viewed as the Coppa crowd leader. Xavier Martinez stenciled a frieze of black cats, underneath which was a border with the names of many of the Coppa Bohemians, along with those of well-known writers and philosophers. This was known as the "Temple of Fame".

Xavier Martinez

Painter and etcher Xavier Timoteo Orozco Martinez (1869-1943) was born in Guadalajara, Mexico. He studied art in San Francisco and then in Paris for several years during the late 1890's. While he lived there, he picked up many Bohemian ways and clothing styles from the Latin Quarter. Martinez was known for his thick, black hair and was nicknamed, "the Aztec" or "Marty". Since 1895, he made regular visits to Monterey for subject material for his artwork.

Perry Newberry

San Francisco journalist, editor, illustrator, and political reformer, Perry Newberry (1870-1938) was born in Michigan. Newberry's wife, Bertha Bair Brubaker Newberry (1874-1934) also from Michigan, was a poet. (She was nicknamed "Buttsky" because she allegedly saved her partially smoked cigarette butts to smoke later.) Perry and Bertha Newberry moved to San Francisco in 1897 and rented a studio in the Montgomery Block Building. He worked for several newspapers in San Francisco and the Bay Area from 1897 through 1905, including the *San Francisco Examiner*, where he was in the art department, and the *Sketch* in San Jose. Perry Newberry purchased *The Wave*, a weekly, literary magazine in 1901, and was the publication's last owner and editor until it went out of business.

Nora May French

Journalist and poet Nora May French (1881-1907) was another member of the Coppa crowd, one of the few women along with Bertha Newberry to be part of the coterie. She was from New York but grew up on a Southern California ranch from the late 1880's onwards. Around the age of 12, Nora May French began writing poetry. She put herself through school, where she studied art in Los Angeles, and later in New York. At the age of 18, back in Los Angeles, Nora May French's poetry started to be published in Charles Fletcher Lummis' influential Los Angeles magazine, *Land of Sunshine*. She became part of his literary group and met many of his Bohemian friends. By her mid-twenties, Nora May French left Los Angeles and moved to San Francisco. Most people described her as tall and beautiful, with blond hair and blue eyes. She was known as

"Phyllis". French had many male admirers, but few female friends. She had experienced several bad relationships with married men. French had an affair with and was later briefly engaged to a wealthy, married, Santa Cruz timber rancher, Captain Alan Hiley. She also had an affair with San Francisco editor Henry Lafler, who published some of her poetry. (He planned to divorce his first wife at the time.) Nora May French's poems were described as sorrowful and she went through periods of depression.

Henry Anderson Lafler

Poet, writer, journalist, and literary editor Henry ("Harry") Anderson Lafler (1878-1935) also sold real estate. He wanted to set up a Bohemian colony south of Carmel in the rugged, scenic, and remote Big Sur area. He tried to convince others such as fellow Bay Area journalist Perry Newberry and poet Herman Scheffauer to settle in the area. Lafler ended up being the only one among them who built a house along the Big Sur coast. The home, constructed by hand, had a redwood shake roof and one large room made of local, white marble, with a large marble fireplace, many bookshelves, and large redwood furnishings. Lafler didn't stay there for long, and he ended up back to San Francisco, where he took part in other real estate opportunities following the 1906 earthquake.

George Sterling

Poet George Sterling (1869-1926) was born in Sag Harbor, Long Island, New York. His father was a prominent physician. Members of his family had converted to Roman Catholicism. While he studied to join the priesthood at St. Charles College, a Baltimore area seminary school, George Sterling first expressed an interest in poetry, which he ultimately pursued. In 1890, at the age of 21, Sterling arrived in California to work for his uncle, a wealthy, East Bay real estate developer, Frank Colton Havens (1848-1917). Havens had a Piedmont real estate office and a San Francisco insurance business. (Frank Havens would support George Sterling financially throughout most of his life.) In 1896, Sterling married Caroline ("Carrie") Rand. (Carrie's sister, Lila Rand Havens, had married Frank Havens in 1892.) Carrie worked as a stenographer for Havens; she was an attractive, tall blonde. Sterling was physically fit, and described as slim and handsome. On George Sterling's daily ferry commute from the East Bay to San Francisco, he wrote poetry. During this time in the 1890's, he also became acquainted with some well-known literary figures in the San Francisco Bay Area, who provided encouragement, praise, and guidance for his work. One of these was literary critic, newspaper correspondent, and satirist Ambrose Bierce (1842-1914?), who became his powerful mentor. Another one was Bohemian poet Joaquin Miller (1841?-1913). In 1895, George Sterling became one of Bierce's disciples, and over the next decade, Bierce helped publish and promote Sterling's work through his connections in the literary world. [Another disciple of Ambrose Bierce was the up-and-coming, San Francisco architect-turned-poet Herman Scheffauer (1878-1927).] With Bierce's support, George Sterling assembled and published his first book of collected poetry, *The Testimony of the Suns and Other Poems* (1903). It was successful and he received many compliments for his work, and thus Sterling decided to pursue his writing full time and leave the business world of his uncle. As he was now a published poet, George Sterling fully adopted the Bohemian lifestyle.

Mary Austin visits Coppa's

George Sterling wrote to Southern California based author Mary Austin in 1903, and told her he liked her work. He had read her essays in the *Atlantic Monthly* from *The Land of Little Rain*, which described life in the Owens Valley in the Southern California desert, where she lived. During the summer of 1904, on a visit to Northern California to do research for her upcoming novel, *Isidro*, a romance set during the mission era, Austin spent time in Monterey and Carmel, and went to see Mission San Carlos Borroméo. She visited San Francisco as well, where she met Sterling and was invited by him to dinner at Coppa's. Mary Austin made the acquaintance of many of his Bohemian friends, several of whom would become Carmel residents or frequent visitors, such as James Hopper, Henry Lafler, Perry and Bertha Newberry, and Xavier Martinez.

Mary Hunter Austin

Mary Hunter Austin (1868-1934) was born in Carlinville, a small Illinois town. She grew up in a Methodist family. At an early age, she knew that she wanted to be a writer. After college she moved to California in 1888 with her family. They settled in the Southern San Joaquin Valley. Mary Hunter became a schoolteacher. In 1891 she married Stafford Wallace Austin (1860-1932), a grape grower and teacher, who also was involved in water irrigation and management projects in the Owens River Valley, in Inyo County. This region, on Eastern edge of Sierra Nevada Mountains, was high desert country. Through the 1890's they lived in several locations in the Owens Valley, though they were not always together during the time because of his work. Their only child, a daughter, Ruth, (1892-1918) who had a mental and learning disability, was born in 1892 and eventually permanently institutionalized in a Santa Clara facility in 1905. While Mary Austin spent time in the desert country, she sought and underwent spiritual experiences. She was viewed as unconventional and not accepted by members of the community for her non-traditional ways. Austin studied the people (Native Americans, European sheepherders, and Mexican settlers) around her in the desert valley and used these observations in her work as she began her writing career. During her lifetime, Mary Austin was a feminist, environmentalist, and a defender of the Native American people of the Southwest and their culture. By the early 1890's, her short stories began to be published in magazines. Austin met and received encouragement from California's literary figures, as she started her career. She transitioned into a serious writer in the early 1900's, and more of her stories and books were published. These included *The Land of Little Rain* in 1903, *Isidro*, in 1905, and *The Flock*, in 1906, about the Basque sheepherders in the southern San Joaquin region.

THE COPPA CROWD ARRIVES IN CARMEL-BY-THE-SEA

George Sterling, who had previously visited Carmel-by-the-Sea several times, was the first member of the Coppa crowd to move to the town in 1905. His decision to locate there led the way for other San Francisco and Bay Area Bohemian writers and artists to join him in the seaside village. Through the rest of 1905 and early 1906, among the other Bohemians who settled in the town were photographer Arnold Genthe, painter Chris Jorgensen, and author Mary Austin. After the Great San Francisco

Earthquake and Fire in April 1906, many residents of the Bay Area came down to Carmel-by-the-Sea. Some stayed for days, while others decided to move to the village permanently, especially those whose homes had been destroyed. Among those who became residents of Carmel-by-the-Sea after the quake were writer James Hopper and journalist Fred Bechdolt.

George Sterling's bungalow

George Sterling purchased one acre of land on a wooded hillside, half a mile from Carmel Bay. It was in the Eighty Acres tract, an undeveloped area of Carmel, to the southeast of Ocean Avenue and Junipero Street. Sterling's property had a view of the Santa Lucia Mountains, Carmel Valley, the Carmel River, and the Carmel Mission, which was about 1000 feet away. Sterling's lot was located on what is now Torres Street between Tenth and Eleventh Avenues. In late June of 1905, Sterling arrived in Carmel-by-the-Sea with two friends from San Francisco, who helped him build his home. While they constructed his house, they all lived in a tent. By the fall of 1905 Carrie came down, as the house had been built. The Sterlings' bungalow was in the Arts and Crafts, or Craftsman style, with a wood-shingled exterior and a porch. There was a very big living room, 30 feet long by 18 feet wide, made of redwood, with a large fireplace. George Sterling regularly chopped pine trees for firewood to burn in his fireplace, which had a chimney made of flagstone (or chalk-stone, also known as chalk rock, which came from Carmel Valley). Outside, Sterling tended to a vegetable garden and he was proud of his efforts to live off of the land. He fished for salmon, gathered abalone and mussels, and hunted birds, rabbits, and squirrels with his shotgun. In the woods behind his house, George Sterling created a "pagan altar", made of cattle or horse skulls, which were hung on the trees. There was a stone fire pit in the center, where he and his Bohemian friends roasted abalone and mussels. While he lived in Carmel, several of George Sterling's books of collected poetry were published. These included his second book, *A Wine of Wizardry: and Other Poems* (1909) and his third book, *The House of Orchids: and Other Poems* (1911).

Arnold Genthe

Arnold Genthe, Ph.D. (1869-1942) was born in Berlin to an academic family; his father was a Latin and Greek professor at a German university. Arnold Genthe was well-educated. In 1894 he received his doctorate in classical philology from the University of Jena. He also studied French literature and art history at the Sorbonne in Paris. Genthe had planned to teach at a German university, but in 1895, he took up an offer to be a tutor for a San Francisco family, and he moved to California. Over the next two years, Arnold Genthe taught himself to be a photographer, as he explored the city, particularly Chinatown. By 1897, he decided to stay in San Francisco and became a portrait photographer. Genthe continued to work on and establish his photographic style, in which he used informal poses for his subjects. His photos had a dream-like quality to them. Arnold Genthe built up his clientele, especially among San Francisco's high society, and he became one of the city's most prominent photographers. He was a member of the San Francisco Bohemian Club and the Coppa crowd. George Sterling and Jack London were among his many Bohemian friends.

Arnold Genthe's bungalow

When Arnold Genthe first came to Carmel-by-the-Sea in 1905, he visited George Sterling. A few months later he decided to move down and started to build his own house, which he designed himself on Camino Real Street and Eleventh Avenue. His rustic bungalow had a wood-shingle exterior and a long porch, with four large redwood tree trunks used as support. Genthe's home had a combined studio and a living room, 30 feet by 60 feet, built entirely of redwood, with solid redwood rafters, and a huge fireplace. It had a high ceiling with two skylights, and he furnished the home with Arts and Crafts (or Craftsman) style furniture. Genthe often invited his friends to his home. His house was the only one in the entire town with a cellar or cement basement, which he used as a darkroom, to process his color photographic film. (It was around this time in Carmel, that Arnold Genthe became one of the first photographers to do color photography.) Genthe happened to be in San Francisco when the 1906 earthquake hit. He lost almost everything he owned, not only his personal belongings, but nearly all of his professional materials: his negatives and thousands of photographic plates. For days afterwards, with a borrowed camera, he captured the devastation he saw around him on film.

Mary Austin arrives in Carmel-by-the-Sea

Mary Austin visited Carmel-by-the-Sea again in the late summer of 1905, at the time when George Sterling had already settled there. When she arrived in Carmel-by-the-Sea in January 1906, she rented a log cabin on North Lincoln Avenue, in the northern part of the town. In March 1906 she paid $1,602.50 for 11 lots in the town, on a steep, heavily wooded hill near her rental, where she planned to build a house. (However, it would be about six years later before she had her own cottage, "The Rose Cottage", built on the property she had purchased.) The location she chose gave her a lot of privacy, but it didn't have much of a view of the Pacific Ocean. Around the town, Mary Austin was known for her eccentric appearance, clothing, and unconventional ways. Her long hair flowed down to her waist and at times she wove it in long braids. She often wore lengthy Grecian robes or a beaded Native American dress made out of leather. Austin had an elaborate tree house called a "Wick-I-Up", built near her home. A ladder led up to the platform where she wrote, high among the trees. The name, Wick-I-Up (or "Wickiup") was a Native American word for shelter, and her structure was modeled on one used by the Paiute group of Native Americans. Unlike most of the Bohemians around her, Mary Austin didn't drink alcohol. *[Carmel-by-the-Sea was also a "dry" town, although liquor could be obtained from the local drugstore. There was a clause in the deeds that prohibited alcohol sales, which remained until the 1930's, when a court ruled it was not applicable, as exceptions to it had been made.]* Austin was in San Francisco, on publishing-related business in April of 1906 when the quake struck. A few days afterwards, she left the battered city and came back to Carmel-by-the-Sea.

James Marie Hopper

Bohemian writer, journalist, and member of the Coppa crowd, James Hopper, moved with his family to Carmel-by-the-Sea in 1906, a few months after the San Francisco earthquake. (They rented a cottage located on Dolores Street and Ninth Avenue.) Hopper had been in the city when the April 18th disaster occurred, and reported on it as a journalist first in newspapers and subsequently in magazines. Paris-born writer James ("Jimmy") Marie Hopper (1876-1956) moved to the Bay Area with his mother at the age of ten. He attended public school in Oakland. From 1894 to 1898 Hopper studied at the University of California at Berkeley, where for a brief while Jack London was a classmate of his. Hopper was very athletic; he was the football team's star quarterback and he also rowed for the crew team. While an undergraduate, he began to write short stories and edited a college magazine. After graduation, he studied at the University of California, Hastings College of Law, and passed the bar in 1900. Instead of practicing law, Hopper decided to be a newspaper reporter for several years in San Francisco in the early 1900's. Afterwards, he spent a few years in the Philippines, where he taught French. He traveled with his wife, Mattie, and used the time he spent there as the basis for some of his short stories and his book, *Caybigan* (1906), a collection of fiction stories. Hopper's work was published in West Coast-based magazines, such as *Sunset* and the *Pacific Monthly*. James Hopper remained athletic all his life and he was known to be a great swimmer. In Carmel he took hikes and swam daily. No matter how chilly or rough the water was in Carmel Bay, he would swim out to a rock in the bay, which became known as "Hopper's Rock".

Frederick Bechdolt

Journalist and Western fiction writer Frederick ("Fred" or "Beck") Ritchie Bechdolt (1874-1950) was born in Pennsylvania. He earned his college degree at the University of Washington in 1896, where his father was a German professor. Afterwards, Bechdolt took part in the 1897 Klondike Gold Rush and drove a dog sled in Alaska. He also spent time in California's Death Valley and Mohave desert, where he explored mines and lived on ranches. Back in the state of Washington, he took part in drilling the Cascade Tunnel, so that railroad track could be laid down through the Cascade Mountains. All of these experiences would become subject matter for his Western fiction and cowboy works. Bechdolt's stories were published in magazines including *McClure's*, *Collier's*, *The Saturday Evening Post*, and *Popular*. In 1900, Fred Bechdolt became a journalist, and he worked as a reporter at *The Seattle Star*, *Los Angeles Times*, and *(The San*

Francisco) Morning Call. He reported on daily criminal activity. Bechdolt conducted research at San Quentin and Alcatraz prisons in the Bay Area, and he took up the cause of prisoners' rights. In 1906, Fred Bechdolt met James Hopper and the two began what would be a friendship that lasted through the next several decades. Soon thereafter Bechdolt became a lifelong Carmel resident, as well. When he arrived in Carmel in 1907, Bechdolt discussed working with Hopper. Together, the two wrote a fictional novel, *9009* (1908) about the condition of American prisons and the brutal effect prison life had on those confined in the Alcatraz and San Quentin facilities, along with the need for reform of the prison system. Their prison exposé was serialized in *The Saturday Evening Post.* (*9009* was a controversial book at the time and it fit in with the investigative journalism of the Muckraking period of the early 20th century.) In 1908, Fred Bechdolt married musician Adele Hale (1873-1945) and they built a home in the Eighty Acres tract of Carmel, where they were neighbors of the Sterlings.

GEORGE STERLING'S GUESTS
IN CARMEL-BY-THE-SEA

George Sterling was the center of the Bohemian group in Carmel-by-the-Sea. The Sterlings' home was most often the focal point of social activities. Many of George and Carrie's Bohemian friends from the Bay Area frequently visited. These included Jack London and his wife, Charmian, who made two visits to Carmel, once in 1906 and again in 1910. Another regular guest, Nora May French, usually came down to Carmel-by-the-Sea with Henry Lafler. As some of the Sterlings' friends remained for extended stays, tents were set up outdoors as a place to house the out-of-town visitors.

Jack London

Author Jack London (1876-1916) was born in San Francisco on January 12, 1876. He grew up in Oakland, left school in his youth, and took on various jobs. London worked in a cannery, a factory (jute mill), and a coal power plant. He was also an oyster pirate and a sailor. After these work experiences, in 1895, London finished his education at Oakland High School and briefly attended the University of California at Berkeley, before he dropped out in his freshman year for financial reasons. He read many books by philosophers and thinkers and studied on his own. In 1896 London joined Oakland's Socialist Labor Party. From mid-1897 to 1898, during the Klondike Gold Rush, Jack London went to the Yukon and worked as a miner. When he returned back to California, he immersed himself in writing and used his adventures in his stories. Despite numerous rejection letters, London broke into the literary world in 1899, with his first published magazine stories in the *Overland Monthly* and the *Atlantic Monthly*. Jack London's first book, *The Son of the Wolf*, a collection of eight stories, was published in 1900. By the early 1900's, with his books *The Call of the Wild* (1903), followed by *The Sea-Wolf* (1904), and *White Fang* (1906), London had become one of the country's most successful, widely-read, and highly paid authors.

In 1900, Jack London married his first wife, Elizabeth ("Bess(ie)") Maddern, and they had two young daughters. During the early 1900's, Jack London lived in Piedmont, in a house rented from George Sterling's uncle, Frank Havens. London and Sterling became close, lifelong friends. They took hikes in Piedmont. The two had nicknames for each other: George called Jack, "Wolf" and Jack called George, "Greek". In the years to come, they corresponded through letters. Sterling would often read over and edit London's manuscripts. Jack London invited many of the Bohemian artists, writers, and poets from the region to his Piedmont home regularly. Among his guests were Sterling, James Hopper, and Xavier Martinez. In June 1905, Jack London bought 129 acres of ranch and farm land north of San Francisco, in Glen Ellen, Sonoma County. His "Beauty Ranch" was located in what London called the "Valley of the Moon", and through the years he would subsequently add additional acreage.

Bessie filed for divorce in 1904. Jack London married Charmian Kittredge (1871-1955) who was from Berkeley, on November 19, 1905, the day after he received the final divorce decree. At the time he was on a nationwide tour, in which he gave lectures on socialism, including one at Yale University in January 1906. The Londons made their first visit to Carmel-by-the-Sea in late 1906 before they set sail on the *Snark* in April 1907, for what was to be a seven-year voyage. The trip was cut short because of illnesses and other problems to just over two years. During the voyage, London's book, *The Iron Heel* (1908) was published, as was his partially autobiographical novel, *Martin Eden* (1909). Jack and Charmian London had returned to their ranch in Glen Ellen by July 1909. They invited many of their Bohemian friends to stay with them at the Beauty Ranch. Those who made the trip up north included Harry Leon Wilson, Arnold Genthe, James Hopper, Fred Bechdolt, and Xavier and Elsie Martinez.

Xavier and Elsie Martinez

Xavier Martinez made regular trips to the Monterey Peninsula to visit with his Bohemian friends, such as George Sterling in Carmel-by-the-Sea and many of the artists who lived in Monterey. One of those trips to Carmel was in the winter of 1906. In October 1907, Xavier Martinez married Elsie Whitaker (1890-1984) who was twenty years younger than Martinez. They had their honeymoon in Carmel. She was the daughter of Bay Area journalist and author Herman ("Jim") Whitaker (1867-1919). Xavier and Elsie Martinez rented a house in Carmel during the summers from 1909 through 1914, when he taught summer art classes at the Hotel Del Monte in Monterey and at the Arts and Crafts Club in Carmel. While they were in town, the couple spent time with their friends and took part in cultural activities in Carmel. *[Xavier and Elsie Martinez's only child, a daughter Micaela Martinez DuCasse (1913-1989) was born on August 26, 1913, and she also became an artist.]*

The death of Nora May French

Nora May French spent considerable time in Carmel-by-the-Sea and Henry Lafler often accompanied her there. They went together in August 1906, and again in December 1906. In her mid-twenties, Nora May French had difficulty establishing herself in San Francisco and earning enough money through her poetry. The following year, Nora May French lived with George and Carrie Sterling in Carmel in the summer and fall of 1907. Nora May French became part of the Bohemian colony in Carmel-by-the-Sea. Sterling often edited her poems. In 1907, she resumed her previous relationship with Captain Alan Hiley, was engaged to him again, and planned to marry him in the spring of 1908. As her troubles increased, Nora May French's poetry, which had already been described as sad and melancholy, became darker and "death-obsessed". In addition to financial difficulties, she suffered from poor health (possibly tuberculosis). Those around her observed that she had mood swings, and had become more emotional, depressed, and despondent. They viewed her as fragile and even suicidal.

On November 14, 1907, in the early morning at George Sterling's house in Carmel, while he was away in Oakland, Nora May French swallowed a fatal dose of potassium cyanide. Carrie Sterling discovered her body. Nora May French was 26 years old. George Sterling, James Hopper, Alan Hiley, and Henry Lafler were among those who attended the funeral service at Point Lobos. (Hiley and Lafler were said to have glared at one another). There was a dispute among Hopper, Lafler, and Sterling as to who would scatter her ashes into the Pacific Ocean; Sterling was ultimately the one who did. (Thereafter, to mark the anniversary of her death, George Sterling returned to that site at Point Lobos every November.) In 1910, Lafler and Sterling put together and posthumously published a book with a collection of seventy of French's poems, titled, *Poems*. It included a portrait photograph of Nora May French by Arnold Genthe.

DEPARTURES

In 1907, Mary Austin's husband, who had remained in Southern California, accused her of desertion. That fall, she left Carmel-by-the-Sea for about five years. She traveled in Italy and England, and then New York. At the time Austin left, she thought she was dying of breast cancer. She wanted to spend her last days in Rome, yet through intensive prayer there, her symptoms disappeared. (There is a question if she may have been misdiagnosed originally). Mary Austin continued to write and several more of her books were published while she was in Europe: the novel *Santa Lucia* (1908), *Lost Borders* (1909), a book of folk stories about the Native American inhabitants of the Desert Southwest, and *Outland* (1910). Her novel *Outland* was written under a pseudonym and set in a fictionalized town, similar to Carmel-by-the-Sea. Austin corresponded with James Hopper and the two saw each other in London. While she was away, Austin and Sterling also wrote to each other; his nickname for her was "Coyote Woman". In 1911, Mary Austin's Native American play, *The Arrow Maker* was produced at the New Theatre in New York. During her time away, she became involved in feminism, women's suffrage, and labor movements. At the end of 1912, she returned to California.

By 1908, James Hopper left Carmel-by-the-Sea and moved to New York, where he continued to write. His work appeared in magazines including *McClure's*, *The Saturday Evening Post*, and *Collier's*. While he was away, his books *The Trimming of Goosie* (1909) and *The Freshman* (1912) were published. Hopper corresponded with many of his Bohemian friends from Carmel, including George Sterling and Mary Austin. In 1910, he traveled to England and France. He missed life in Carmel-by-the-Sea and after about five years away, Hopper returned to Carmel in 1913.

In 1911, Arnold Genthe decided to leave California altogether and he moved to New York, where he opened a photography studio.

9

The Muckrakers and the Helicon Home Colony Arrivals in Carmel, 1908 and 1909

THE MUCKRAKERS

The Muckraking era began in the late 19th and early 20th century in the United States, as an investigative, journalistic movement which exposed corruption and graft in business and in government. The muckraking reporters pointed out how the privileged and wealthy held control over political and economic systems. They also exposed the harsh plight of working men, women, and children. The muckraker's exposés, many of which appeared in magazines such as *McClure's*, and also *Munsey's* and *Collier's Weekly*, led to social and political reforms across the country. Among the well-known muckrakers who visited Carmel-by-the-Sea briefly in its early years were Lincoln Steffens, Ray Stannard Baker, Will Irwin, and Upton Sinclair.

Lincoln Steffens

Muckraking journalist, author, Socialist, and political activist Joseph Lincoln Steffens (1866-1936) was born in San Francisco, but grew up in Sacramento. He lived in the famous house, which later became the governor's mansion, first owned by businessman Albert Gallatin. Steffens graduated from the University of California at Berkeley and then studied in Europe, before he began his journalistic career in New York. He was a reporter and editor in the 1890's and early 1900's. From 1902 to 1906, his muckraking articles for *McClure's Magazine* in New York City exposed corruption and graft in numerous cities, including St. Louis, Minneapolis, Pittsburg, Philadelphia, Chicago, and New York. These articles later appeared in the book, *The Shame of the Cities* (1904). Steffens also revealed political corruption in several states in his book, *The Struggle for Self Government* (1906). In 1906, he left *McClure's*, along with fellow muckrakers, reporters Ida M. Tarbell (1857-1944) and Ray Stannard Baker (1870-1946), and they founded *The American Magazine*. Steffens also wrote for *Everybody's Magazine* from 1906 to 1911. His book, *Upbuilders*, (1909) contained several articles on reformers in the United States. Lincoln Steffens visited Carmel-by-the-Sea in 1907, and most likely first met Mary Austin at that time, and they became friends. (Another two decades would pass before Steffens would move to Carmel-by-the-Sea permanently and spend his remaining years in the town.)

Perry Newberry

Between 1905 and 1908, journalist Perry Newberry along with other civic reformers was involved in fighting political corruption in San Francisco, which led to the imprisonment of city boss Abe Ruef for bribery. Newberry and his wife Bertha moved to Carmel-by-the-Sea in 1910, where they would spend the rest of their lives. They purchased two lots close to the beach, where they built a house.

John Kenneth Turner and Ethel Duffy Turner

A short time after the Newberrys arrived, journalist John Kenneth Turner and his wife, Ethel Duffy Turner, also a writer, moved to Carmel. Muckraker author, journalist, and Socialist John Kenneth Turner (1878-1948) was born and grew up in Portland, Oregon. His father worked for the *Oregonian* newspaper in Portland as a printer. The family moved to California's Central Valley when he was a youth, and they became farmers. John Kenneth Turner began his career as a schoolteacher. He took courses at the University of California at Berkeley.

Writer, poet, and editor Ethel Duffy Turner (1885-1969) was born in San Pablo, California. When she was a child, her father, William Joseph Duffy took a job as a prison guard and eventually became the warden at San Quentin State Prison in Marin County. (Her brother, Clinton T. Duffy later was the warden at the prison.) She was raised in San Rafael, California. In the early 1900's, Ethel Duffy was an English major at the University of California at Berkeley. John Kenneth Turner and Ethel Duffy met there. They were married in March 1905. The Turners lived in Fresno briefly afterwards and were in San Francisco at the time of the April 1906 earthquake. The Turners spent the rest of the decade in Los Angeles. John Kenneth Turner worked at various newspapers on the West Coast as a journalist (reporter and sports editor). His jobs were in California's Central Valley, Portland, and also Los Angeles. (The Turners had a daughter Juanita, born in 1909, in Los Angeles.) John Kenneth Turner had traveled through Mexico before the Revolution of 1910, and wrote a book, *Barbarous Mexico* (1911) about the almost slave-like working conditions of the people of Mexico under the country's political and economic system led by Porfirio Díaz. His exposure of these conditions was an attempt to bring labor reform. (Part of his book was published as articles in the fall of 1909 in *The American Magazine*.) Ethel Duffy Turner accompanied her husband in his travels through Mexico, and she was also interested in the country's political issues.

The Turners had first visited Carmel in 1910 and they moved there in 1911. John Kenneth Turner became a good friend of George Sterling, as they shared beliefs in socialism. (In 1913, Turner was arrested, imprisoned, and almost executed in Mexico. Through the efforts of Carmel Highlands writer Harry Leon Wilson and especially those of George Sterling, who helped bring publicity to Turner's plight through the newspapers, along with the intervention of the United States government, John Kenneth Turner was released.)

§

UTOPIAN COMMUNITIES

As word of Carmel-by-the-Sea spread amongst writers, artists, poets, and other creative free-thinkers, Bohemians and intellectuals from other parts of the country were enticed to come to the seaside town. Some of them were looking for a peaceful, quiet place to live, where they could have the freedom to create an idealistic, utopian community with like-minded people. Many who had been part of the short-lived, Helicon Home Community (Helicon Hall) literary commune on the East Coast, founded by Upton Sinclair, made their way to Carmel-by-the-Sea in late 1908, in the months after its abrupt, unplanned end.

Upton Sinclair

Journalist, author, Socialist, and social crusader Upton Beall Sinclair, Jr. (1878-1968) was born in Baltimore, Maryland in 1878. He received a Bachelor of Arts degree from the College of the City of New York in 1897, and then took graduate classes at Columbia University. He became a professional writer while still in his teens. He submitted his jokes and articles to magazines, followed by the publication of his first "dime novels", which paid for his education. Afterwards, from 1901 to 1904, while at Columbia, Upton Sinclair's first novels were published, including *King Midas* (1901) and *Manassas* (1904). He married his first wife, Meta Fuller, and became a socialist in the early 1900's. They had a son, David, and they moved to Princeton, New Jersey.

The Jungle

Upton Sinclair's book, *The Jungle* (1906), a novel based on facts obtained from undercover reporting in 1904 at the Chicago stockyards, exposed the unsanitary meat packing industry practices in America along with the poor conditions of the workers. The book was successful and brought him fame instantly. It also resulted in nationwide attention to these conditions. This led to federal legislation: the Pure Food and Drug Act of 1906, which required labeling of all ingredients in food and medicines for consumer safety and the Federal Meat Inspection Act of 1906, which brought federal inspection to ensure sanitary slaughtering and processing of livestock.

Helicon Home Colony

In 1906, with the $30,000 in royalties he received from his book, *The Jungle*, Upton Sinclair made plans for, publicized, and established a utopian cooperative, Helicon Home Colony. He created it in the socialist spirit, as a commune for writers, teachers, and other professional workers. Sinclair bought 400 acres in Englewood, New Jersey, across the Hudson River and New York City. The location was chosen so that it would be far enough away from the city, but still close enough to New York for professional contacts. (Helicon Hall, the three-story building where the residents lived, had been a former boarding school for boys.) There were about 70 members in Upton Sinclair's communal living experiment; the members raised and grew their own food, brought up their children through the community, and did their own daily, domestic chores, as they decided not to have servants to assist them with tasks. Helicon Home Colony ran for five months in the winter from November 1906 through March of 1907. Along with Upton Sinclair, his wife Meta, and their young son, David, the other writers who lived at Helicon Hall were short story author and newspaperman, Michael Williams and his wife Margaret ("Peggy"), with their young son and daughter. Additionally, authors Alice MacGowan and Grace MacGowan Cooke, who were sisters, resided there with MacGowan Cooke's two children Helen and Katherine, as did a college-aged, aspiring writer, who worked in the cellar, Sinclair Lewis.

Michael Williams

Journalist, writer, and editor Charles Michael Williams (1877-1950) was born and grew up in Halifax, Nova Scotia, and was Catholic. His father, a sailor, died at sea when Michael was a teenager, and his family went into poverty. For the next five years, Williams, who had left school, worked at a warehouse until he moved to Boston. There he had a job in the basement of a "five and dime store", and during this time he sent stories and poems he wrote to magazines, but they were rejected. He also experienced his first of many recurrent, health problems with blood in his lungs. Michael Williams began his newspaper career in the South, where he edited a weekly newspaper. Some of his stories began to be published; then he returned back to Boston to be a writer. (He wrote stories and rewrote stories others had written for *Black Cat* magazine.) Afterwards, Williams began his career as a newspaperman, first in Boston, then in New York, and later in San Francisco. He spent over five years in New York as a reporter while he tried to establish himself as a writer. Due to more health problems (tuberculosis) he went to Texas with his wife and two children, to regain his health. Afterwards they moved to San Francisco, where he continued his newspaper career. He was the city editor of the *San Francisco Examiner* when the April 1906 earthquake and subsequent fires occurred. He lost a manuscript he had written which burned in the fire. The evening before the quake, he had eaten at Coppa's with friends James Hopper and Xavier Martinez. Six weeks later, he returned to New York, where he wrote stories for magazines such as *Everybody's*, and other publications. Late in 1906, Michael Williams went to New Jersey and became part of Upton Sinclair's Helicon Home Colony. The two became friends and shared socialist beliefs.

Alice MacGowan and Grace MacGowan Cooke

The MacGowan sisters, Alice MacGowan (1858-1947) and Grace MacGowan Cooke (1863-1944) were both born in Ohio towns, Perrysburg and Grand Rapids, respectively, but were raised in Tennessee. During the Civil War, their father, John E. MacGowan was a Colonel in the Union Army. The family moved to Chattanooga, Tennessee in 1865, and remained there after the war ended. Colonel MacGowan worked as a lawyer, and then in 1872, he became the editor of the *Chattanooga Times* newspaper, where he remained until his death in 1903. The MacGowan sisters were "self-educated"; both married and were schoolteachers before they became writers. Alice had a brief marriage to a man who was much older than she was. Grace married William Cooke in 1887, and they remained married for close to two decades. She worked at a print shop, MacGowan & Cooke, which was owned by their brother, Frank, and her husband. Grace was a bookkeeper during the day, and she wrote articles in the evening. By 1888, her first stories were published in magazines. During their long writing careers, the MacGowan sisters wrote books, whose subject matter varied and ranged from historical romances to social novels to Westerns and mysteries; they also wrote short stories, poems, essays, and magazine articles. The two authors dictated all of their work and always employed private secretaries who typed their material. The MacGowans often worked together and also collaborated with other authors on their writings. The sisters' first books were published in the 1900's. Grace wrote the historical novel, *Mistress Joy, A Tale of Natchez in 1798* (1901), with Knoxville writer, Annie Booth McKinney. Alice MacGowan's *The Last Word* (1902) was her first published book, a novel, said to be autobiographical, based on letters written while she traveled through Texas on horseback. Next Grace wrote *A Gourd Fiddle* (1904) and *The Grapple: A Story of the Illinois Coal Region* (1905). Together Grace and Alice wrote *Huldah, Proprietor of Wagon-Tire House and Genial Philosopher of the Cattle Country*, (1904) and *Return: A Story of the Sea Islands in 1739* (1905). They also wrote fiction stories for children and books for young adults.

Grace and William had two daughters, Helen Cooke (1895-1945) and Katherine Cooke (1901-1972), who were both born in Chattanooga. Grace MacGowan Cooke, her two daughters, along with Alice, left Tennessee in March of 1906 and made their way to the Helicon Home Colony in New Jersey, later that year. Grace had left her husband at this time. (William Cooke filed for divorce, under the grounds of desertion, and the divorce was granted in 1908.)

Sinclair Lewis

Journalist, short story author, novelist, and playwright Harry Sinclair Lewis (1885-1951) was born in Sauk Centre, Minnesota, the youngest of three sons. His father was a doctor; his mother died in 1891, when he was six years old, and his father remarried about a year later. Harry Lewis, as he was known at the time, attended Oberlin Academy, a college preparatory school in Ohio, before he began Yale University in 1903. As a teenager, Lewis described himself as "tall, ugly, thin, (and) red-haired..."[13] a description shared by others who knew him. His classmates viewed him as a provincial, "gawky Midwesterner", who stood out because of his lanky and gangling physique. While at Yale, Harry Lewis wrote prose poems and was interested in literature. He contributed to the campus publications: *The Yale Literary Magazine*, the *Courant*, and the *Record*. He

---

13   Richard L. Lingeman, *Sinclair Lewis: Rebel from Main Street*, p. 16

also worked part time for the New Haven newspaper, *Journal Courier*, where he rewrote stories on the night desk shift. By 1905, his first work was published in magazines, such as *The Critic*. As part of a speaking tour, author and Socialist Jack London gave a lecture at Yale in January 1906. (According to London's biographer, Russ Kingman, Lewis met London there, and he would develop a friendship with the established author.) Among Lewis's friends at the university were other like-minded, literary students, such as Bill Benét. *[Poet, novelist, editor, and Pulitzer Prize winner in 1942, William Rose Benét (1886-1950) was born at Fort Hamilton (army base) in Brooklyn, New York. His father and grandfather were both officers in the U.S. Army. As an undergraduate, he was involved with the* Yale Courant *and the* Yale Record, *where he became editor. William Rose Benét received his degree in 1907.]* Harry Lewis didn't like Yale, and he dropped out at the end of October 1906. During some of his time off, he became part of the Helicon Home Colony, where he operated the furnace, in exchange for room and board. He met Alice MacGowan and Grace MacGowan Cooke. After about a month at Upton Sinclair's utopian commune, Lewis left because he wanted more time to write.

Fire at Helicon Hall

In the early morning of March 16, 1907, a fire broke out at Helicon Hall, where all the members lived, and the entire building burned down. Among the 70 occupants, there were numerous injuries, some serious, and one fatality; a carpenter was found dead in his room. When the fire started, Upton Sinclair went up and down the hallways of Helicon Hall and knocked on doors to awaken the residents. He, his wife, and son got out safely, as did Michael Williams, his wife, and two children, who fled the smoke-filled building. Some of the residents jumped from windows to escape the flames and smoke, and were hurt in doing so. Among those whose lives were saved, Grace MacGowan Cooke's two daughters, Helen and Katherine, were dropped from a window into the arms of rescuers on the ground below. Afterwards, their mother and aunt each jumped from the window, onto a blanket held by Upton Sinclair and other men, but it gave out under their weight and the women both fell to the ground. They were hospitalized for their internal injuries and suffered back problems. As with the other writers who lived in Helicon Hall, the MacGowan sisters lost all of their personal possessions and manuscripts; it was the same case for Upton Sinclair and Michael Williams.

"Helicon Hall on the hoof"

In addition to the socialist cause, Williams and Sinclair also shared a newly found passion in natural, healthful food and simple living to cure them of their ills and to become well. Both had experienced health problems and had opted for healthier lifestyles and natural foods as a remedy. Michael Williams would later admit in his autobiography that he drank too much; he changed his diet, turned to vegetarianism, and stopped drinking. (He had previously earned the nickname, the "Wild Irishman".) Upton Sinclair became a health faddist to combat his multiple ailments, including his stomach problems and nervous disorders. He, too, became a strict vegetarian, didn't drink alcohol, coffee, or tea, and didn't smoke. After the Helicon Hall disaster, Sinclair did not rebuild the commune. Instead, for a while, he and Michael Williams considered the possibility of forming a traveling literary colony, "...a perambulating colony, a Helicon Hall on the hoof..."[14] as described by Williams. They planned to take it on the road from place to place out West along the Pacific Coast and in the mountains, with stops in Bohemian locales such as Point Loma, Carmel, San Francisco, Berkeley, and Yosemite. The members would live outdoors and live off the land. Michael Williams explained, "It will be a health pilgrimage, a pæan to the outdoor life... We are worshippers of sunshine and fresh air and cold water and the simple life; we use no alcohol nor tobacco, tea nor coffee, nor the corpses of our fellow-creatures."[15] Along with their planned journey, Sinclair and Williams had proposed a series of magazine articles about the traveling colony and its healthful ways. However, none of it ever happened, as their wives didn't like the idea and it was also made fun of in the press.

---

14 Michael Williams, *The Book of the High Romance, A Spiritual Autobiography*, p. 187

15 *ibid.*, p. 188

Good Health, and How We Won It

Nonetheless, Sinclair and Williams did team up to write a health book based on their visit in the fall of 1907, to the Battle Creek Sanitarium ("the San") in Michigan. (Upton Sinclair's wife had arrived first, he joined her there, and then Williams followed in October 1907.) *[The facility was run by John Harvey Kellogg (1852-1943), a physician, surgeon, author, lecturer, and health advocate. He influenced thousands of health-seekers. Kellogg promoted exercise along with simple, healthful eating, a vegetarian diet, and the avoidance of drugs, tobacco, alcohol, and caffeine. His brother, Will Keith Kellogg, managed the business. In the 1890's, John Harvey Kellogg invented health foods, such as ready-to-eat cereal flakes. Will Keith Kellogg began the Battle Creek Toasted Corn Flake Company in 1906, which was the start of the eventual Kellogg's breakfast cereal corporation, the Kellogg Company.]* After the Michigan visit, Upton Sinclair and Michael Williams went to Bermuda with their families, in late 1907 until early 1908, where they spent the winter. They wrote their book about diet education and reform, *Good Health, and How We Won It*, during this time, but it wasn't published until 1909. (Upton Sinclair had used advance money from his book *The Metropolis* (1908), to pay for the Bermuda trip. Sinclair wrote *The Moneychangers* (1908), as a sequel to *The Metropolis*, and dedicated the book to Jack London. The two novels were based on the world of Wall Street bankers and the wealthy.)

FORMER HELICON HOME COLONY MEMBERS COME TO CARMEL

The first arrival, Michael Williams in 1908

After the stay in Bermuda, Michael Williams returned to New York, where he shared a residence for a while with his friend James Hopper, who had recently left Carmel-by-the-Sea. Hopper is said to have convinced Williams to go to the seaside town. While he was on the East Coast, Michael Williams experienced more problems with his lungs (he coughed blood). In 1908, he decided to go to the Desert Southwest and California to restore his health. He acknowledged that by his early 30's, his body had been "...shaken and racked and badly damaged by tuberculosis...

nicotine and alcohol."[16] Michael Williams, his wife and family were the first of the former Helicon Home Colony residents to arrive and settle in Carmel-by-the-Sea, sometime around the summer of 1908. During his years in the town, Williams continued to work as a writer; he wrote plays and edited the *Carmel Whirl*, a newspaper of the Arts and Crafts Club. (In the *Carmel Whirl*, he published the poetry of George Sterling, Henry Lafler, and Sinclair Lewis.) For his first three and a half decades, Michael Williams admitted he had wandered through life, and had been on a spiritual quest. Along with the influence of the Carmel Mission, he eventually returned to his Catholic roots, as he later documented in his autobiography.

Upton Sinclair follows in November 1908

Upton Sinclair headed out to California in September of 1908. In early November, he arrived in Carmel-by-the-Sea, where he stayed for three months, during the winter of 1908 to 1909. It is most likely that Sinclair had learned of Carmel-by-the-Sea from his friend, George Sterling, who urged him to visit. It would be the first time Sterling and Sinclair would meet in person; the two had corresponded by letters for some time, as was Sterling's practice of communicating with other writers whom he admired. They also shared a common bond of their socialist beliefs. Upton Sinclair was welcomed to Carmel-by-the-Sea by George Sterling and he stayed at Arnold Genthe's home. (Genthe had gone on a trip to Japan for six months in 1908.) While in town, Upton Sinclair kept physically active and spent much time outdoors: he took longs walks, played tennis, went horseback riding, and swam early in the morning. He maintained his strict, vegetarian diet regime. Sinclair mostly ate fruit, salads, nuts, and shredded wheat or graham crackers, something he himself and the Carmelites jokingly referred to as a "squirrel diet". Yet it didn't take long for Upton Sinclair to become upset at George Sterling and the rest of the Bohemians for their drinking. His rigid ways did not fit in well with the easygoing lifestyle in Carmel. In early January 1909 Sinclair left for San Francisco, where he remained for the next four months.

---

16   *ibid.*, p. 219

The MacGowans relocate in December 1908

In the summer of 1908, Alice MacGowan and Grace MacGowan Cooke spent time in a Missouri sanitarium for ongoing health problems from their injuries in the Helicon Home Colony fire rescue. Afterwards, they lived in New York, where Sinclair Lewis visited them. The MacGowan sisters were in search of another writer's colony where they could relocate. Peggy Williams, Michael Williams' wife, convinced them to move to Carmel-by-the-Sea, which they did in December 1908. At that time, Alice was 50 years old, Grace was 45 years old, and daughter Helen was entering her teenage years, while younger daughter Katherine (or "Kit") was seven. In Carmel-by-the-Sea, the MacGowan sisters bought and moved into a large, two-story house on Thirteenth Avenue, 2 Northeast of San Antonio Street. It had been built in 1905 by architect Eugenia Maybury, as her own residence. (Carmel has had a history of female builders.) The house was constructed in the Tudor Revival style, with half-timbering. The MacGowan residence was about one block up from Carmel Beach; that part of the beach became known as "Cooke's Cove". Though the MacGowan sisters became part of the Bohemian group focused around George Sterling, both of the authors were known for being serious, hard workers, who went to bed early, seldom attended parties, and abstained from alcohol. (The sisters continued to work together and had a pattern to their writing collaboration. After their typist typed their dictation in a triple spaced format, to make their edits, Alice literally cut the typed paper, sometimes sentence-by-sentence, and pasted it together in a new order. This work was then re-typed by the typist, and they read it aloud after dinner.) The next books that Alice MacGowan wrote included: *Judith of the Cumberlands* (1908), *The Wiving of Lance Cleaverage* (1909), and *The Sword in the Mountains*, (1910), a novel set during the Civil War, with Emma Bell Miles as a contributor and artist. Grace MacGowan Cooke wrote the children's book, *Son Riley Rabbit and Little Girl* (1908), in which her younger daughter "Kit" posed for the book's illustrations. Cooke wrote *The Power and The Glory* (1910), a novel set in Appalachia, which addressed feminist issues, as well as poor cotton mill working conditions. (Grace MacGowan Cooke also wrote for *The Nautilus*, a New Thought movement magazine, which published articles on self-help, wellness, and health fads. She wrote the article, "The Spiritual Meaning of Fletcherism" (the practice of chewing one's food many times, as a purported health benefit), which appeared in the January 1908 issue. The editor and publisher of *The Nautilus*, Elizabeth Towne and her husband, William Towne, frequently updated readers on the latest news about the two sisters, and visited them in Carmel in 1909.)

Sinclair Lewis arrives in January 1909

In 1907, Harry Sinclair Lewis spent time in New York, where his writing career began, mostly with freelance work. His short pieces and verse were published in children's, humor, and literary magazines. These included *Puck, Life*, and *The Smart Set*. For a while he worked as an assistant editor for *Transatlantic Tales*; he translated German stories into English for the publication. Lewis obtained an agent in 1907. That same year his adventures included travel to Panama, where he wanted to help build the Panama Canal, but he didn't get a job there. He returned to New Haven, Connecticut in late December 1907. At that point Lewis decided to go back to Yale and he completed his final exams in June 1908. Harry Lewis earned his Bachelor of Arts degree and graduated with the class of 1908. In the summer of 1908, he worked at a newspaper in Waterloo, Iowa as an editorial writer and proofreader, but he was fired after a few months. His agent sold a story of his for $75 to *Redbook* magazine and Lewis used the money to buy a train ticket to California. He would go to Carmel, where Grace MacGowan Cooke offered him a part-time job to work as a secretary, for herself and her sister. [There is some discrepancy as to whether Lewis paid for the train ticket out to California himself, as his biographer, Richard Lingeman states, or whether the MacGowan sisters paid for his ticket, as others have written, such as Kay Baker Gaston, their biographer.] The young college graduate, 23-year old Harry Sinclair Lewis arrived in Carmel-by-the-Sea on January 5th, 1909. (Though he still went by the name of "Harry" at the time, he was also called "Red" because of his red hair, and was nicknamed "Hal" by the MacGowans.) Lewis lived in a small cabin, which he rented for five dollars a month. It was close by to the beach and to his employers, the MacGowans.

William Rose Benét arrives later in January 1909

William Rose Benét had gone to California in 1909. His father, Colonel James Walker Benét was in the U.S. Army, stationed in Benicia, in the East Bay region, where he was commander of the Benicia Arsenal. Lewis's friend, Bill Benét arrived in Carmel-by-the-Sea in late January 1909 and became his roommate. Benét began his career as a freelance writer; he wrote for *Sunset* magazine. The two young, carefree bachelors were well-known around town as partygoers. They were regulars at the picnics on Carmel Beach. Photographer Arnold Genthe recalled in his autobiography, *As I Remember*, that in Carmel-by-the-Sea he took walks with Harry Sinclair Lewis through the woods and they had long discussions. He, Lewis, and Benét all liked Helen Cooke, who would turn 14 that year. (Arnold Genthe used Helen Cooke as a model for some of his photographs on the beach, in which the women were dressed in classical, silk, flowing gowns, which made them look as if they were "Greek goddesses". He also photographed Helen in a field of poppies in Carmel during this time.) As an expression of his fondness for Helen Cooke, Sinclair Lewis often flirted with her. On one occasion, he was said to have made an inappropriate remark, in German, about the teenager and was promptly fired by her mother, Grace MacGowan Cooke. (At the time he still owed money to the family.) Thus, six months after Lewis's arrival, he and Benét left Carmel and went up to the Bay Area. Lewis stayed with William Rose Benét and his family in Benicia during the summer of 1909. Afterwards, Harry Lewis moved to San Francisco, where George Sterling helped him get a job at the *San Francisco Evening Bulletin* newspaper. He was a copy editor and reporter, but he was soon fired from that job, as well. Lewis then worked at the AP (Associated Press) wire service, a night job, but he resigned right as he learned he was to be fired from that position. He wrote articles for *Sunset* magazine and received free railroad passes on the Southern Pacific Railroad to travel, as the magazine was owned by the railroad. Sinclair Lewis also wrote for *The Nautilus*, which published two of his works, a story and a serial. (He had met magazine's editors, the Townes, when they visited the MacGowans in Carmel earlier in the year.)

10

The Simplicity of Life and A Typical Day in Carmel-by-the-Sea

SIMPLICITY OF LIFE IN CARMEL

The Bohemians in Carmel-by-the-Sea enjoyed a relatively uncomplicated and carefree lifestyle, filled with the fundamental joys of friendship and the pleasure of the company of others. They often marched to the beat of their own drummers and had freedom to express themselves in free-spirited, idiosyncratic, unconventional, and other eccentric ways. The Carmel-by-the-Sea Bohemians were away from life in the cities and the complexities it entailed. Carmel historians Daisy Bostick and Dorothea Castelhun observed, "Things that mattered so vitally in the cities such as bank accounts, conventional clothing, keeping up appearances--seemed no longer of much importance."[17] Furthermore, in addition to the simplicity of life in Carmel-by-the-Sea, it was inexpensive to live in the village, and one could survive off the land. There was plenty of food to be obtained by hunting, fishing, gathering seafood (abalone and mussels), and growing fruit and vegetable gardens. Mary Austin remarked how basic activities such as the pursuit of food, chopping trees for firewood, and building a home brought satisfaction in life. She recalled in her autobiography, *Earth*

---

17   Daisy Bostick and Dorothea Castelhun, *Carmel at Work and Play*, p. 51

Horizon, of the early days in Carmel-by-the-Sea with George Sterling, "It was the simplest occupations that gave us the most pleasure and yielded the richest harvest of impressions, observations and feeling responses."[18] The Bohemians in Carmel-by-the-Sea appreciated nature around them, spent much time outdoors, and were aware that they lived in one of the most beautiful areas on the West Coast. This beauty that surrounded them: the Pacific Ocean, the beach, the trees, the mountains and the valley brought them happiness and pleasure. It also provided inspiration for their work, such as their poetry, art, and writing.

A typical day in Carmel-by-the-Sea

Carmel-by-the-Sea has always had a mild climate year-round. On a typical day, the morning fog blanketed most of the town. In the early part of the day many of the Bohemians did their work. They wrote, painted, or read. On weekdays some kept themselves on strict work schedules and weren't to be interrupted for socializing. Yet some others often shared in the creative process; for example, they collaborated on writing or they edited each other's work. By the afternoon, when the fog had usually burned off, the Bohemians frequently spent time outdoors in the fresh air. They took horseback rides or long walks in the area, and sometimes even made longer hikes south to Point Lobos, which was a rugged trek. Before the trip back to Carmel-by-the-Sea, they fortified themselves with a picnic lunch. They relished foods such as enchiladas, shrimp salad, and fried fish. Sometimes on weekends, a group occasionally hiked as far south as Big Sur, or they camped out in the Santa Lucia Mountain Range. In the evenings, if they weren't gathered at the beach, the Bohemians entertained guests at their homes. They ate seafood stew or fish chowder ("Thackeray stew" which was like a Bouillabaisse) and drank ale and muscatel. The Carmelites sat around the fireplace in their living room, where they talked, laughed, and drank into the early hours of the morning. Another place where the Carmel Bohemians often met was at the Pine Inn, especially if the weather was bad. They played cards or charades, sang songs, and engaged in long, free-spirited, intellectual discussions and debates on a variety of subjects, such as socialism.

18   Mary Austin, *Earth Horizon*, p. 298

Frequently during the daytime the Bohemians went to Carmel Beach to have a picnic, fly a kite, or swim in the chilly water. Some searched for abalone along the rocks or dove for it in Carmel Bay. (Abalone is a mollusk, with a large flat, oval-shaped shell, which was abundant in Carmel Bay at the time.) George Sterling and James Hopper were among those who collected abalone. (It is said that Hopper, who was a good swimmer, was the one who taught Sterling how to search for it.) The shellfish, such as abalone and mussels that they gathered, would afterwards be cooked on an open fire at the beach. This was done during their legendary parties, which came to symbolize and demonstrate the enjoyment of life by the Bohemians in Carmel-by-the-Sea during its first years, and the memorable times they spent together. The group gathered around a driftwood fire, drank alcohol, smoked, talked (what Mary Austin described as "ambrosial, unquotable talk"),[19] laughed, and sang songs, as they prepared and then roasted the shellfish, under the moonlight, with the sound of a steady crash of waves in the background. In Jack London's fictional book, *The Valley of the Moon* (1913) the two main characters, Billy and Saxon Roberts, spend some time with the Bohemians in Carmel-by-the-Sea. London's descriptions of the Bohemians and their daily lives were based on his real-life friends and recollections of his stays in the seaside town. London wrote of the dreamlike atmosphere at a group picnic on Carmel Beach.

> "Saxon's enjoyment was keen, almost ecstatic, and she had difficulty convincing herself of the reality of it all. It seemed like some fairy tale or book story come true...What impressed [Saxon] most was their [the Bohemians'] excessive jollity, their childlike joy, and the childlike things they did. This effect was heightened by the fact that they were novelists and painters, poets and critics, sculptors and musicians."[20]

The Abalone Song

The abalone meat needed to be flattened to tenderize it, so the Bohemians would pound the abalone for about an hour before they grilled it over

---

19   Mary Austin, "George Sterling at Carmel", *American Mercury*, Volume XI, Number 41, May 1927, p. 66

20   Jack London, *The Valley of the Moon*, p. 315-316

the fire. As they prepared the abalone, the Bohemians created and sang a song, the "Abalone Song". This ode to the shellfish delicacy ended up with ninety verses, as new ones were added while they drank and waited for the abalone to be ready to eat. George Sterling along with Michael Williams and visitor Sinclair Lewis were among several of the Carmel Bohemians who are credited with composing some of the original verses. Most of the song was a compilation of silly, at times farcical phrases that rhymed with the refrain that ended in "abalone". In a section of *The Valley of the Moon*, Billy and Saxon Roberts took part in one of the beach get-togethers with the "Tribe of Abalone Eaters" of Carmel, as the Bohemians were referred to in the book. London described the carefree days the characters spent at the beach in Carmel, as they gathered and prepared their abalone feast. He wrote of the "Abalone Song", which he called, "Hymn to the Abalone". (The verses that Jack London used in his book were many of the popular ones in the actual song, sung by the real Carmel Bohemians.) The character "Mark Hall", in *The Valley of the Moon*, who was said to have been based on George Sterling, explained the song to the guests:

> "'Now, listen; I'm going to teach you something,' [Mark] Hall commanded, a large round rock poised in his hand above the abalone meat. 'You must never, never pound abalone without singing this song. Nor must you sing this song at any other time. It would be the rankest sacrilege. Abalone is the food of the gods. Its preparation is a religious function. Now listen, and follow, and remember that it is a very solemn occasion.'"[21]

"The stone came down with a thump on the white meat, and thereafter arose and fell in a sort of tom-tom accompaniment to the poet's song:

> 'Oh, some folks boast of quail on toast.
>   Because they think it's tony;
> But I'm content to owe my rent
>   And live on abalone...'

---

21   *ibid.*, p. 310-315

'Some stick to biz, some flirt with Liz
    Down on the sands of Coney
But we, by hell, live in Carmel,
    And whang the abalone.'

'We sit around and gaily pound
    And bear no acrimony,
Because our ob--ject is a gob
    Of sizzling abalone.'

'Oh! Some like ham and some like lamb
    And some like macaroni;
But bring me in a pail of gin
    And a tub of abalone.'

'Oh! Some drink rain and some champagne
    Or brandy by the pony;
 But I will try a little rye
    With a dash of abalone.'

Some live on hope and some on dope
    And some on alimony;
But my tom-cat, he lives on fat
    And tender abalone.

'The more we take, the more they make,
    In deep sea-matrimony;
Race-suicide cannot betide
    The fertile abalone.'"[22]

May 22, 1910 *Los Angeles Times* article

The routine beach picnics at Carmel-by-the-Sea were characterized and even satirized in a May 22, 1910 illustrated article about the town and its Bohemian residents, which appeared in the *Los Angeles Times*. It was

---

22   *ibid.*

titled, "Hot Bed of Soulful Culture, Vortex of Erotic Erudition. Carmel in California, where Author and Artist Folk are Establishing the Most Amazing Colony on Earth". The article's author, Willard Huntington Wright ridiculed many of the Carmel Bohemians and their eccentric and even pretentious traits and ways. Wright spent a week in Carmel-by-the-Sea doing research for the piece. He derided what he perceived as the Carmelites taking themselves and their intellectual abilities too seriously. Wright mocked, "The plumber of Carmel has subscribed to the Harvard Classics; the butcher reads Browning, and the liveryman wears long hair."[23] He divided the Carmel Bohemian writers and artists into two groups: "The Respectables", whose members George Sterling, Jack London, James Hopper, Fred Bechdolt, "Harry" Lafler, Bert Heron, and Xavier Martinez drank alcohol and enjoyed themselves. While Wright labeled those who did not drink, went to bed early, and were more serious about their work, as the "Eminently Respectables". That group consisted of the MacGowan sisters, Arnold Genthe, Arthur Vachell, Mary Austin, and Upton Sinclair. There were cartoons that accompanied the article. One of the illustrations was of a large group of most of the well-known Carmel Bohemians, while on a picnic at Point Lobos, all drawn as caricatures of themselves. For example, even though Upton Sinclair was no longer in Carmel-by-the-Sea, he was shown eating a tomato. Mary Austin, who was also away at this time, was pictured wearing her hair down, dressed in a long gown, and on a walk in the woods. George Sterling was illustrated cutting firewood. *[Harvard educated journalist, critic, and editor Willard Huntington Wright (1888-1939) later wrote under the pseudonym, S. S. Van Dine. He became best known for his fictional mystery stories about a detective named Philo Vance.]*

§

---

23   Kevin Starr, *Americans and the California Dream 1850-1915*, p. 269

VISITORS AND NEW ARRIVALS IN 1910

Sinclair Lewis and Jack London return to Carmel again, early in 1910

Harry Sinclair Lewis came back again to Carmel-by-the-Sea in the late winter and early spring of 1910. It was at the same time Jack London happened to be visiting, for two weeks in late February through March. Once again, London and his wife Charmian were guests of George and Carrie Sterling. During the time the Londons were in town, a large group of the Carmel Bohemians and their wives walked to the Point Lobos area, where they enjoyed a big picnic at the beach. Among those who attended were Arnold Genthe, Fred and Adele Bechdolt, and Peggy Williams. Though it would be years before he authored his first novels, Sinclair Lewis had the creative ability to come up with inventive ideas for stories on the spot, and as he noted them down, he compiled a huge file of story plots. Lewis impressed the Bohemians with this skill and he made a profit from it, too, when he sold some of these plots to fellow writers, such as Jack London. Twice in 1910, Lewis sold story plots to him. It was said that Jack London needed ideas, while Sinclair Lewis needed the money. The charge was about $5 for each, and Lewis sold a combined total of around two dozen plots to London on two occasions, bringing him a sum of about $120. [There is lack of consistency among biographers as to exactly the number of plots sold to London and the total dollar amount Lewis was paid, depending on different accounts by Franklin Walker, Russ Kingman, and others, so this is an approximate estimation.] Only a few of the plots were used by London. One of these became his work, *The Assassination Bureau, Ltd.*, a novel, which London never finished; he had written about 20,000 words. (In 1963, a sci-fi author, Robert Fish, bought it and finished writing it.) A second one of Lewis's plots became London's novelette: *The Abysmal Brute*. Lewis used the money he received from London in March 1910 to leave California and go to Washington D.C., where he worked at a magazine, *The Volta Review*. Subsequently, his next job was in New York, the place where he wanted to be, as a manuscript reader for publisher Frederick A. Stokes. Lewis lived in Greenwich Village, and his roommate again was William Rose Benét. Later Sinclair Lewis worked as editor of *Adventure* magazine, and began to have his stories published in *The Saturday Evening Post*. This was all before he became a successful novelist in the 1920's. In 1921, George Sterling recalled, that during the time Harry Sinclair Lewis was in Carmel-by-the-Sea, he was their "ugly duckling", while Sterling admitted he used to be the "giddy swan" of the seaside town.[24]

Ambrose Bierce's one and only visit, 1910

After numerous invitations, George Sterling's mentor, Ambrose Bierce, finally decided to make a trip to Carmel-by-the-Sea in August of 1910. It was his one and only visit. He stayed for a week at the Pine Inn. Bierce had frequently dismissed Carmel's Bohemian colony with descriptions of its members as a "nest of anarchists", radicals, Socialists, and "cranks and curios".[25] He was contemptuous of the Carmel Bohemians and their lifestyles. Sterling served his guest the Carmel staples: mussels and abalone, and he boasted that Bierce, a difficult man to please, liked them.

John Fleming Wilson

One of the writers who joined the Bohemian colony at Carmel-by-the-Sea around 1910 was John Fleming Wilson, known as "Jack". He had been part of the Coppa Bohemian group in San Francisco, while he was a newspaperman there. When he settled in Carmel, Wilson lived in a bungalow around Carmel Point. Journalist, novelist, and short story writer John Fleming Wilson (1877-1922) was born in Erie, Pennsylvania. His father was a reverend, who later became the president of the Portland (Adventist) Academy in Oregon, and thus the family lived in the state for some time. In 1900 John Fleming Wilson received his B.A. from Princeton University. He returned to Portland, where he taught for two years at his father's school. Then Wilson began his newspaper career with jobs in Oregon, California, and Hawaii. He worked at *The Oregonian* in Portland, and went on to be editor of the *San Francisco Argonaut*. Wilson also wrote for the *Honolulu Advertiser*. His early, published works included

---

24   *From Baltimore to Bohemia, The Letters of H. L. Mencken and George Sterling*, Edited by S. T. Joshi, p. 124

25   George Sterling, "A Memoir of Ambrose Bierce", *The Letters of Ambrose Bierce*, Edited by Bertha Clark Pope, p. xxxix, p. 121

The Amateur Revolutionist (1906), which was a collection of his stories from the *Argonaut* and *South Sea Stories* (1907). John Fleming Wilson had a long-time interest in the sea; he was very familiar with sailing, different types of sailing vessels, and the entire West Coast and its ports. He used his knowledge and experience with the sea frequently as the subject matter for his writing. When he came to Carmel, he gave up newspaper work and became a short story writer. Many of his fiction stories appeared in magazines such as the *Pacific Monthly, Sunset,* and later *The Saturday Evening Post* and *Cosmopolitan*. During his lifetime, John Fleming Wilson authored about a hundred short stories. The books he wrote while he spent time in Carmel were *Across the Latitudes* (1911), a collection of twelve sea stories, *The Land Claimers* (1911), his book about frontier life in Oregon, *The Man Who Came Back* (1912), which became a play, *The Princess of Sorry Valley* (1913), and *The Master Key* (1915).

John Fleming Wilson also wrote short stories and books that appealed to younger audiences. His boy scout adventure stories, which were centered around the character, Tad Sheldon, and set on the Pacific Coast, appeared in *Boys' Life* magazine. The stories were also collected and published as books, such as *Tad Sheldon, Second Class Scout* (1913), which first appeared in *The Saturday Evening Post, Tad Sheldon, Boy Scout: Stories of His Patrol,* (1913), and *Tad Sheldon's Fourth of July: More Stories of His Patrol,* (1913), which was illustrated by Norman P. Rockwell.

Grant Wallace

Also about this same time, journalist and magazine writer Grant Wallace became a resident of Carmel-by-the-Sea. Artist, reporter, war correspondent, essayist, and lecturer Grant Wallace (1867-1954) was born in Hopkins, Missouri. He graduated from Western Normal College in Shenandoah, Iowa, with a B.S. degree in 1889 and he taught school in the Midwest. Wallace also studied art in New York at the Art Students League. He worked as a newspaper artist and writer in St. Paul, Minnesota at the *St. Paul Pioneer Press,* before he moved to San Francisco in the 1890's. Wallace spent several years working for various newspapers in the city: the *Examiner, Chronicle,* and *Evening Bulletin*. At these papers, Wallace was a reporter, editorial writer, and illustrator. (For example, while at the *San Francisco Examiner*, he drew the cartoons that accompanied Ambrose Bierce's editorials.) Wallace later became a lead editorial and feature writer at the *Evening Bulletin*. During the Russo-Japanese war in 1904, Grant Wallace was a war correspondent for the *Bulletin* and his articles were syndicated in other papers, as well. After his return back to California, he tried to cross over from journalism into fiction writing. Wallace wrote short stories and illustrated them, but was not as successful in this endeavor. In the early 1910's, he became a Carmel resident with his wife and children.

Harry Leon Wilson

When Harry Leon Wilson settled in the Carmel area in 1910, at the age of 43, he was already one of the most accomplished and financially well-off writers to live in the community, yet his most successful work was still to come. Writer, novelist, and humorist Harry Leon Wilson (1867-1939) was born in Oregon, Illinois, a small town in the northern part of the state. His father was a newspaper publisher and Harry Leon Wilson learned the skills of the trade early on, such as type setting. He went to public schools and liked to read Bret Harte and Mark Twain, which led to his interest in the West. After Wilson learned shorthand and secretarial skills, he left school at age sixteen, and made his way out west. Harry Leon Wilson worked for the Union Pacific Railroad as a stenographer, first in Omaha and then in Denver between late 1884 through late 1885. After that position, he then worked in the Denver office of the Bancroft History Company. *[H. H. (Hubert Howe) Bancroft was the author and publisher of history books about the American West.]* Wilson collected pioneer histories and sold subscriptions as a traveling salesman for the company for a year in 1886. While still working at Bancroft, he went to California for the first time in 1887, initially to San Francisco and afterwards to Los Angeles. In 1889 Wilson went back to work for the Union Pacific Railroad in Omaha, this time as the secretary for the Chief Engineer, Virgil G. Bogue.

During his lifetime, Harry Leon Wilson would be married and divorced three times. In the late 1890's, when he was in his early 30's in Denver, he entered into his first marriage, to journalist, author, and recent young widower, Wilbertine Nesselrode Teters Worden (1867-1949). The marriage was brief and they divorced in 1900.

While he lived out west, Harry Leon Wilson took notes on his humorous observations and used them for his stories, which he sent to magazines on the East Coast, in hopes of having them published. His first story, "The Elusive Dollar Bill", was picked up in 1886 by one of the main humor magazines in the country, *Puck*, a weekly, which was based in New York City. Wilson studied the magazine's format and submitted other contributions to *Puck*. He worked his way up from a staff writer to assistant editor in 1892, and eventually to editor in 1896, where he stayed through 1902. Wilson chose jokes, and wrote stories and some editorials. He spent most of the 1890's in New York while at *Puck*. His first book, *Zigzag Tales from the East to the West*, a collection of short stories was published in 1894. Harry Leon Wilson spent ten years living in New York, but he wanted to move away and be able to write full time. He wrote his first novel, *The Spenders: A Tale of the Third Generation* (1902), and used the book's advance money to quit his job and leave New York.

At that time, in 1902, Harry Leon Wilson married his second wife, a divorcee, Rose Cecil O'Neill Latham (1874-1944). She was a professional artist who contributed drawings to many well-known magazines, including *Collier's*, *Cosmopolitan*, *Harper's*, and *Life*, and she worked on the staff of *Puck* as an illustrator. O'Neill also wrote short stories and verse for *Puck*, and wrote and illustrated a novel, *The Loves of Edwy* (1904). They settled in the Ozarks in Southern Missouri, where Rose had built a large house for her family, called "Bonniebrook". Harry Leon Wilson wrote his next three novels there between 1903 and 1905, including *The Lions of the Lord* (1903), (which he had researched in Colorado and Salt Lake City), *The Seeker* (1904), and *The Boss of Little Arcady* (1905). Rose illustrated four of his books including *The Spenders* and *The Lions of the Lord*.

Harry Leon Wilson met author Booth Tarkington in New York in 1904. They became friends and would collaborate as playwrights in the years to come. [Novelist and playwright Newton Booth Tarkington (1869-1946) was born in Indianapolis and he lived there throughout much of his life. He studied at Purdue University and Princeton University. Tarkington became a best-selling and popular author of forty books, along with poetry, novels, short stories, and more than twenty plays. His "Penrod" series of novels about a boy coming of age were as widely known in popular culture as Mark Twain's *The Adventures of Tom Sawyer*. Tarkington later won Pulitzer Prizes in 1919 and 1922 for his novels, *The Magnificent Ambersons* (1918) and *Alice Adams* (1921). Much of his work included humorous observations of the places he spent time in, including Europe and the Midwest.]

In 1905, Wilson and Tarkington traveled with their wives to Europe, where they began to write plays together over the next half decade. In 1905 they all went to Capri, Italy, and then they spent 1906 through 1909 in Paris. While the couples were in Europe, Rose studied art in Italy and France, and exhibited her artwork at the Paris Salon in 1906 and 1907. Harry Leon Wilson and Booth Tarkington's first collaboration, *The Man from Home* (1908) was based on their perceptions of Americans in Europe. *The Man from Home* became a very successful play and was produced on Broadway, as well as at other theaters around the United States. Together they earned more than $600,000 from the play. Wilson and Tarkington wrote half a dozen plays jointly through 1910, including *Cameo Kirby* (1908), *Foreign Exchange* (1909), *Springtime* (1909), *If I Had Money* (1909), and *Your Humble Servant* (1910).

While he was still in Europe, Harry Leon Wilson's fifth novel, *Ewing's Lady* (1907) was published. After five years of marriage, Harry and Rose separated in Europe and divorced in 1907. (Later, she went on to make the popular Kewpie Doll in the 1920's, based on her cartoons, and she earned over a million dollars at the time.) In 1908, Harry Leon Wilson was elected as a member of the National Institute of Arts and Letters. After his return from Europe, Wilson spent several months hunting and fishing in the Canadian Rockies, and then he went on to San Francisco. He joined the San Francisco Bohemian Club in 1910 and became friends with fellow members George Sterling and Jack London. Shortly afterwards that same year, he arrived by boat down the coast to Carmel-by-the-Sea. Wilson's description of Carmel was that it had "...the scenic beauty of

Capri...the climate is perfection of the Italian climate."[26] Harry Leon Wilson decided he wanted to live in the Carmel Highlands, five miles south of Carmel-by-the-Sea, and he chose a location along the coast, high on a hillside, where he built a large home. The ocean front site had an expansive view of the Pacific Ocean and the Santa Lucia Mountains on the other side. He wrote to a friend that he loved the scenery and the climate, which both reminded him of the Riviera. Wilson's residence was called "The Ocean Home"; the big, brown, redwood-shingled house had 12 rooms and was located on eight acres of land. It had gardens and a pool. He lived in Carmel-by-the-Sea until the construction of the house was completed in 1912.

Harry Leon Wilson was a friend of many of the Carmel Bohemians. George Sterling would often make the one hour long walk down to the Highlands for a visit. (Mary Austin recalls that Sterling had originally wanted to live a few miles down the coast when he first came to Carmel-by-the-Sea, but he decided against it as it was too far from town.) Wilson liked to drink fine whiskey and play cards: bridge and poker. He was described as a country gentleman, more so than a true Bohemian in appearance, who was reserved and was known to always be well-dressed. His nickname was "Old Ironsides" for his rugged facial feature of a square jaw.

Harry Leon Wilson's third marriage in 1912

In June of 1912, Harry Leon Wilson married Helen Cooke in San Francisco. It was his third marriage. He was 45 years old; he met and married her when she was 17 years old. Their marriage took place around the same time as his new house was ready. Within two years, as Helen was still in her late teens, they had two children, both born in San Francisco. Their son, Harry Leon Wilson Jr. (1913-1997) was born in 1913, and their daughter, Helen Charis Wilson (1914-2009) was born in 1914.

---

26   Franklin Walker, *op. cit.*, p. 104

11

The Forest Theatre

CARMEL'S GROWTH INTO A SMALL VILLAGE

In less than a decade since Frank Devendorf and Frank Powers began the Carmel Development Company and started to sell lots in Carmel-by-the-Sea, the town had grown into a small village. Around $200,000 worth of lots had been sold; there were 400 houses and three hotels. More than a dozen shops were in business and provided necessities for residents and visitors, including a grocery, hardware store, lumberyard, and two livery stables. Frank Devendorf's vision of a town made up of "brain workers" was coming to fruition. The Carmel Development Company released a promotional brochure in 1911 which stated: "Over 60% of the residents of the town are devoting their lives to work connected with the aesthetic arts..."[27] The population of Carmel-by-the-Sea reflected this: "...the citizenry included '18 college professors, 9 leading artists, 3 newspaper editors, 3 ministers, 2 leading photographers, and over 100 other families'."[28] From the early days since the town had been founded, Carmel-by-the-Sea had firmly set its reputation as an artists' and writers'

---

27   Sharron Lee Hale, *A Tribute to Yesterday*, p. 22

28   Scott Shields, *Artists at Continent's End, The Monterey Peninsula Art Colony 1875-1907*, p. 199-200, p. 317 footnote 93

colony, characterized by an easy-going, intellectual, Bohemian lifestyle amidst the natural scenery. The establishment of Carmel's Forest Theatre furthered the town's artistic and creative reputation, usually united the community, and brought even more notoriety to the seaside village. The Forest Theatre productions brought out mostly the best and sometimes the worst among the Bohemians in Carmel-by-the-Sea. The rifts that developed in connection with the Forest Theatre served as a sign that in spite of the beauty and camaraderie around them, there were indications that life in Carmel-by-the-Sea wasn't as idyllic as its residents had expected it to be.

§

OUTDOOR DRAMA IN NORTHERN CALIFORNIA AND THE LITTLE THEATRE MOVEMENT

When the 20th century began, Northern California had three drama centers and all of them were outdoor theatres: the Greek Theatre at the University of California at Berkeley, the open air stage amongst the redwoods at the Bohemian Grove in Sonoma County, and the Forest Theatre in Carmel-by-the-Sea. All three were established within a decade of each other. In 1902, the San Francisco Bohemian Club began its tradition of the Grove Play, at its annual summer encampment along the Russian River. From mid-to-late July, members produced original works on an open stage, flanked by two large redwood trees. This natural amphitheater was set on a hillside among the redwood trees and redwood logs were used for seating. George Sterling's, *The Triumph of Bohemia* was performed as the Grove Play in 1907. The open-air Hearst Greek Theatre on the University of California at Berkeley campus opened in 1903. The theatre was a gift to the school from William Randolph Hearst. It, too, was situated among the trees, in a natural amphitheater, yet could seat about 8,000 people. (Architect John Galen Howard (1864-1931), who was in charge of much of the construction on the University of California at Berkeley campus, modeled the Hearst Greek Theatre on the classic architectural ones found in Greece.) The Little Theatre Movement began to develop across the country around the time Carmel's Forest Theatre was established. The movement by small theatre groups was a departure from what had been considered the formality of traditional stage productions and was a turn towards more experimental and cutting edge work.

Herbert Heron

Through the decades, the man who was most associated with the establishment of Carmel's Forest Theatre and its continuity was Herbert ("Bert") Heron. As a California Bohemian poet, actor, and aspiring playwright, Heron used the U. C. Berkeley Greek Theatre and the open-air theatre at the Bohemian Grove as models for his vision of an outdoor theatre in Carmel-by-the-Sea, founded in the spirit of the Little Theatre movement. In 1910, he and several other Bohemians helped start the Carmel landmark institution. Herbert Heron Peet (1883-1968) was born in New Jersey, but raised in Los Angeles. (*Heron's mother, Jeanie Spring MacKaye Johns Peet, was a sculptor and writer who married three times. Her first husband was Broadway actor, Steele MacKaye, whose children from his second wife, after he divorced Heron's mother, included Percy MacKaye. Herbert Heron's step-brother, dramatist Percy MacKaye (1875-1956), followed in his father's footsteps and became a well-known actor; he also produced outdoor plays and was involved in the Little Theatre movement nationally. A son of Jeanie Spring MacKaye Johns Peet, Cloudsley Johns, Herbert Heron's older step-brother, was a journalist and very good friend of Jack London.*) Heron studied at Stanford University, yet did not graduate; he left to train as a Shakespearean actor. He acted in Los Angeles and San Francisco. During the time he spent in the Bay Area, he became friends with many of the Coppa Bohemians. In 1908 Heron visited George Sterling in Carmel. Not long afterwards he bought land in the Eighty Acres tract and built a redwood house for his family, which included his wife, Opal, and their young daughter, Helena. (In 1905, Heron had married his first wife, Opal Piontkowski, who came from a Polish background.) He also wrote poetry, which was published in the *Overland Monthly* and other magazines. Heron wanted to write plays, as well as to act in and produce plays, which he would do for decades at Carmel's Forest Theatre.

John Northern Hilliard

Another dramatist who wrote and produced plays at the Forest Theatre and was involved in the Little Theatre Movement was John Northern Hilliard. He collaborated with Herbert Heron on productions at the Forest Theatre during its first decade. Journalist and author John Northern Hilliard (1872-1935) was born in Palmyra, New York. He didn't have much of a formal education. He began his career in his teens, as a newspaper reporter and critic in Chicago and in New York. *[Hilliard was a friend of author Stephen Crane, (1871-1900) who was a reporter and writer in New York from 1890 to 1895, and became best known for his second book,* The Red Badge of Courage *(1895).]* From 1895 to 1911 John Northern Hilliard was a reporter, and later a drama critic, editorial writer, and literary editor for newspapers in Rochester, New York. He continued to write freelance articles for magazines and newspapers. Hilliard wrote the book of poetry, *Underneath the Rose* (1894). He edited Thomas Nelson Downs's book, *The Art of Magic* (1908) and became interested in magic himself. Around the time the Forest Theatre was established, John Northern Hilliard lived in Carmel, as a writer. He resided in a large redwood bungalow in town with his family, along with author Grace Sartwell Mason and her family. During this time Hilliard and Mason collaborated on several fiction books including *The Bear's Claws* (1913) and *The Golden Hope* (1916), which was dedicated to Mary Austin.

THE FOREST THEATRE

In 1910, the Carmel Development Company provided an entire city block of wooded property on a hillside that formed a natural amphitheater as the site for the Forest Theatre. The outdoor theatre was located at Mountain View Avenue at Santa Rita Street. Frank Devendorf embraced the plan for Carmel's Forest Theatre as he saw its marketing possibilities; it was another way to promote Carmel-by-the-Sea as an artistic and cultural town. He also viewed its potential to strengthen the community's spirit. Devendorf was equally generous with money and supplies to build this outdoor theatre among the pine trees. (The Carmel Development Company also paid for the production costs of one play each year; this annual play was usually held in July.) Construction on the theatre began in February 1910 and continued through the spring. The structure was very basic architecturally, with a simple raised wooden floor stage (32 feet deep by 44 feet wide) on the bare ground. The stage was flanked by two tall pine trees. Rows of logs were used for seats that could hold an audience of 1,000 people. (Through the years, the Forest Theatre underwent several renovations; the stage was expanded in 1912 and was eventually set on a stone foundation.) Theatergoers carried homemade lanterns, which consisted of lit candles held in tin cans (also familiarly known as "bugs") to illuminate their path. A bon fire on Ocean Avenue led the way to the theatre. On fogless nights, the moonlight was the only source of light in the early years, as there was no electricity there yet. (It would be several years later, between 1913 and 1914, when electricity would be established at the Forest Theatre and in Carmel-by-the-Sea.) Since it was often cold in the evenings, the audience members had to dress warmly and bring their own blankets.

Participants in the Forest Theatre

Along with construction of the theatre, Herbert Heron and about 20 other members formed the Forest Theatre Society, which selected the plays that would be put on stage. Though the aim was to promote the work of local and statewide playwrights, this was not always reflected in the works ultimately performed. Additionally, participation in the Forest Theatre productions was open to all residents who wanted to be involved in one way or another, depending on their skills and interests (such as set design and construction, as well as acting, playwriting, directing, etc.). This semi-amateur approach was seen as a way to foster new talent. Along with Herbert Heron, among the Carmelites (or part-time Carmelites) who would be actively involved in the Forest Theatre during its formative years were Opal Heron, Perry Newberry, Bertha Newberry, George Sterling, Carrie Sterling, Mary Austin, Xavier Martinez, John Fleming Wilson, Grant Wallace, James Hopper, Fred Bechdolt, Vernon Kellogg, Charlotte Kellogg, Grace MacGowan Cooke and Alice MacGowan. Several of Carmel-by-the-Sea's bohemian artists who created set designs for the Forest Theatre productions were Ferdinand Burgdorff, Mary DeNeale Morgan, Arthur Vachell, and others, including Perry Newberry. Many of the town's children also had parts acting in the productions, such as

Frank Devendorf's youngest daughter, Marion (who went on to become a professional actress) and both of Grace MacGowan Cooke's daughters, Helen and Katherine.

Early Forest Theatre performances

The Forest Theatre opened on July 9, 1910. The first performance was *David*, based on the Biblical story, and many prominent Carmelites made up the cast. Herbert Heron had the title role. Other players included Grace MacGowan Cooke, Alice MacGowan, Helen Cooke, and Ferdinand Burgdorff, who not only acted in it, but also designed the set. *David* was presented to an audience of at least a thousand who came from around Northern California. Newspapers from San Francisco and Los Angeles sent their drama critics to review the performance and the Forest Theatre gained much attention. The play *David* was written by Constance Lindsay Skinner. (*Canadian-born and raised Constance Lindsay Skinner (1877-1939) was a friend of Herbert Heron from his days in Los Angeles. She was also Jack London's friend. Constance Lindsay Skinner began as a journalist and a dramatic critic, and became a well-known writer, historian, and editor. She often wrote about the Northwest frontier. In her lifetime, Skinner wrote short stories, novels, poetry, and plays.*) *David* was directed by Garnet Holme. Englishman Garnet Holme taught drama at the University of California at Berkeley. He wrote and directed plays and pageants at the Greek Theatre. Holme, a Cambridge University graduate, had extensive experience staging and directing Shakespearean plays. During the Forest Theatre's first decade he directed about 11 plays including *David*, *Twelfth Night*, *The Toad*, and *The Serra Pageant*. In 1911, rather than a locally written play, Shakespeare's *Twelfth Night* was performed as the annual play at the Forest Theatre. Around one hundred performers made up the large cast and they included Herbert Heron, as well as Grant Wallace and his wife, Harry Leon Wilson, and Helen Cooke. (From 1911 onwards, Ethel Duffy Turner collected photographs and other memorabilia, which she compiled into scrapbooks from her days in Carmel-by-the-Sea and later San Francisco. She chronicled productions at the Forest Theatre with photos of George Sterling, Mary Austin, and others. Her scrapbooks are now at the University of California at Berkeley Bancroft Library.)

Children's plays

During most years, children's plays were also produced at the Forest Theatre. For example, in 1912, *Alice in Wonderland* was staged. This version had been written by Perry Newberry and Arthur Vachell, though it was based on the children's book by Lewis Carroll, *Alice's Adventures in Wonderland*. Katherine Cooke had the leading role. Garnet Holme was the director. The play also brought a lot of publicity to the Forest Theatre.

Historical pageants

Around the 4th of July each year, annual historical pageants were performed, which were often based on Carmel and Monterey's historic past. These grand outdoor, summer productions had casts in the hundreds, and they brought in audiences by the thousands. The most noted was the *Serra Pageant*, which recounted the story of how Father Junípero Serra founded the mission in Carmel. The first *Serra Pageant* was performed on the 4th of July in 1911 and it was produced again in the years to come. The pageant was written by John Fleming Wilson, Perry Newberry, Fred Bechdolt, and Grant Wallace. Garnet Holme produced the 1911 *Serra Pageant*, and he had also collaborated with the writers. As part of the main cast, Grant Wallace played Portola. Perry Newberry and Fred Bechdolt also acted in it, as did Grace MacGowan Cooke, Alice MacGowan, and Helen Cooke. Soldiers from Monterey and local townspeople filled many of the roles as extras.

The Toad and its aftermath

Usually the theatrical productions at the Forest Theatre united the Carmelites, but once in a while there was discord. In 1912, the members of the Forest Theatre Society had a disagreement over which play to produce that year, and the selection of a play caused a considerable rift among Carmel's acting community. Herbert Heron's *Montezuma* was not selected and instead, *The Toad*, a play submitted by an anonymous writer was chosen. It turned out that Bertha Newberry had written *The Toad*, which was set in ancient Egypt and written in verse. However Heron claimed it resembled a play he had written, and George Sterling took his side. Bertha Newberry was accused of plagiarizing the work. Perry Newberry backed his wife and their faction won out. *The Toad* was staged in 1912 and was directed by Garnet Holme. Perry Newberry had the title role and Xavier Martinez also had a part. (He gave a memorable, humorous performance as he played the main assassin.) This production at the Forest Theatre led to a cast performance of *The Toad* at the University of California at Berkeley's Greek Theatre in 1912.

Yet the rift that had developed caused George Sterling, Herbert Heron, James Hopper, and several other Bohemians to split away from the Forest Theatre Society and start their own group, the Western Drama Society. It originally had twelve members, but the membership eventually grew to 50. The Newberrys, along with others, remained in the Forest Theatre Society. Also at this time, the Arts and Crafts Club produced plays in Carmel-by-the-Sea, as well.

Mary Austin returned to Carmel in 1912, around the time of the split over the Forest Theatre. She became involved with several productions. Her play, *Fire*, which was written in rhythmic verse about the Native American legend of the discovery of fire was presented at the Forest Theatre in 1913 by the Western Drama Society. Austin produced the play. Herbert Heron had the leading role, and other Carmelites including George Sterling, John Kenneth Turner and his wife, Ethel Duffy Turner, Vernon Kellogg and his wife, Charlotte Kellogg, and Bert Heron's wife, Opal Heron acted in the production. George Sterling played a Native American and wielded a club.

During this time within the Western Drama Society, George Sterling and Mary Austin fought over which plays should be produced. The Sterling faction preferred pageants that were historical or mythological, while Mary Austin's supporters wanted mystical or Native American dramas, which were to be performed in a true manner with Native American dialogue. She won out, and in 1914 the Western Drama Society performed her play, *The Arrow Maker*, at the Forest Theatre. It was also a Native American drama in authentic cadence. Austin produced it; Charlotte Kellogg had the starring role and Helen Cooke was in it. In August of 1914, Herbert Heron starred in *Montezuma*, which he had previously written. After a wait of a few years, it was finally staged by the Western Drama Society at the Forest Theatre. In the first years since the Forest Theatre was established, there were three theatrical groups whose members were all producing plays in Carmel-by-the-Sea on the Forest Theatre stage: The Forest Theatre Society, The Western Drama Society, and the Arts and Crafts Club.

§

THE DECLINE AND DESPAIR OF THE ORIGINAL GROUP OF CARMEL BOHEMIANS

The disagreements at the Forest Theatre were a sign that things were not as idyllic in Carmel-by-the-Sea for the Bohemians as they had appeared. Underneath the surface there was unhappiness, failed hopes and dreams, and even despair, which began to reveal itself among the members within the first decade of the colony's founding. Though Carmel-by-the-Sea's artists and writers continued to turn out material, its quality and substance sometimes could be viewed as mediocre. For example, when the Forest Theatre first opened, virtually every Carmelite either wrote and submitted plays or performed in them. However, the end result of their efforts may not have been as good as they had perceived their work to be. California historian Kevin Starr noted that serious work in Carmel-by-the-Sea could be undermined by, "...an atmosphere of pretension and trivial artiness [that] continually threatened to dominate."[29] For example, in 1910, writer Harry Leon Wilson harshly found fault with his fellow Carmelites for their inflated sense of self. "The town is a hot bed of gossip and all uncharitableness, with a Forest Theatre complicated by amateur acting and amateur authorship...", he lambasted.[30] He punctuated his remarks with, "[Carmel's]...post-office handles more rejected manuscripts than any other of this size in the country."[31] (As the legend went at that

---

29 Kevin Starr, *Americans and the California Dream 1850-1915*, p. 268-269

30 Lawrence Clark Powell, *California Classics, The Creative Literature of the Golden State*, p. 336

31 *ibid.*

time, there was a huge oil drum located outside of the Carmel post office for writers to dump all of the manuscripts they received back marked as rejected.)

For some of the Bohemians who lived in Carmel-by-the-Sea, it was difficult to work amidst the natural distractions the outdoors presented. Procrastination was common; George Sterling called Carmel, 'the "Land of day-after-tomorrow."'[32] Furthermore, the often-available temptation of food, drink, and camaraderie meant that more hours were spent in the pursuit of enjoyment and day-dreams, rather than in the dedication to hard work. Sterling, as the center of the group of Carmel Bohemians, epitomized this way of life. Through the years, he was known for his drinking and his numerous marital infidelities. Carrie Sterling was upset with his actions and the public embarrassment he brought upon the two of them. In early 1912, she left George in Carmel-by-the-Sea after a public scandal in which he was accused of having an affair with a 23-year old woman. Carrie returned to Piedmont and stayed with her sister, Lila Havens for the next year, while George Sterling remained in Carmel. He moved out of their bungalow and lived in the guest quarters instead, for the rest of 1912 through 1913. With Carrie gone, Sterling had a new group of Bohemian friends in town that provided him company and kept an eye on him, as he was living alone. These friends included writers Michael Williams, John Fleming Wilson, John Kenneth Turner, Ethyl Duffy Turner, and Harry Leon Wilson. George Sterling invited 19- year old, aspiring poet Clark Ashton Smith to stay for a month in Carmel in June 1912. *[Northern California ("Gold Rush country") born and raised poet, and later science fiction writer and artist Clark Ashton Smith (1893-1961) was mentored by George Sterling, as a young adult. Sterling helped him get his first book of poetry published,* The Star-Treader and Other Poems *(1912). Sterling wrote the preface to Smith's second book of poetry,* Odes and Sonnets *(1918).]* Carrie Sterling came back to Carmel later in 1913 to give the marriage another chance. However, their reconciliation was brief, and in November

---

32   Agnes Foster Buchanan, "The Story of a Famous Fraternity of Writers and Artists" *The Pacific Monthly*, Volume XVII, January 1907, p. 65-83

1913 Carrie left permanently. She went back to Piedmont and filed for divorce, which was granted in January 1914. While he mostly lived in Carmel-by-the-Sea for close to a decade, 1905 to 1914, George Sterling kept track of his daily activities in a journal. Historian Kevin Starr wrote that,

> "[George] Sterling's Carmel Diaries record a trivial existence, odds and ends of puttering days which never really amounted to much: days which seem imprisoned in a suspension which was neither rest nor creative leisure: days to no purpose: Carmel days under the sun and by the peacock-blue Pacific."[33]

Looking back on those days, writer Van Wyck Brooks described George Sterling's appearance as "Dante in hell".[34] (In his youth George Sterling had been compared to the Italian poet, Dante, both in his looks and talent.) Author Van Wyck Brooks, in his mid-twenties at the time, made his first visit to Carmel-by-the-Sea in 1911. Brooks later became one of the critics of the Carmel Bohemians and their way of life. *[Cultural and literary historian, biographer, and critic Van Wyck Brooks (1886-1963) was born in Plainfield, New Jersey. After he graduated from Harvard University in 1907, he moved to England, where he worked as a journalist. His first book,* The Wine of the Puritans: A Study of Present-Day America, *was published in 1908. Brooks returned to the United States that same year, and worked for a magazine in New York. In 1911, he moved to California, where Brooks became an English Professor at Stanford University that fall. Earlier in the year, in late April, he married his first wife, Eleanor Stimson, a Wellesley graduate, who lived with her mother in Carmel at the time. Afterwards, the newlyweds spent several months in the town, as part of their honeymoon. Brooks and his family would return and have lengthy stays in Carmel-by-the-Sea throughout his lifetime.]* In his book, *Scenes and Portraits: Memories of Childhood and Youth* (1954), the first of three autobiographies he wrote, Van Wyck Brooks looked back on the initial time he spent in Carmel. Though he described the town as beautiful, he noted the contradictions and melodramas that immersed

---

33   Kevin Starr, *op. cit.*, p. 280

34   James Hoopes, *Van Wyck Brooks, In Search of American Culture*, p. 130

the Bohemian way of life. He saw wasted effort, squandered time, and failure among the Bohemian residents. Brooks wrote,

> "...[They came] from the East to write novels in this paradise... [and] found themselves becalmed and supine. They gave themselves over to day-dreams while their minds ran down like clocks, as if they had lost the keys to wind them up with, and they turned into beachcombers, listlessly reading books they had read ten times before and searching the rocks for abalones. For this Arcadia lay, one felt, outside the world in which thought evolves and which came to seem insubstantial in the bland sunny air."[35]

A dark side of life sometimes emerged despite the Carmel Bohemians' seemingly carefree existence. As they faced the reality of careers that didn't reach their full potential, along with their personal difficulties, they developed feelings of hopelessness and despondency. As some lost their creativity and were drained of ambition and drive, they edged into apathy, depression, philosophical pessimism,[36] and even nihilism. Suicide was discussed, especially following Nora May French's death. Through the years, George Sterling, as well as a few other Bohemians during that time, was said to have always carried cyanide, (potassium cyanide) with him. Sterling did not want to experience pain or suffering. In *The Valley of the Moon*, Jack London through one of his fictional characters, notes the conflict within the Bohemians' existence:

> "But what she [Saxon] could never comprehend...was the pessimism that so often cropped up...At such times Saxon was oppressed by these sad children of art. It was inconceivable that they, [the artists and writers] of all people, should be so forlorn."[37]

---

35 Van Wyck Brooks, *Scenes and Portraits: Memories of Childhood and Youth*, p. 191

36 Kevin Starr, *op. cit.*, p. 285

37 Jack London, *The Valley of the Moon*, p. 328

Chris Jorgensen's home and stone tower studio, built in 1905, later became the La Playa Hotel, on Eighth Avenue and Camino Real Street, Carmel-by-the-Sea. Photo c. 1906 to 1916. (Courtesy of Henry Meade Williams Local History Department at the Harrison Memorial Library, Carmel, California.)

Artist Ferdinand Burgdorff, Carmel. Photo by Lewis Josselyn, c. 1930.
(Courtesy of Pat Hathaway, California Views Photo Collection.)

Artist Arthur Vachell seated in his garden outside of his house in Carmel.
Photo c. 1905 to 1926. (Courtesy of Henry Meade Williams Local History
Department at the Harrison Memorial Library, Carmel, California.)

Poet George Sterling, "King of Bohemia". Photo c. 1905 to 1914.
(Courtesy of Henry Meade Williams Local History Department
at the Harrison Memorial Library, Carmel, California.)

Poet Nora May French. Photo by Arnold Genthe, c. 1903 to 1907. (Courtesy of Wikipedia; U.S. public domain.)

Author Mary Hunter Austin. No date given. (Courtesy of George Grantham Bain Collection, Library of Congress.)

Photographer Arnold Genthe, c. 1911 to 1942. (Courtesy of Arnold Genthe Collection, Library of Congress.)

Interior of Arnold Genthe's bungalow in Carmel. Photo by Arnold Genthe, c. 1906 to 1911. (Courtesy of Arnold Genthe Collection, Library of Congress.)

Aftermath of 1906 San Francisco Earthquake and Fire, view of the destruction in Chinatown. (Titled, "On the Ruins (April 1906), San Francisco", also "End of Old Chinatown, San Francisco" and "Last of Old Chinatown, San Francisco". A similar image appeared in *Old Chinatown, A Book of Pictures*, Photos by Arnold Genthe, Text by Will Irwin, 1913. Foreward, p. 3.) Photo by Arnold Genthe, April 1906. (Courtesy of Arnold Genthe Collection, Library of Congress.)

On the porch at the Sterlings' house in Carmel-by-the-Sea: (from left to right) Charmian London, Jack London, Carrie Sterling, and George Sterling. Photo c. 1906 or 1910. (Courtesy of Henry Meade Williams Local History Department at the Harrison Memorial Library, Carmel, California.)

Authors James Hopper and Mary Austin at her "Wick-i-up" in Carmel-by-the-Sea. Photo c. 1907. (Courtesy of Henry Meade Williams Local History Department at the Harrison Memorial Library, Carmel, California.)

Illustration from *Puck* magazine, titled, "The Crusaders", which depicted the numerous muckracking journalists of the early 1900's, who fought against corruption and graft. Illustration by Carl Hassman, *Puck* magazine, Volume 59, Number 1512, February 21, 1906. Copyright 1906 by Keppler & Schwarzmann. (Courtesy of Library of Congress.)

Journalist and author Lincoln Steffens at Union Square, New York City. Photo, April 1914. (Courtesy of George Grantham Bain Collection, Library of Congress.)

Author Upton Sinclair in New York City. No date given. (Courtesy of George Grantham Bain Collection, Library of Congress.)

Writers Fred Bechdolt, James Hopper, Michael Williams (from left to right) on horseback on Ocean Avenue in downtown Carmel-by-the-Sea. Photo by L. S. Slevin, c. 1908 to 1913. (Courtesy of Henry Meade Williams Local History Department at the Harrison Memorial Library, Carmel, California.)

Looking north from the south end of Carmel Beach, with the two-story, Tudor Revival, MacGowan-Cooke house on the right. Photo by L. S. Slevin, c. 1912. (Courtesy of Pat Hathaway, California Views Photo Collection.)

Author Sinclair Lewis, who achieved career success in the 1920's. Photo by Harris & Ewing, no date given. (Courtesy of Harris & Ewing Collection, Library of Congress.)

Writer John Kenneth Turner. Photo c. 1922. (Courtesy of Henry Meade Williams Local History Department at the Harrison Memorial Library, Carmel, California.)

George Sterling on the rocks at Carmel Beach. Photo c. 1905 to 1914. (Courtesy of Henry Meade Williams Local History Department at the Harrison Memorial Library, Carmel, California.)

Arnold Genthe at Carmel Beach preparing to photograph a group of the Bohemians, to his right. (Seated from left to right) George Sterling, Mary Austin, Jack London, and James Hopper. The Carmel Bathhouse is in the background. Photo c. 1906 to 1910. (Courtesy of Arnold Genthe Collection, Library of Congress.)

Author John Fleming Wilson, with his dog, in Carmel. Photo c.
1910. (Courtesy of Henry Meade Williams Local History Department
at the Harrison Memorial Library, Carmel, California.)

Herbert Heron with his wife, Opal and their daughter, Helena.
Photo c. 1908. (Courtesy of Henry Meade Williams Local History
Department at the Harrison Memorial Library, Carmel, California.)

Helen Cooke with George Manship, in the play *David*, the first
production at Carmel's Forest Theatre. Photo 1910. (Courtesy
of Pat Hathaway, California Views Photo Collection.)

Mary Austin (center) with the cast of her play, *Fire*, which she directed at
the Forest Theatre. George Sterling is seen in the upper right, holding
a club. Photo 1913. (Courtesy of Henry Meade Williams Local History
Department at the Harrison Memorial Library, Carmel, California.)

12

Epilogue

EPILOGUE FOR CARMEL'S BOHEMIAN RESIDENTS AND VISITORS

By around 1913 or so, some members of the first group of Bohemians who had established the town began to disperse. As they left and moved elsewhere, new Bohemian artists, writers, poets, and other free-spirited individuals would make Carmel-by-the-Sea their home in the years to come. They, too, would be drawn by the beauty of the natural surroundings and the inspiration they provided. However, those early days of Carmel-by-the-Sea would never be recreated in another era. This is what happened to the rest of the Carmel Bohemians, visitors, and prominent residents from its founding days...

Jack London, d. 1916, Charmian London d. 1955

Through the years, Jack London bought more land and grew the size of his Beauty Ranch in Sonoma County's Glen Ellen. His property, the Valley of the Moon, eventually totaled 1,400 acres by 1914. London also took part in the Eucalyptus tree craze of the time in California, and spent tens of thousands of dollars on the purchase and planting of 35,000 of the trees on his land. He wanted to be a super-rancher and even started a Grape Juice Company in 1914. However, Jack London experienced numerous problems on his ranch due to natural events, and he was continually losing money on it. He also focused his attention and a large amount of resources on the construction of his residence, "Wolf House", starting in 1911. The large, four-story, 15,000 square foot home was made of local building materials, built to last a thousand years, and was thought to be fireproof and able to withstand earthquakes. On August 22, 1913, just as the house was nearly completed it burned down. Only the stone walls remained; Wolf House was never rebuilt.

Jack and Charmian London continued to travel through the years; in 1912 they took a trip around Cape Horn. In 1913, his novel *John Barleycorn*, which was said to be semi-autobiographical, was published, as was *The Valley of the Moon*. London reported on the Mexican Revolution for *Collier's* magazine in 1914. During the summers of 1915 and 1916, the Londons made their last boat trips to Hawaii. Charmian London wrote several books about her experiences with Jack London, including the *Log of the Snark* (1915) and *Our Hawaii* (1917).

From 1913 onwards, Jack London's medical ailments increased, which stemmed from his kidney problems (uremia). His health declined through his heavy diet and drinking along with overwork and lack of exercise. In the last months of his life, as his health had further deteriorated, London relied on morphine for his kidney pain. On October 22, 1916, his Shire stallion died and the loss hit him hard. Exactly one month afterwards, on November 22, 1916, Jack London died at age 40 at his home in Glen Ellen. Most likely, his death was caused by uremic-kidney failure. However, as London had also taken an overdose of morphine, it is possible that it was an accidental death or deliberate suicide. One of his closest friends, George Sterling attended the funeral service and burial. Jack London's ashes were interred at his grave on top of the knoll at the Valley of the Moon in Glen Ellen.

Five years after Jack London's death, Charmian London's two-volume, *The Book of Jack London* (1921) was published. She remained on their ranch for the rest of her life. She lived in a house designed for her, "House of Happy Walls", and built in memory of Jack London. It was a stone house, like the Wolf House that was destroyed, but it was smaller. Charmian London died there on January 13, 1955. She was 84 years old.

Frank Powers, d. 1920, Jane Gallatin Powers, d. 1944

Frank Powers traveled to the Spanish island of Mallorca (Majorca) in 1913, to attend the 200th birthday celebration of Father Junípero Serra. He was there to represent California. In 1920, Frank Powers sold the massive family property, "The Dunes", in Carmel-by-the-Sea. He died later that year, at age 56.

After her husband died, Jane Gallatin Powers burned all of her paintings and went to Europe, where she would spend the rest of her life. She took three of her adult children with her to France, where she further studied art in Paris and exhibited her work. Jane Gallatin Powers had studios in Paris, Capri, and Rome. During World War II, she spent her last years in Rome, on her own, with little money. Jane Gallatin Powers died there on December 18, 1944, at the age of 76.

John Fleming Wilson, d. 1922

John Fleming Wilson left Carmel-by-the-Sea and served in the Canadian Army during World War I, for two years in France. One of the last books he wrote was *Scouts of the Desert* (1920). John Fleming Wilson died in Southern California at age 45, on March 5, 1922, after a freak accident at his home. (The previous day, he was shaving and his bathrobe caught fire.) His book, *Somewhere at Sea and Other Tales* (1923) was published posthumously, with an appreciation of the author written by Raymond Blathwayt.

George Sterling, d. 1926, Carrie Sterling, d. 1918

From 1914 onwards, after she divorced George Sterling, Carrie lived in Piedmont. Lila Havens, her sister, helped her find a job as curator of the Piedmont Art Gallery, which was established by Lila's husband, George Sterling's uncle, Frank Havens. (The Piedmont Art Gallery contained Frank C. Havens' private art collection of hundreds of paintings.) Right after the divorce, George Sterling left Carmel-by-the-Sea and California altogether for New York, in early 1914. He lived in Greenwich Village until 1915. Without finding career success on the East Coast, he came back to San Francisco, where he spent the rest of his life. He lived in a room at the San Francisco Bohemian Club, which was paid for anonymously by a benefactor, Thomas Barbour Lathrop. Around this time, George Sterling's fourth book of collected poetry, *Beyond the Breakers and Other Poems* (1914), and his fifth one, *The Caged Eagle and other Poems* (1916) were published. Through the years, Sterling wrote many articles and reviews of poetry in numerous publications. Carrie and George Sterling are said to have both had regrets about ending their marriage. These feelings of depression and despair stayed with Carrie for four years. On November 17, 1918, at home in her bedroom in Piedmont, Carrie Sterling wore an elegant gown, took a dose of cyanide, and ended her life. She had put Chopin's "Funeral March" to play on the gramophone.

In the early 1920's, as George Sterling was in his fifties, he continued to have his poetry published including two books of dramatic verse: *Lilith: A Dramatic Poem* (1920) and *Rosamund: A Dramatic Poem* (1920). A book of collected poetry, *Sails and Mirage and Other Poems* (1921) contained "Spring in Carmel", a poem written for Carrie after his first return to their home in Carmel following her death. The book also contained the poems "Autumn in Carmel" and "The Cool, Grey City of Love", a tribute to San Francisco, his adopted city. From 1925 through 1926 George Sterling was a contributing editor at the *Overland Monthly* magazine and he wrote a column, "Rhymes and Reactions" for the periodical. As the Jazz Age came about during the 1920's, styles changed and new, up-and-coming writers and poets gained popularity. George Sterling stayed with his classical style and was not part of this new movement. His youthful days were long behind him and he had not achieved the literary accomplishments and widespread acceptance he had once hoped for. During his last years, those who knew him said Sterling was lonely, sad, pessimistic, and depressed, as well as being broke. He began to experience health problems when he drank heavily. He became ill and was even hospitalized on several occasions. Most of Sterling's original group of friends from San Francisco, Piedmont, and Carmel-by-the-Sea were no longer a part of his life. He continued to travel in California and made trips to Carmel and Los Angeles. He visited Carmel-by-the-Sea with author Sinclair Lewis in early 1926. As with poet Clark Ashton Smith, earlier, George Sterling appreciated and became acquainted with new literary talent. Another such rising Northern California poet was Robinson Jeffers (1887-1962) who had made Carmel-by-the-Sea his home since 1914, the year Sterling left. In mid-1926 Sterling made another trip to Carmel, during which he stayed for a week with Jeffers. In late August 1926 Sterling wrote *Robinson Jeffers, the Man and the Artist*. (It was to be Sterling's last book.) Several of those closest to him, Nora May French, Jack London, and Carrie Sterling, had all died in November. Prior to an event at the San Francisco Bohemian Club in mid-November 1926, in honor of writer, editor, and critic H. L. Mencken (1880-1956), who was also a good friend of his, Sterling went on a drinking binge. (Several months earlier, Sterling had stopped drinking altogether.) He did not attend the festivities of the occasion that night, and instead Sterling locked himself inside of his room at the Bohemian Club. He set his papers on fire. George Sterling took potassium cyanide, which he had carried with him for years. Most likely Sterling died in the early morning of November 17, 1926, the same date as Carrie's suicide, eight years earlier. George Sterling was 57 years old. When his body was discovered in the morning, there were scraps of burnt paper found, a few with writing which was still discernible. One read,

> "I walked with phantoms that ye know not of"[38]
> and another,
> "Deeper into the darkness can I peer,
> Than most, yet find the darkness still beyond."[39]

---

38   Lawrence Ferlinghetti and Nancy J. Peters, *Literary San Francisco, A Pictorial History from Its Beginnings to the Present Day*, p. 106-107

39   *ibid.*

Arthur Vachell, d. 1933

Arthur Vachell held art receptions at his home and was involved in Carmel-by-the Sea's art and social communities through the 1920's. In 1926, he left the town to go back to England, despite the pleas of many Carmelites for him to stay. He and his brother, Horace Annesley Vachell bought a large 18th century, English country estate, Widcombe Manor, in Bath, England. Arthur Vachell, who suffered from a heart problem, died in England on June 1, 1933, at age 68.

Mary Austin, d. 1934

After her return to Carmel-by-the-Sea and her participation in the Forest Theatre for a few years from 1912 to 1914, Mary Austin spent less time in the village. She was divorced from her husband, Stafford Wallace Austin in 1914. (In Mary Austin's autobiography, *Earth Horizon*, she indicated the last time she was in Carmel was in the summer of 1918, before her daughter, Ruth, died that fall in Santa Clara, at age 26. Ruth had remained institutionalized there since 1905, and Mary never saw her daughter again after that year.) After Ruth's death, Austin made her first visit to Santa Fe, New Mexico in 1918, where she would eventually make her home in the last decade of her life. For part of period between 1914 through 1924, she lived in New York, and she also gave lectures on college campuses across the country. In the early 1920's, Mary Austin went back to Europe. After her return around 1924, she permanently moved to Santa Fe, where she built a house "La Casa Querida" in 1925. In Taos, New Mexico there was a literary and artistic colony centered around socialite and art patron, Mabel Evans Dodge Sterne Luhan (1879-1962) and her fourth husband, Antonio Lujan ("Tony Luhan"), who was a Native American. Austin was a friend of theirs. Mary Austin's familiarity with the Desert Southwest recurred as a theme and setting in her books, *California, Land of the Sun* (1914) and *The Land of Journeys' Ending* (1924). She continued her involvement in the preservation of Spanish and Native American art, culture, and heritage. In 1929, she wrote the forward for the book, *Taos, Pueblo* (1930) with photographs by Ansel Adams (1902-1984). Austin's experience with the controversial Owens Valley water rights issue was the basis of her novel, *The Ford* (1917). She remained active in feminist and women's suffrage movements. Her novels *A Woman of Genius* (1912), *The Lovely Lady* (1913), and *26 Jayne Street* (1920) were considered feminist works. In 1929, despite the onset of health problems, Mary Austin started to write her autobiography, *Earth Horizon*. It was published in late 1932. Austin suffered her first heart attack the next year, in 1933. She died at her home in Santa Fe of a heart attack on August 13, 1934, at the age of 65.

Frank Devendorf, d. 1934

More than a decade after Frank Devendorf and Frank Powers founded Carmel-by-the-Sea, Devendorf turned his attention to the development and acquisition of water for the Carmel Highlands, about five miles south of Carmel. The Carmel Development Company had purchased the land in 1906 from ranchers along the coast; it was a very rugged area with magnificent views of the Pacific Ocean. Starting in 1915, Devendorf decided to develop the Carmel Highlands, with the Highlands Inn, a resort hotel, as its center part. The hotel was finished in 1917 and it opened in 1918. (Initially the hotel consisted of a few cabins and a residence). Devendorf sold the Highlands Inn in 1922. He spent part of his later years traveling on his own to countries such as Mexico, Panama, Canada, and Egypt, though he continued to be involved with Carmel-by-the-Sea and the Carmel Highlands, particularly in the search for a water supply there. In May of 1934, Devendorf, who was in his late seventies, visited the Wildcat Canyon area of the Carmel Highlands on horseback, along with his assistant, on a quest for a source of water. Devendorf suffered a heart attack following the excursion. A few months later, in poor health, he went back to Oakland, where he still had a family home. He died there on October 9, 1934, at the age of 78. [*Devendorf Park, located on Ocean Avenue across from the Carmel Plaza, at the entrance to the town, is named in his honor. In the park, there is a bronze bust of him on a large granite boulder, which was made by his daughter, Edwina, a sculptor.*]

John Northern Hilliard, d. 1935

For about a decade while he lived in Carmel-by-the-Sea, John Northern Hilliard was involved with several productions at the Forest Theatre including *Tusitala, A Masque of Robert Louis Stevenson*, which was performed by the Western Drama Society at the Forest Theatre on July 28, 1916. (He wrote it with Herbert Heron, and it was based upon Stevenson's works.) Hilliard also took part in another production of *Alice in Wonderland*, *Kismet*, and *The Yellow Jacket* at the Forest Theatre in the early 1920's. After leaving Carmel-by-the-Sea, John Northern Hilliard continued to pursue his interest in magic. Beginning in the mid-1920's he worked with his friend, magician Howard Thurston (1869-1936). Hilliard followed him on the road, made preparations, handled publicity, and wrote press releases for him as he toured with his show across the country. During one of these stops, Hilliard, in his early sixties, died suddenly on March 14, 1935 in Indianapolis, Indiana. At the time, he had spent his last three years working on a very lengthy sequel to the first magic book he edited, *The Art of Magic* (1908). *Greater Magic* was published posthumously, in 1938.

Chris Jorgensen, d. 1935, Angela Ghirardelli Jorgensen, d. 1936

After the death of their niece Alida Ghirardelli, in 1909, the Jorgensens found themselves unable to continue to live in Carmel-by-the-Sea, as it reminded them of the loss, so they moved to Pebble Beach. They leased and eventually sold their Carmel home and studio to Agnes Signor several years subsequently. (The house later was expanded and transformed into the La Playa Hotel, with the addition of rooms.) In Pebble Beach, the Jorgensens built a log cabin style home and studio with ten rooms on the Seventeen Mile Drive, across from the Pebble Beach Lodge. Through the late 1910's, they divided their time between their homes and studios in Piedmont, San Francisco, and Yosemite. After 1921, the Jorgensens left the Monterey Peninsula and moved to their newly constructed home in Piedmont, where they spent the rest of their lives. Chris Jorgensen continued to paint and exhibit his artwork. He died in Piedmont on June 24, 1935, at age 74.

Angela Ghirardelli Jorgensen died several months following her husband's death, on January 19, 1936 in Riverside, California. She was in her mid-seventies. She left nearly 200 of her husband's paintings to the United States Department of the Interior, which placed them on exhibit at the Yosemite National Park Museum.

Lincoln Steffens, d. 1936

After his muckraking reporting in the United States, journalist Lincoln Steffens traveled to Mexico and Russia, during their revolutions. He reported on these events through the 1910's. Steffens became a proponent of communism, and was well-known for the statement, "I've seen the future and it works", in regards to the Russian Communist system after the 1917 Revolution.[40] Steffens married his second wife, writer Ella Winter (1898-1980) in Paris in 1924. (His first wife, Josephine Bontecou, whom he married in 1891 had died in 1911.) He and Ella had one child, a son named Peter, who was born in 1926. In 1927, Steffens and his family moved to Carmel-by-the-Sea. Lincoln and Ella Steffens divorced on friendly terms in 1929. He spent his last years writing at home, where he completed his two-volume autobiography, *The Autobiography of Lincoln Steffens* (1931). Lincoln Steffens died on August 9, 1936 of a heart attack at his residence in Carmel, at age 70.

Perry Newberry, d. 1938, Bertha Newberry, d. 1934

Perry Newberry was heavily involved in Carmel-by-the-Sea's political and cultural life since his arrival in 1910. He had strong ideas about the town's future, and he expressed them through writing and politics. Newberry wanted to keep Carmel-by-the-Sea residential and quaint; he was against growth and commercialization of the town. In the 1920's, Perry Newberry ran for office based on his "Don't Vote for Perry Newberry" campaign, which emphasized his anti-development stance. Newberry was elected twice to Carmel's Board of Trustees and became President of the

---

40   Justin Kaplan, *Lincoln Steffens, A Biography*, p. 8

Board of Trustees (which was the equivalent to mayor). He resumed his journalism career in Carmel-by-the-Sea as editor of *The Carmel Pine Cone*, the town's weekly paper, in 1927. Newberry later owned the newspaper and was its co-publisher until he sold it in 1935. He continued to participate in the productions at the Forest Theatre; he wrote, directed, and acted in the theater's plays throughout the years. Perhaps one of the most remarkable performances Perry Newberry was involved in was *The Serra Pageant* in 1915. He wrote and performed in it, along with Fred Bechdolt, John Fleming Wilson, and Grant Wallace. The large, outdoor production about the story of how Father Junípero Serra founded the Carmel Mission was also subsequently presented at the end of the Panama-Pacific International Exposition in San Francisco, in July 1915. Through the years, Perry Newberry wrote children's stories, short stories, and mystery novels. Some of his books were *Tom Westlake's Golden Luck: A Story of Adventure in California* (1913), *The Last Mayor of Las Pasturas* (1918), *Castaway Island* (1920), *Black Boulder Claim* (1921), and *Forward Ho! A Story of the Argonne* (1927). He also wrote five mystery novels with Carmel author Alice MacGowan in the 1920's. Additionally, along with his politics, journalism, and theater work, Newberry built houses. As a builder he designed and constructed cottages in Carmel, but some of the homes he built had flaws, such as problems with the roofs and chimneys.

Through her lifetime, Bertha Newberry also remained involved with drama, poetry, and politics in Carmel-by-the-Sea. In the early 1930's several of her poems were chosen as part of *The Anthology of California Poets* (1932). Bertha Newberry suffered from health problems and she died in January 1934.

Two years after his first wife's death, in 1936, Perry Newberry married a bohemian writer from San Francisco who lived in Carmel-by-the-Sea, Ida Brooks. Newberry had heart problems and other ailments that stemmed from his service in World War I. Perry Newberry died in Carmel on December 6, 1938, at age 68. The town mourned his death. *[There is a street in Carmel, "Perry Newberry Way", named after him.]*

Harry Leon Wilson, d. 1939, Helen Cooke Wilson Peabody, d. 1945

As he settled into his new home in the Carmel Highlands, in his first decade there, 1912 to 1922, Henry Leon Wilson returned to writing fiction: short stories and novels. He was a dedicated writer and wrote eight hours a day. This was the most successful period of his career. His short stories were often serialized and regularly appeared in *The Saturday Evening Post.* His best known, most popular, and widely read novels, which were written as humorous, light fiction, came out during this time. They were *Bunker Bean* (1913), which had been serialized in *The Saturday Evening Post* in 1912, *Ruggles of Red Gap* (1915), *Somewhere in Red Gap* (1916), *Ma Pettingill* (1919), and *Merton of the Movies* (1922). (He wrote *Merton of the Movies* after he lived in Hollywood during the early 1920's.) In all of these works, Harry Leon Wilson created widely known characters that became part of the popular culture. Several of his books were turned into movies and some of them became films even more than once. (For example, *Bunker Bean* was made into a movie three times: in 1918, 1925, and 1936. *Ruggles of Red Gap* was filmed in 1923, again in 1935 with actor Charles Laughton, and in 1950, the film was called *Fancy Pants,* with Bob Hope and Lucille Ball. *Merton of the Movies* also became a film three times, first as a silent film in 1924, and later as a movie in 1932 and 1947.) Wilson attended the summer encampments at the Bohemian Grove regularly, and his play, *Life,* was selected as the annual Grove Play in 1919. Once again, Harry Leon Wilson co-authored several works with writer Booth Tarkington, including *The Gibson Upright* (1919), *Tweedles, A Comedy* (1924), and *How's Your Health?* (1930). Some of Wilson's other books written during the 1920's, which never reached the levels of popularity of his earlier ones, were *The Wrong Twin* (1922), *So This is Golf* (1923), *Professor How Could You!* (1924), and *Cousin Jane* (1925).

Harry Leon Wilson was also known to have had a temper. In 1922, Wilson accused his Carmel Highlands neighbor, painter Theodore Criley of flirting with his wife, Helen, while they worked together on a play at the Forest Theatre. Wilson challenged him to a duel, which was fought as a fistfight, and Criley won. This incident made its way into *The New York Times.* Harry and Helen divorced in 1927. The divorce proceedings revealed that at the height of his career, he made close to $100,000 a year from his writing and royalties. Initially, Helen had custody of Charis, while Leon stayed with his father, but both children were later raised by their aunt, Katherine Cooke, grandmother, Grace MacGowan Cooke, and great aunt, Alice MacGowan in Carmel. After the divorce Harry Leon Wilson spent some time in Oregon and then came back in 1929 to his home in the Carmel Highlands. He lived there alone, although he had a nurse who took care of him. His last works were *Lone Tree* (1929), written in Oregon after his split with Helen, and *Two Black Sheep* (1931). Despite his great earnings at the peak of his career, after the divorce and during the time of the Great Depression, Harry Leon Wilson had financial problems late in his life. In 1932, when he was in his mid-sixties, he was a passenger in a serious car accident south of Carmel, in car driven by his nurse. His injuries affected his eyesight and memory, and he suffered from health problems through the rest of his life. In spite of these difficulties, he continued to write during his last years. Harry Leon Wilson died in his sleep at home in the Carmel Highlands on June 29, 1939, at age 72. His children, Charis and Leon, along with Grace and Alice MacGowan completed and then helped to posthumously publish his last work, *When In The Course* (1940), which was unfinished at the time of his death.

After her divorce, Helen Cooke Wilson opened a dress shop, "The Carmelita", on Ocean Avenue in Carmel. About three years later, because of the Great Depression, it failed. In 1934, Helen met Colonel Paul E. Peabody, who was stationed at the Monterey Presidio. The next year, 1935, she moved to Washington D. C., where he was transferred and they were married. (He was promoted to brigadier general.) Helen Cooke Wilson Peabody was terminally ill with cancer and died at Walter Reed General Hospital (now Walter Reed Army Medical Center) in Washington, D. C., in July 1945, at age 49.

[Harry Leon Wilson Jr. worked for a Hollywood studio and was also an author. He died in 1997. Helen Charis Wilson Weston Harris, married and later divorced photographer Edward Weston (1886-1958), who was much older than she was. Charis posed as a model for him and also wrote several books. She died in Santa Cruz at age 95 in 2009.]

Arnold Genthe, d. 1942

Arnold Genthe was successful in his New York photography studio, where he continued to take portrait photographs of prominent members of society. [Between 1912 and 1917, a young, up-and-coming photographer, Dorothea Lange (1895-1965) began her career as Genthe's assistant.] He continued his travels around the world. Several more books of his photographs were published, including *The Book of the Dance* (1916), *Impressions of Old New Orleans: A Book of Pictures* (1926), and *Isadora Duncan: Twenty-Four Studies* (1929). Genthe's autobiography, *As I Remember*, was published in 1936, which included more than 100 of his photographs. Arnold Genthe died at age 73 in Connecticut, on August 10, 1942.

Xavier Martinez, d. 1943, Elsie Whitaker Martinez, d. 1984

In 1923, Xavier and Elsie Martinez divorced. Their daughter, Michaela, lived with Elsie in Piedmont. Xavier Martinez continued to paint, do etchings, and exhibit his artwork through the years. For three decades he taught at the California School of Arts and Crafts (later renamed the California College of Arts and Crafts) in the East Bay, until he retired in 1942. Around 1940 Elsie Martinez had moved to Carmel-by-the-Sea, where she took care of her former husband during the last year of his life, as his health failed. He died of a heart attack at age 73 in Carmel, on January 13, 1943. Xavier Martinez was buried in Monterey at San Carlos Cemetery.

Elsie Martinez remained in Carmel through 1980, where she had many friends and pursued cultural interests. In the 1960's she was interviewed about her recollections of the early Bohemians in the Bay Area and Carmel, and the transcript, *San Francisco Bay Area Writers and Artists*, was published through the Bancroft Library at the University of California at Berkeley. In 1981, the year after she celebrated her 90th birthday in Carmel, she moved to San Francisco. Elsie Martinez died there at the age of 93, on January 31, 1984. She, too, was buried at San Carlos Cemetery in Monterey.

Grace MacGowan Cooke, d. 1944, Alice MacGowan, d. 1947, Katherine Cooke, d. 1972

Around the middle of 1910, the MacGowan sisters stopped writing together. Several years later, when they resumed they wrote *The Straight Road* (1917) and subsequently, *The Trail of the Little Wagon* (1928). During their split, Alice collaborated with other writers; she worked with Garnet Holme on a play, a dramatization of her Civil War novel, *The Sword in the Mountains*, which was titled *Chattanooga*. Grace and her daughters took a trip to the Desert Southwest to do research on the life and customs of the Hopi Native Americans who lived in the Arizona desert. They spent several months there in 1910. The information was used for her upcoming novel, *The Joy Bringer* (1913). Along with author Caroline Wood Morrison, she co-wrote *William and Bill* (1914). Grace MacGowan Cooke's book *Wild Apples, A California Story* (1918) about a woman who raises her illegitimate child touched on feminist issues. Her last book was *The Fortunes of John Hawk: A Boy of Old New York 1781* (1928). In the 1920's, Perry Newberry and Alice McGowan wrote five mystery novels together, set in San Francisco. They were *The Million Dollar Suitcase* (1922), *The Mystery Woman* (1924), *Shaken Down* (1925), *The Seventh Passenger* (1926), and *Who Is This Man?* (1927). After the 1920's, the sisters' literary works became less popular. During the Great Depression, they lived in a home in Carmel's Hatton Fields. In 1935, the MacGowans sold their house and they moved to Los Gatos, with Grace's daughter, Katherine. Grace MacGowan Cooke died in Los Gatos, on June 24, 1944 at age 82. Alice MacGowan died there at age 89, on March 10, 1947. Katherine Cooke died in 1972, at age 71.

Charles Chapel Judson d. 1946

Charles Chapel Judson and his wife, Besse continued to make trips to Carmel-by-the-Sea during the summer and other times of the year. They permanently moved to the town in 1926, a few years after his retirement, where they lived for the next twenty years. Judson was a member of the Carmel Art Association, which began in 1927 and he continued to participate in the local art community. In poor health during his last years, Charles Chapel Judson died on November 4, 1946, at age 82 in Carmel.

John Kenneth Turner, d. 1948, Ethel Duffy Turner, d. 1969

John Kenneth Turner and his wife Ethel Duffy Turner separated. He remained in Carmel and remarried in the 1920's. His second wife, Adriana Spadoni (1879-1953) was a socialist writer. She was the author of *The Swing of the Pendulum* (1920) and *The Noise of the World* (1921). Turner remained interested in Mexico and wrote *Hands Off Mexico* (1920). Following World War I, he authored *Shall It Be Again?* (1922). John Kenneth Turner continued to write articles for newspapers. In his later years, he sold real estate in Carmel and wrote a book that examined communism, *Challenge to Karl Marx* (1941). John Kenneth Turner died in Carmel on July 31, 1948, at the age of 70.

After she separated from her husband, Ethel Duffy Turner went to San Francisco, where she wrote poetry and pursued other literary interests. She edited a poetry magazine, *The Wanderer*, in the 1920's. In 1930, Ethel Duffy Turner wrote a novel, *One-Way Ticket*, which was turned into a movie. She moved to Mexico in 1955 and spent her remaining years there alone. Ethel Duffy Turner wrote a book, *Revolution in Baja California: Ricardo Flores Magón's High Noon*, which was published in Mexico in 1960. In 1966 and 1967 she was interviewed by the Regional Oral History Office of the Bancroft Library at the University of California at Berkeley; the transcript was titled, *Writers and Revolutionists*. Ethel Duffy Turner died in 1969, at age 84 in Mexico.

Mary DeNeale Morgan, d. 1948

Mary DeNeale Morgan continued to play a significant role in Carmel-by-the-Sea's artistic and cultural communities, as well as in its civic affairs. She remained active in the Arts and Crafts Club through the 1920's and helped to establish the Carmel Art Association in 1927. Morgan was also involved with the Forest Theatre, where she designed sets for the productions. At the Panama-Pacific International Exposition in San Francisco in 1915, she was awarded a silver medal for her painting, "The Summer Sea". During the 1920's, Mary DeNeale Morgan's artwork was exhibited in major U.S. cities, including New York City in 1922, as well as in Washington, D.C., Baltimore, Chicago, and Cincinnati. In 1928, *Scribner's Magazine* named her one of the country's top female artists. Morgan continued to exhibit at the Hotel Del Monte since it had opened. In 1934, 60 of her paintings went on display there in a large, solo exhibit of her artwork. Mary DeNeale Morgan was well-known for her generosity and she often opened her home and studio to visitors. Morgan painted up to the very end of her life. Her last work was an unfinished painting of a cypress tree at Point Lobos. She painted it four days before she died in Carmel at age 80, on October 10, 1948.

Frederick Bechdolt, d. 1950

Throughout his long, literary career, Frederick R. Bechdolt continued to write numerous short stories and novels with Western themes, set in the days of the pioneers, often going back to his adventures and activities as a young man in the West. Bechdolt's next book after *9009* was *The Hard Rock Man* (1910), which also appeared in *The Saturday Evening Post*. It recounted how transcontinental railroad track was laid through a mountain tunnel, based on his own experiences. Bechdolt's many other books included *Hill Racketeers* (1918), *When the West Was Young* (1922), *Tales of the Old Timers (Texas after the Alamo)* (1924), *Mutiny: An Adventure Story* (1927), *Giants of the Old West* (1930), *Riders of the San Pedro* (1931), *Horse Thief Trail* (1932), *Prairie Rider* (1935), *The Tree of Death* (1937), *Danger on the Border* (1940), *Bold Raiders of the West* (1940), *Bold Riders Out of Santa Fe* (1940), *Hot Gold* (1941), *Riot at Red Water* (1942), *The Hills of Fear* (1943), *The Great Mogul Murders* (1946), and *Drygulch Canyon* (1949). During his several decades as a Carmel resident, Frederick Bechdolt was involved in local politics and civic service. He had two terms on the Carmel City Council. Bechdolt later was Carmel's postmaster and police commissioner. He also was involved with police reform. Fred and Adele Bechdolt were married for over 35 years. She died in 1945. Frederick Bechdolt died at age 75 in Carmel, on April 12, 1950.

William Rose Benét, d. 1950

After he left California, William Rose Benét returned to the East Coast. He joined *The Century Magazine* staff in New York City in 1911, and in 1914 became an assistant editor of the magazine. During World War I, he was in the U.S. Army Air Force, where he was a second lieutenant. Afterwards, William Rose Benét worked as the associate editor for *The New York Evening Post Literary Review* from 1920 to 1924. In 1924, he was an associate editor at *The Saturday Review of Literature*. He became a contributing editor in 1929 and wrote a regular column for the publication. Benét authored many volumes of verse and edited several anthologies, such as *The Reader's Encyclopedia* (1948), *The Oxford Anthology of American Literature*, and *The Poetry of Freedom, An Anthology*. In 1942, William Rose Benét won the Pulitzer Prize for Poetry for his autobiographical, *The Dust Which is God: A Novel in Verse* (1941), in which he described his Carmel-by-the-Sea days and the life of the Bohemians. William Rose Benét had been married four times. (He had three children with his first wife. His first two wives died, he divorced the third, and the fourth survived him.) William Rose Benét died on May 4, 1950, in New York City at age 64.

[*His younger brother, Stephen Vincent Benét (1898-1943), also a Yale graduate, poet, short story writer, and novelist, had won the Pulitzer Prize for Poetry in 1929 for his most famous book-length, Civil War narrative poem,* John Brown's Body *(1928). Stephen Vincent Benét posthumously won a Pulitzer Prize for Poetry in 1944 for* Western Star *(1943), also a lengthy, historical narrative poem, which he had not completed at the time of his death.*]

Michael Williams, d. 1950

Michael Williams resided in Carmel-by-the-Sea for about five years. He then went to Mexico in 1913 as war correspondent. He came back to Carmel to write his autobiography, *The Book of the High Romance, A Spiritual Autobiography* (1918), which had been 20 years in the making. Williams returned to the East Coast. In 1924, he founded and became the editor of the New York based, Catholic magazine, *The Commonweal*. He remained editor of the publication until 1938. Through the years he continued to write books: among them were *American Catholics in the War: The National Catholic War Council, 1917-1921* (1921), *The Little Flower of Carmel* (1926), *Catholicism and the Modern Mind* (1928), *The Shadow of the Pope* (1932), and *The Catholic Church in Action* (1935). Towards the end of his life, Michael Williams was ill for some time and had been hospitalized. He died at age 73, in Connecticut on October 12, 1950.

Sinclair Lewis, d. 1951

Sinclair Lewis married Grace Livingston Hegger in 1914. She worked for *Vogue* magazine. *(Their son, named after author H. G. Wells, Wells Lewis (1917-1944), was killed in World War II.)* Through the years, Lewis continued to visit Carmel-by-the-Sea, and he remained friends with George Sterling. In 1916, Sinclair Lewis drove across the country to California with Grace. They spent time in San Francisco, and met with Sterling. Grace and Sinclair drove down to Carmel and they stayed for two months in a rented bungalow, where he wrote stories for *The Saturday Evening Post*. However, he really wanted to write novels. Between 1914 and 1920 Sinclair Lewis authored five novels, but they were unsuccessful. These early works were *Our Mr. Wrenn* (1914), *The Trail of the Hawk* (1915), *The Job* (1917), *The Innocents* (1917), and *Free Air* (1919). Lewis did not achieve popularity until the 1920's, beginning with his novel, *Main Street* (1920), which was followed by other successful books: *Babbitt* (1922), *Arrowsmith* (1925), *Elmer Gantry* (1927), and *Dodsworth* (1929). These acclaimed, widely read, satirical novels depicted small-town, Midwestern, middle class life in 1920's America. *Arrowsmith* was awarded the Pulitzer Prize for the best novel of the year in 1926, but Lewis turned down the honor. In 1930, Sinclair Lewis became the first American to win the Nobel Prize for Literature, which he did accept in Stockholm. Sinclair and Grace divorced in 1925. Sinclair Lewis remarried; his second marriage was to newspaper correspondent and journalist Dorothy Thompson (1894-1961) in 1928. *(They had a son, Michael Lewis (1930-1975), who became an actor.)* In the 1920's and 1930's, Lewis made additional return trips to Carmel-by-the-Sea, as a famed author. He stayed in Carmel in February 1926, and spent time drinking with George Sterling. Sinclair and Dorothy rented a house in Monterey for several months in 1930; during that time he visited Carmel, where he met with Lincoln Steffens. Sinclair Lewis wrote plays and also acted in some of them in the 1930's. Although he continued to write, his writing career declined after the mid-1930's, and his novels were not as lucrative or as popular as the ones he had written in the 1920's. Among his later works were *Ann Vickers* (1933), *Work of Art* (1934), *It Can't Happen Here* (1935), a novel about fascism coming to the United States, *The Prodigal Parents* (1938), *Bethel Merriday* (1940), *Gideon Planish* (1943), *Cass Timberlane* (1945), *Kingsblood Royal* (1947), and *The God-Seeker* (1949). During the 1940's Lewis spent time in Europe. Sinclair and Dorothy divorced in 1942. He resided in Italy in his later years, where he lived in a villa near Florence. Through the years, Sinclair Lewis had suffered from health problems tied to his alcoholism. He spent his last months mostly alone and in ill health. Sinclair Lewis died in a hospital in Rome of a heart attack, on January 10, 1951, at the age of 65. His last novel, *World So Wide* (1951) was published posthumously.

Grant Wallace, d. 1954

In the 1910's, Grant Wallace wrote screenplays for movies. He did cartoon animation and also edited a movie magazine in the 1920's. Later in life Grant Wallace studied, wrote, and lectured on occultism. He was interested in communication with extraterrestrial life and made drawings of such. After he left Carmel, Grant Wallace resided in the Bay Area. He died on August 12, 1954 in Berkeley, at age 87, after a short illness. He left behind his wife, Margaret McVicker Wallace, two sons and a daughter.

James Hopper, d. 1956

During his lifetime, James Hopper wrote hundreds of short stories, many of which appeared through the years in national publications. Aside from the time he spent on the East Coast or overseas for work, as he occasionally left for some journalistic assignments, Hopper made Carmel-by-the-Sea his home. He, his wife, and their four children moved into George Sterling's house in 1914, the year Sterling left Carmel-by-the-Sea.

(The house burned down in 1922, and a new one was built at the same location.) While Hopper was back in Carmel, a collection of children's stories, *What Happened in the Night and Other Stories* (1913) was published, as was *Coming Back with the Spitball: A Pitcher's Romance* (1914), his last novel. But he did not stay in town for long; with the start of World War I, Hopper returned to his journalistic roots and became a war correspondent for *Collier's* magazine in France and Mexico. After the war, James Hopper returned to Carmel-by-the-Sea, where he spent most of the rest of his life. He remained physically active and was involved in the community. Three years after the death of his first wife, Mattie, Hopper remarried in 1938. His second wife, Elayne Lawson, was a Monterey musician. In the last year of his life, Hopper had been working on his memoirs. He suffered from a heart problem and was sick until his death, on August 28, 1956 in Carmel, at age 80.

M. J. Murphy, d. 1959

In 1914, M. J. Murphy became a general contractor. A decade later, he opened a construction supply business, M. J. Murphy, Incorporated. He also had a lumberyard on Ocean Avenue and Junipero Street, the block that would become the Carmel Plaza. His wife Edna managed the business. Through the years, M. J. Murphy constructed over 300 structures in Carmel; many were homes, while others were commercial buildings. Among those he worked on were the La Playa Hotel, the Highlands Inn, the Sundial Lodge, and the Harrison Memorial Library. M. J. Murphy remained one of the most well-known and influential builders in Carmel-by-the-Sea for over 30 years, until his retirement in the early 1940's. In 1941, after Edna died, Murphy moved up to Oregon, where he retired. He lived there until his death in 1959, when he was in his mid-seventies.

Van Wyck Brooks, d. 1963

Van Wyck Brooks remained at Stanford University where he taught English until 1913. The books he wrote while he lived in California were *The Malady of the Ideal* (1913), *John Addington Symonds: A Biographical Study* (1914), and *The World of H. G. Wells* (1915). After he left California, Brooks spent time living in Europe and New York, but ultimately settled in Connecticut, where he resided for most of the rest of his life. During his lifetime Van Wyck Brooks authored about 30 books, and he remained a longtime literary critic on the East Coast. He also translated several dozen books from French into English throughout his career. In the late 1910's through the early 1920's, Van Wyck Brooks, along with his wife and two sons would make return trips to Carmel-by-the-Sea to visit, and even made their home there for several years. They also made a lengthy return visit to the town in 1945. Van Wyck Brooks wrote about American authors such as Mark Twain, Henry James, Ralph Waldo Emerson, and others in the books: *The Ordeal of Mark Twain* (1920), *The Pilgrimage of Henry James* (1925), and *Emerson and Others* (1927). Most of these first two books (the one on Mark Twain, and also the book on Henry James) were written in Carmel, during the late 1910's and early 1920's, while he lived there with his family at his mother-in-law's home. On their return visit, twenty years later in 1945, Van Wyck Brooks rented a house in Carmel-by-the-Sea, which was on the coast, with a view of Point Lobos. His first wife, Eleanor died in 1946. Overall, Van Wyck Brooks is best known for his five-volume series, *Makers and Finders: A History of the Writer in America, 1800-1915*. He won the Pulitzer Prize in History in 1937 for his book, *The Flowering of New England, 1815-1865* (1936), which was one of the five books in the series. [The others were *New England: Indian Summer, 1865-1915* (1940), *The World of Washington Irving* (1944), *The Times of Melville and Whitman* (1947), and *The Confident Years, 1885-1915* (1952).] Van Wyck Brooks wrote three memoirs: *Scenes and Portraits* (1954), *Days of the Phoenix: The Nineteen Twenties I Remember* (1957), and *From the Shadow of the Mountain: My Post-Meridian Years* (1961). (These three books were joined into one, *An Autobiography* (1965), which was published posthumously.) Van Wyck Brooks died at age 77, at his longtime home in Bridgewater, Connecticut on May 2, 1963. His second wife, Gladys, survived him.

Laura Wasson Maxwell, d. 1967

Laura Wasson Maxwell came back to Carmel-by-the-Sea permanently in 1918 with her husband, Navy Captain William Lindsay Maxwell. They lived in a house on Carmelo Street and Santa Lucia Avenue. In 1929, after her husband's death, she moved to Carmel Valley, where her garden was often the subject of her paintings. Maxwell's artwork was exhibited around the United States, in New York and San Francisco, and in international cities such as Paris and Peking, China. She remained involved in Carmel's art community, and participated in the 1927 establishment and operation of the Carmel Art Association. Laura Wasson Maxwell died on the Monterey Peninsula on August 7, 1967, at age 89, two months short of her 90th birthday.

Herbert Heron, d. 1968

Through his lifetime, Herbert Heron was actively part of Carmel-by-the-Sea's cultural and later business and political activities. Heron continued to write poetry and plays, and to act in and direct productions at the Forest Theatre. Additionally, he was involved in the Bohemian Grove productions during the summers. In 1916, he spent time in Los Angeles with his family, where he was director of a Little Theatre. After their return to Carmel, he and his wife, Opal, divorced. In 1918, Heron opened a bookshop; he sold books, art materials, pottery, and antiques. He became a professional book dealer and added rare books to his store. Heron also did printing. His shop was later moved to The Seven Arts building, which he owned in downtown Carmel. (The Seven Arts building was constructed in 1925, on the southwest corner of Ocean Avenue and Lincoln Street. Heron sold the Seven Arts Building in 1940.) In 1924, Herbert Heron married Helena Conger. The previous year, he had partnered with her in his business. Heron was involved in politics and real estate; he served on the City Council and was mayor of Carmel-by-the-Sea in the 1930's. Heron started Carmel's Shakespeare Festival in 1926, and it continued through most of the 1940's. In 1949, he set up the Forest Theatre Guild, which produced plays through the 1950's. After a brief illness, Herbert Heron died on January 8, 1968. He was 84.

Upton Sinclair, d. 1968

In 1911 after a scandal, Upton Sinclair divorced his first wife, Meta. He married his second wife, Mary Craig Kimbrough in 1913, and remained with her until she died in 1961. (After her death, he married his third wife, Mary Willis, the following year, and was married to her until her death in 1967.) Upton and Mary Craig moved to Southern California in the mid-to-late 1910's. They first lived in Pasadena, and later settled in Monrovia, near Los Angeles. Sinclair spent the next several decades living in Southern California, where he continued his healthful eating and daily physical exercise, namely playing tennis. During the 1920's, Upton Sinclair established the ACLU (American Civil Liberties Union) branch in Southern California. He ran for office in California many times, including for the House of Representatives in 1920 and the U.S. Senate in 1922. Sinclair was a candidate for governor in 1926 and 1930, as a Socialist. In 1934, he ran for governor of California as a Democrat. He lost all of his electoral bids. (His platform in 1934 was known as "EPIC", which stood for End Poverty in California.) Sinclair wrote *I, Candidate for Governor* (1935) after his failed 1934 bid for the office. Throughout his life Upton Sinclair remained politically involved. He fought for and promoted issues and causes he believed in through his writing, lectures, and political campaigns. Sinclair wrote nearly 100 books and pamphlets. Among his more notable books were *King Coal* (1917), a novel about the working conditions and a strike at the Colorado coal mines, *The Brass Check, A Study of American Journalism* (1919), *The Goose Step, A Study of American Education* (1923), *Oil* (1927), about the California oilfields, and *Boston* (1927), a novel about the Sacco-Vanzetti case. [*His book,* Oil, *was the basis of the 2007 movie,* There Will Be Blood.] Upton Sinclair also wrote historical fiction, centered on a main character named, "Lanny Budd". There were eleven books in the series, which he wrote in the 1940's and 1950's, mostly during the Cold War. The first book was *World's End* (1940). In 1943, when he was in his mid-sixties, Upton Sinclair won the Pulitzer Prize for the Novel category, for *Dragon's Teeth* (1942), which was part of the "Lanny Budd" series. In 1962, *The Autobiography of Upton Sinclair* was published. Upton Sinclair spent his last months in a New Jersey nursing home; he died on November 25, 1968, at age 90.

Ferdinand Burgdorff, d. 1975

In 1911, after his artwork was exhibited in Cleveland, Ferdinand Burgdorff used money from the sale of his works to fund his world travels, during the 1910's, which he in turn used for the subject matter of his paintings. Burgdorff continued to make frequent painting trips to the Desert Southwest (Arizona and New Mexico) through 1924. He visited the Grand Canyon, and spent time with the Hopi and Navajo Native Americans. In 1920, when he returned to the Monterey Peninsula, he built a home in Pebble Beach, designed by well-known Bay Area architect Bernard Maybeck. Ferdinand Burgdorff was a member of the Carmel Art Association. He continued to paint and was the oldest artist in Monterey Peninsula's art community at the time he died, at the age of 93, on May 12, 1975.

BIBLIOGRAPHICAL NOTES

Chapter 1

The Early History of the Monterey Peninsula and the Establishment of Mission San Carlos Borroméo

General California history: Dale L. Walker, *Bear Flag Rising, The Conquest of California, 1846*; James D. Hart, *A Companion to California, New Edition, Revised and Expanded*; Kevin Starr, *California: A History*; Andrew Rolle, *California, A History, Fifth Edition*; Office of Historic Preservation, *California Historical Landmarks*; *California, A Literary Chronicle*, Edited and Commentaries by W. Storrs Lee; W. W. Robinson, *Land in California*; Roy Nickerson, *Robert Louis Stevenson in California, A Remarkable Courtship*; Daniel P. Faigin, webmaster@cahighways.org, California Highways: Trails and Roads: El Camino Real, www.cahighways.org/elcamino.html, © 1996-2006; Ernest Peixotto, *Romantic California*, 1914 [Google Digitized Book]; Edwin Markham, *California the Wonderful*, 1914 [Google Digitized Book]; Nellie Van De Grift Sanchez, *Spanish and Indian Place Names of California, Their Meaning and Their Romance*, 1914 [Google Digitized Book]

Carmel and Monterey Peninsula history: Writers' Program of Work Projects Administration in Northern California, *Monterey Peninsula*; *Illustrated History of Monterey County, California*; *History of Monterey, Santa Cruz, and San Benito Counties, California, Cradle of California's History and Romance*; Laura Bride Powers, *Old Monterey, California's Adobe Capital*; Augusta Fink, *Monterey County, The Dramatic Story of Its Past*; Harold and Ann Gilliam, *Creating Carmel*; Sydney Temple, *Carmel by-the-Sea*; John Walton, *Storied Land*; J. D. Conway, *Monterey Presidio, Pueblo, And Port, The Making Of America Series*; Scott Shields, *Artists at Continent's End, The*

Monterey Peninsula Art Colony 1875-1907; Helen Spangenberg, *Yesterday's Artists on the Monterey Peninsula*

Native Americans, California missions, and Father Serra: Alfred L. Kroeber, *Handbook of the Indians of California*, 1953; *Monterey in 1786, Life in a California Mission. The Journals of Jean Francois de La Pérouse*, Introduction by Malcolm Margolin; *The California Missions, A Complete Pictorial History and Visitor's Guide*, Sunset Books; Don DeNevi and Noel Francis Moholy, *Junípero Serra, The Illustrated Story of the Franciscan Founder of California's Missions*; Francisco Palóu, George Wharton James, *Francisco Palóu's Life and Apostolic Labors of the Venerable Father Junípero Serra, Founder of the Franciscan Missions of California (1913)*; L. S. and M. E. Slevin, *Guide Book to the Mission of San Carlos at Carmel and Monterey, California*, 1912 [Google Digitized Book], George R. Stewart, Jr., Introduction to "San Carlos Day, An Article in a California Newspaper by Robert Louis Stevenson," *Scribner's Magazine*, Volume LXVIII, August 1920, p. 209-211 [Google Digitized Book]; Robert Louis Stevenson, "The Old Pacific Capital", *Across the Plains, with other Memories and Essays*, 1892, p. 77-107 [Google Digitized Book]; Kevin Howe, "San Carlos Cathedral statue coming home with face-lift Statue to be on display inside church before return to niche", *Monterey Herald*, October 9, 2009; Laura Poole, "Seismic retrofit under way at Carmel Mission Basilica, Carmel Basilica retrofit project expected to be finished by next fall", *Monterey Herald*, October 3, 2012

Architectural history: Kent Seavey, *Images of America, Carmel: A History in Architecture*; Sally Woodbridge, *California Architecture*; Richard Janick, Laurie Boone, and Kent Seavey, *Architecture of the Monterey Peninsula*; G. E. Kidder Smith, *Sourcebook of American Architecture, 500 Notable Buildings from the 10th Century to the Present*

General history: *The Oxford History of the American West*, Edited by Clyde A. Milner II, Carol A. O'Connor, Martha A. Sandweiss

Chapter 2

Mexican California and California Statehood

General California history: Kevin Starr, *Americans and the California Dream 1850-1915*; W. W. Robinson, *Land in California*; Dale L. Walker, *Bear Flag Rising, The Conquest of California, 1846*; James D. Hart, *A Companion to California, New Edition, Revised and Expanded*; Kevin Starr, *California: A History*; Andrew Rolle, *California, A*

History, Fifth Edition; Office of Historic Preservation, *California Historical Landmarks*; *California, A Literary Chronicle*, Edited and Commentaries by W. Storrs Lee; *Historic Spots in California, Fourth Edition*, Revised by Douglas E. Kyle; Leonard Pitt, *The Decline of the Californios, A Social History of the Spanish-Speaking Californians, 1846-1890*, Updated with a new Foreword by Ramon A. Gutierrez; Lawrence Clark Powell, *California Classics*; Richard Henry Dana, Jr. *Two Years Before the Mast, A Personal Narrative*, (1840); Ella Sterling Cummins, *The Story of the Files, A Review of Californian Writers and Literature* [Google Digitized Book]; Charles Warren Stoddard, *In the Footprints of the Padres* [Google Digitized Book]; Franklin Walker, *San Francisco's Literary Frontier*; William Deverell, *Railroad Crossing, Californians and the Railroad, 1850-1910*; Philip L. Fradkin, *The Great Earthquake and Firestorms of 1906, How San Francisco Nearly Destroyed Itself*

Carmel and Monterey Peninsula history: Writers' Program of Work Projects Administration in Northern California, *Monterey Peninsula*; *Illustrated History of Monterey County, California*; *History of Monterey, Santa Cruz, and San Benito Counties, California, Cradle of California's History and Romance*; Laura Bride Powers, *Old Monterey, California's Adobe Capital*; Augusta Fink, *Monterey County, The Dramatic Story of Its Past*; Harold and Ann Gilliam, *Creating Carmel*; Sydney Temple, *Carmel by-the-Sea*; John Walton, *Storied Land*; J. D. Conway, *Monterey Presidio, Pueblo, And Port, The Making Of America Series*; Scott Shields, *Artists at Continent's End, The Monterey Peninsula Art Colony 1875-1907*; Helen Spangenberg, *Yesterday's Artists on the Monterey Peninsula*; *Adobes in the Sun, Portraits of a Tranquil Era*, Text by Augusta Fink with Amelie Elkinton

Native Americans, California missions, and Father Serra: Don DeNevi and Noel Francis Moholy, *Junípero Serra, The Illustrated Story of the Franciscan Founder of California's Missions*; Francisco Palou, George Wharton James, *Francisco Palou's Life and Apostolic Labors of the Venerable Father Junípero Serra, Founder of the Franciscan Missions of California (1913)*; *The California Missions, A Complete Pictorial History and Visitor's Guide*, Sunset Books; *Monterey in 1786, Life in a California Mission. The Journals of Jean Francois de La Pérouse*, Introduction by Malcolm Margolin

General history: *The Oxford History of the American West*, Edited by Clyde A. Milner II, Carol A. O'Connor, Martha A. Sandweiss; Stuart Eliot Morison, Henry Steele Commager, William E. Leuchtenburg, *A Concise History of the American Republic*; John Steele Gordon, *An Empire of Wealth, The Epic History of American Economic Power*

Architectural history: Sally Woodbridge, *California Architecture*; G. E. Kidder Smith, *Sourcebook of American Architecture, 500 Notable Buildings from the 10th*

Century to the Present; Richard Janick, Laurie Boone, and Kent Seavey, *Architecture of the Monterey Peninsula*; Rachel Carley, *The Visual Dictionary of American Domestic Architecture*; Marcia Reiss, *Architectural Details*; Susan Dinkelspiel Cerny, *An Architectural Guidebook to San Francisco and the Bay Area*

Dictionaries and other reference guides: *Webster's New Collegiate Dictionary*, G. and C. Merriam Company Publishers, Springfield Massachusetts, 1940 Edition; *Webster's Biographical Dictionary*, First Edition; Edan Hughes, *Artists in California 1786-1940, Volume 1, A-K*, 3rd Edition

Chapter 3

The Decline of Monterey and David Jacks

General California history: W. W. Robinson, *Land in California*; Andrew Rolle, *California, A History, Fifth Edition*; Kevin Starr, *California: A History*; Leonard Pitt, *The Decline of the Californios, A Social History of the Spanish-Speaking Californians, 1846-1890*, Updated with a new Foreword by Ramon A. Gutierrez; James D. Hart, *A Companion to California, New Edition, Revised and Expanded*; William H. Brewer, *Up and Down California in 1860-1864, The Journal of William H. Brewer*, 4th Edition with Maps; *California, A Literary Chronicle*, Edited and Commentaries by W. Storrs Lee; Charles Warren Stoddard, *In the Footprints of the Padres*, New and Enlarged Edition, 1912 [Google Digitized Book]; Kevin Starr, *Americans and the California Dream 1850-1915*; *Historic Spots in California, Fourth Edition*, Revised by Douglas E. Kyle; Major Ben C. Truman, *Tourists' Illustrated Guide to the Celebrated Summer and Winter Resorts of California Adjacent to and Upon the Lines of the Central and Southern Pacific Railroads* [Google Digitized Book]; Benjamin C. Wright, *San Francisco's Ocean Trade. A Story of the Deep Water Service of San Francisco, 1848 to 1911. Effect the Panama Canal Will Have Upon It*, 1911 [Google Digitized Book]

Carmel and Monterey Peninsula history: Sydney Temple, *Carmel by-the-Sea*; J .D. Conway, *Monterey Presidio, Pueblo, And Port, The Making Of America Series*; John Walton, *Storied Land*; Augusta Fink, *Monterey County, The Dramatic Story of Its Past*; Elizabeth Barratt and the Carmel Valley Historical Society, *Images of America Carmel Valley*, Laura Bride Powers, *Old Monterey, California's Adobe Capital*; Writers' Program of Work Projects Administration in Northern California, *Monterey Peninsula*; Harold and Ann Gilliam, *Creating Carmel*; Scott Shields, *Artists at Continent's End, The Monterey Peninsula Art Colony 1875-1907*; Robert Louis Stevenson, "The Old Pacific Capital", *Across the Plains, with other Memories and Essays*, 1892, p. 77-107 [Google

Digitized Book]; Grace MacFarland, *Monterey, Cradle of California's Romance: The Story of A Lost Port That was Found Again and A Dream That Came True*, 1914 [Google Digitized Book]; Ray A. March, *River in Ruin, The Story of the Carmel River*; Julie Cain, *Images of America, Monterey's Hotel Del Monte*; Kent Seavey and the Heritage Society of Pacific Grove, *Images of America, Pacific Grove*; *History of Monterey, Santa Cruz, and San Benito Counties, California, Cradle of California's History and Romance*, Volume II, 1925; *Memorial and Biographical History of the Coast Counties of Central California, Illustrated*, Henry D. Barrows, Editor of the Historical Department, Luther A. Ingersoll, Editor of the Biographical Department, 1893 [Google Digitized Book]; *Santa Cruz County California*, 1879 [Google Digitized Book]; Connie Y. Chiang, Forward by William Cronon, *Shaping the Shoreline: Fisheries and Tourism on the Monterey Coast*; *Illustrated History of Monterey County, California*; *History of Monterey, Santa Cruz, and San Benito Counties, California*; *Historic Context Statement, Carmel-by-the-Sea*, Adopted by the City Council September 9, 2008

California missions and Father Serra: *The California Missions, A Complete Pictorial History and Visitor's Guide*; Sunset Books; Frances Norris Rand Smith, *The Architectural History of Mission San Carlos Borroméo Carmelo, California*, 1921 [Google Digitized Book]; Mrs. Fremont Older, *California Missions and Their Romances*, original Coward-McCann, Inc., 1938, Kessinger Publishing, 2005; L. S. and M. E. Slevin, *Guide Book to the Mission of San Carlos at Carmel and Monterey, California*, 1912 [Google Digitized Book]; *The Catholic Encyclopedia, Knights of Columbus*, Volume One, The Encyclopedia Press, Inc., New York, 1913 [Google Digitized Book]

General history: John Steele Gordon, *An Empire of Wealth, The Epic History of American Economic Power*; *U.S. Congressional Serial Set, 61st Congress, 2nd Session, 1909-1910, Senate Documents*, U. S. Congress, Volume 56, Government Printing Office, Washington, D. C., 1913 [Google Digitized Book]; Stuart Eliot Morison, Henry Steele Commager, William E. Leuchtenburg, *A Concise History of the American Republic*

Architectural history: Richard Janick, Laurie Boone, and Kent Seavey, *Architecture of the Monterey Peninsula*; G. E. Kidder Smith, *Sourcebook of American Architecture, 500 Notable Buildings from the 10th Century to the Present*; Sally Woodbridge, *California Architecture*; Kent Seavey, *Images of America, Carmel: A History in Architecture*; David Gebhard, Robert Montgomery, Robert Winter, John Woodbridge, and Sally Woodbridge, *A Guide to Architecture in San Francisco & Northern California*

Chapter 4

The Railroads and the Hotel Del Monte

San Francisco Bay Area and General California history: Kevin Starr, *California: A History*; James D. Hart, *A Companion to California, New Edition, Revised and Expanded*; W. W. Robinson, *Land in California*; Andrew Rolle, *California, A History, Fifth Edition*; Office of Historic Preservation, *California Historical Landmarks*, California State Parks; Kevin Starr, *Inventing the Dream, California Through the Progressive Era*; *Historic Spots in California, Fourth Edition*, Revised by Douglas E. Kyle; National Park Service: National Historic Landmarks Program website; Tomas Jaehn, "The Southern Pacific Launches a New Vehicle to Develop Its Market", *Sunset Magazine: A Century of Western Living, 1898-1998, Historical Portraits and Bibliography*; Dr. Kevin Starr, "Sunset Magazine and the Phenomenon of the Far West", *Sunset Magazine: A Century of Western Living, 1898-1998, Historical Portraits and Bibliography*; Frank Morton Todd, *The Chamber of Commerce Handbook for San Francisco, Historical and Descriptive, A Guide for Visitors*, 1913 [Google Digitized Book]; Nellie Van De Grift Sanchez, *Spanish and Indian Place Names of California Their Meaning and Their Romance*, 1914 [Google Digitized Book]; Ferol Egan, *Last Bonanza Kings, The Bourns of San Francisco*; Frank Norris, *McTeague: A Story of San Francisco*, Introduction by Kevin Starr, 1982; Ella Sterling Cummins, *The Story of the Files, A Review of Californian Writers and Literature*, 1893 [Google Digitized Book]; Helen Throop Purdy, *San Francisco As It Was, As It Is, and How to See It*, 1912 [Google Digitized Book]; Lawrence Clark Powell, *California Classics, The Creative Literature of the Golden State*; Lawrence Ferlinghetti and Nancy J. Peters, *Literary San Francisco, A Pictorial History from Its Beginnings to the Present Day*; Philip L. Fradkin, *The Great Earthquake and Firestorms of 1906, How San Francisco Nearly Destroyed Itself*

Railroad history: William Deverell, *Railroad Crossing, Californians and the Railroad, 1850-1910*; Stephen E. Ambrose, *Nothing Like It In The World, The Men Who Built the Transcontinental Railroad 1863-1869*; Richard J. Orsi, *Sunset Limited*

Carmel and Monterey Peninsula history: Ray A. March, *River in Ruin, The Story of the Carmel River*; J. D. Conway, *Monterey Presidio, Pueblo, And Port, The Making Of America Series*; John Walton, *Storied Land*; Kent Seavey and the Heritage Society of Pacific Grove, *Images of America, Pacific Grove*; Scott Shields, *Artists at Continent's End, The Monterey Peninsula Art Colony 1875-1907*; Sydney Temple, *Carmel by-the-Sea*; Augusta Fink, *Monterey County, The Dramatic Story of Its Past*; Writers' Program of Work Projects Administration in Northern California, *Monterey Peninsula*; *Memorial and Biographical History of the Coast Counties of Central California, Illustrated*, Henry D. Barrows, Editor of the Historical Department, Luther A. Ingersoll, Editor of the Biographical Department, 1893 [Google Digitized Book]; *Illustrated History of Monterey County, California*; *History of Monterey, Santa Cruz, and San Benito Counties, California*; Burle Willes, *The Monterey Peninsula, A Postcard Journey*; *History of Monterey, Santa Cruz, and San Benito Counties, California, Cradle of California's History and Romance*, Volume II, 1925; *Santa Cruz County California*, 1879 [Google Digitized Book]; Sharron Lee Hale, *A Tribute to Yesterday*; Elizabeth Barratt and the Carmel Valley Historical Society, *Images of America Carmel Valley*; *Historic Context Statement, Carmel-by-the-Sea*, Adopted by the City Council September 9, 2008; Harold and Ann Gilliam, *Creating Carmel*; Bettina Boxall, "$84-million removal of a dam on Carmel River set to begin Dismantling of the Silt-filled San Clemente, to start next month, is being called California's largest-ever dam removal.", *Los Angeles Times*, June 23, 2013

Hotel Del Monte: Julie Cain, *Images of America, Monterey's Hotel Del Monte*; Major Ben C. Truman, *Tourists' Illustrated Guide to the Celebrated Summer and Winter Resorts of California Adjacent to and Upon the Lines of the Central and Southern Pacific Railroads*, "Sea-side Resorts of California", p. 130-170 [Google Digitized Book]; "Mr. Simmons Acquitted", *New York Times*, June 26, 1887; George Wharton James, *The 1910 Trip of the H.M.M.B.A. to California and the Pacific Coast*, Chapter XII, p. 245-268 [Google Digitized Book]; "Famous Times Writer Dies In California, Major Ben C. Truman Served New York Times as Correspondent in Civil War and Was President Johnson's Secretary." *New York Times* obituary, July 30, 1916; Henry Clay Quinby, "The Chapel at Del Monte", *Sunset*, Volume XVI, Number 3, January 1906, p. 298 [Google Digitized Book]

General history: Stuart Eliot Morison, Henry Steele Commager, William E. Leuchtenburg, *A Concise History of the American Republic*; *The Oxford History of the American West*, Edited by Clyde A. Milner II, Carol A. O'Connor, Martha A. Sandweiss; John Steele Gordon, *An Empire of Wealth, The Epic History of American Economic Power*

Architectural history: Sally Woodbridge, *California Architecture*; Richard Janick, Laurie Boone, and Kent Seavey, *Architecture of the Monterey Peninsula*; David Gebhard, Robert Montgomery, Robert Winter, John Woodbridge, and Sally Woodbridge, *A Guide to Architecture in San Francisco & Northern California*; Jeffrey T. Tilman, *Arthur Brown Jr.: Progressive Classicist (Classical America Series in Art and Architecture)*; Susan Dinkelspiel Cerny, *An Architectural Guidebook to San Francisco and the Bay Area*; Peter Booth Wiley, *National Trust Guide--San Francisco: America's Guide for Architecture and History Travelers*; Rachel Carley, *The Visual Dictionary of American Domestic Architecture*; Marcia Reiss, *Architectural Details*; G. E. Kidder Smith, *Sourcebook of American Architecture, 500 Notable Buildings from the 10th Century to the Present*; Kent

Seavey, *Images of America, Carmel: A History in Architecture*; Leslie M. Freudenheim, *Building with Nature, Inspiration for the Arts & Crafts Home*; Robert Winter, Editor, *Towards a Simpler Way, The Arts & Crafts Architects of California*, Chapter 2 on Ernest Coxhead by Jeremy Kotas, p. 23-30; Richard W. Longstreth, *On The Edge of the World: Four Architects in San Francisco at the Turn of the Century*

Dictionaries and other reference guides: Webster's Biographical Dictionary, First Edition

Chapter 5

The Duckworth Brothers and Carmel City

San Francisco Bay Area and General California history: Dr. Kevin Starr, "Sunset Magazine and the Phenomenon of the Far West", *Sunset Magazine: A Century of Western Living, 1898-1998, Historical Portraits and Bibliography*; Kevin Starr, *California: A History*; Carey McWilliams, *Southern California: An Island on the Land*, Chapter IV, "The Growth of a Legend"; Kevin Starr, *Americans and the California Dream 1850-1915*; William H. Gerdts and Will South, *California Impressionism*; Kevin Starr, *Inventing the Dream, California Through the Progressive Era*; Lawrence Clark Powell, *California Classics, The Creative Literature of the Golden State*; Andrew Rolle, *California A History, Fifth Edition*; James D. Hart, *A Companion to California, New Edition, Revised and Expanded*; Philip L. Fradkin, *The Great Earthquake and Firestorms of 1906, How San Francisco Nearly Destroyed Itself*; W. W. Robinson, *Land in California*; Frank Morton Todd, *The Chamber of Commerce Handbook for San Francisco, Historical and Descriptive, A Guide for Visitors*, 1913 [Google Digitized Book]

Railroad history: William Deverell, *Railroad Crossing, Californians and the Railroad, 1850-1910*; Stephen E. Ambrose, *Nothing Like It In The World, The Men Who Built the Transcontinental Railroad 1863-1869*; Richard J. Orsi, *Sunset Limited*

Carmel and Monterey Peninsula history: Augusta Fink, *Monterey County, The Dramatic Story of Its Past*; Elizabeth Barratt and the Carmel Valley Historical Society, *Images of America, Carmel Valley*; Monica Hudson, *Images of America, Carmel-by-the-Sea*; Mission Ranch, Carmel website; Ray A. March, *River in Ruin, The Story of the Carmel River*; *Adobes in the Sun, Portraits of a Tranquil Era*, Text by Augusta Fink with Amelie Elkinton; Writers' Program of Work Projects Administration in Northern California, *Monterey Peninsula*; J. D. Conway, *Monterey Presidio, Pueblo, And Port*,

The Making Of America Series; Sydney Temple, *Carmel by-the-Sea*; *Historic Context Statement, Carmel-by-the-Sea*, Adopted by the City Council September 9, 2008; Scott Shields, *Artists at Continent's End, The Monterey Peninsula Art Colony 1875-1907*; John Walton, *Storied Land*; Harold and Ann Gilliam, *Creating Carmel*; Robert Louis Stevenson, "The Old Pacific Capital", *Across the Plains, with other Memories and Essays*, 1892, p. 77-107 [Google Digitized Book]; Roy Nickerson, *Robert Louis Stevenson in California, A Remarkable Courtship*; Lawrence Clark Powell, *California Classics, The Creative Literature of the Golden State*; Laura Bride Powers, *Old Monterey, California's Adobe Capital*; Michael Orth, "Ideality to Reality: The Founding of Carmel", *The California Historical Society Quarterly*, Volume XLVIII, Number 3, September 1969; Sharron Lee Hale, *A Tribute to Yesterday*; Daisy Bostick and Dorothea Castelhun, *Carmel at Work and Play*; Kent Seavey and the Heritage Society of Pacific Grove, *Images of America Pacific Grove*

California missions and Father Serra: *The California Missions, A Complete Pictorial History and Visitor's Guide*, Sunset Books; L. S. and M. E. Slevin, *Guide Book to the Mission of San Carlos at Carmel and Monterey, California*, Carmel, California, 1912 [Google Digitized Book]; George R. Stewart, Jr., Introduction to "San Carlos Day, An Article in a California Newspaper by Robert Louis Stevenson," *Scribner's Magazine*, Volume LXVIII, August 1920, p. 209-211 [Google Digitized Book]; Helen Hunt Jackson, *Glimpses of California and the Missions*, 1914 [Google Digitized Book]; Helen (Hunt) Jackson, *A Century of Dishonor, A Sketch of the United States Government's Dealings With Some of the Indian Tribes, New Edition Enlarged by the Addition of the Report of the Needs of the Mission Indians of California*, 1917 [Google Digitized Book]

General history: John Steele Gordon, *An Empire of Wealth, The Epic History of American Economic Power*

Architectural history: Kent Seavey, *Images of America, Carmel: A History in Architecture*

Chapter 6

Carmel-by-the-Sea Becomes a Town: Frank Devendorf, Frank Powers, and the Carmel Development Company

San Francisco Bay Area and General California history: Albert Parry, *Garrets and Pretenders, A History of Bohemianism in America*, originally published by Covici-Friede, Inc., New York, 1933; Kevin Starr, *Americans and the California Dream 1850-1915*; James D. Hart, *A Companion to California, New Edition, Revised and Expanded*; Ernest Peixotto, *Romantic California*, 1914 [Google Digitized Book]; Nellie Van De Grift Sanchez, *Spanish and Indian Place Names of California, Their Meaning and Their Romance*, 1914 [Google Digitized Book]; *History of the Bench and Bar of California*, 1912 [Google Digitized Book]; *Historic Spots in California, Fourth Edition*, Revised by Douglas E. Kyle; Office of Historic Preservation, *California Historical Landmarks*; Dr. Kevin Starr, "Sunset Magazine and the Phenomenon of the Far West", *Sunset Magazine: A Century of Western Living, 1898-1998, Historical Portraits and Bibliography*; Tomas Jaehn, "The Southern Pacific Launches a New Vehicle to Develop Its Market", *Sunset Magazine: A Century of Western Living, 1898-1998, Historical Portraits and Bibliography*; Lawrence Ferlinghetti and Nancy J. Peters, *Literary San Francisco, A Pictorial History from Its Beginnings to the Present Day*; Philip L. Fradkin, *The Great Earthquake and Firestorms of 1906, How San Francisco Nearly Destroyed Itself*; Ed Herny, Shelley Rideout, Katie Wadell, *Berkeley Bohemia, Artists and Visionaries of the Early 20th Century*; Kevin Starr, *Americans and the California Dream 1850-1915*; Kevin Starr, *Golden Dreams, California in an Age of Abundance, 1950-1963*; Kevin Starr, *The Dream Endures, California Enters the 1940's*

Carmel and Monterey Peninsula history: Mary Austin, "George Sterling at Carmel", *American Mercury*, Volume XI, Number 41, May 1927, p. 65-72; Mary E. Delport, "The Spell of the Carmel Coast", *Overland Monthly*, Volume LXXIII, Second Series, February 1919, p. 106-115 [Google Digitized Book]; Henry Dumont, "The Pageant at Carmel", the *National Magazine*, Volume XXXV, October 1911, p. 151-157 [Google Digitized Book]; Kathryne Wilson, "The Literary Colony at Carmel", *The Book News Monthly*, Volume 33, Number 7, March 1915, p. 364-367 [Google Digitized Book]; Scott Shields, *Artists at Continent's End, The Monterey Peninsula Art Colony 1875-1907*; Leonore Kothe, "The Monterey Cypress", *Overland Monthly*, Volume LXVI, Second Series, Number 6, December 1915, p. 469-473 [Google Digitized Book]; Josephine Mildred Blanch, "The 'Barbizon' of California, Some Interesting Studios of Old Monterey", *Overland Monthly*, Volume L, Second Series, Number 1, July 1907, p. 63-68 [Google Digitized Book]; George Sterling, "The Islands of the Blest", *A Wine of Wizardry*, p. 21-23 [Google Digitized Book]; Michael Orth, "Ideality to Reality: The Founding of Carmel", *The California Historical Society Quarterly*, Volume XLVIII, Number 3, September 1969, p. 195-210; Sharron Lee Hale, *A Tribute to Yesterday*; Harold and Ann Gilliam, *Creating Carmel*; Augusta Fink, *Monterey County, The Dramatic Story of Its Past*; Franklin Walker, *Seacoast of Bohemia*; *Old Carmel* by Connie Wright, "Frank and Jane Gallatin Powers", *Carmel Residents Association Newsletter* Online, February 2003; Helen Spangenberg, *Yesterday's Artists on the Monterey Peninsula*; Monica Hudson, *Images of America, Carmel-by-the-Sea*; Ray A. March, *River in Ruin, The Story of the Carmel River*; Sydney Temple, *Carmel* by-the-Sea; Burl Willes, *The Monterey Peninsula, A Postcard Journey*; Kim Coventry, *Images of America, Monterey Peninsula, The Golden Age*; Daisy Bostick and Dorothea Castelhun, *Carmel at Work and Play*; Eunice T. Gray, "The Chase School of Art at Carmel-by-the-Sea, California", *Art and Progress*, Volume VI, Number 4, p. 118-120 [Google Digitized Book]; Michael Williams, "The Forest Theater at Carmel, A Dramatic Movement in the Shadow of Junipero Serra's Mission", *Sunset, The Pacific Monthly*, Volume XXIX, Number 3, September 1912, p. 319-325 [Google Digitized Book]; "History of the Pine Inn", Pine Inn Hotel, Carmel-by-the-Sea, California website; *Historic Context Statement, Carmel-by-the-Sea*, Adopted by the City Council September 9, 2008; Louis Stanislas Slevin, M. E. Slevin, *Guide book to the Mission of San Carlos at Carmel and Monterey, California*, 1912 [Google Digitized Book]; Allen Pierleoni, "Travel Spotlight: 102-year-old Carmel Drug Store Holds Its Place in Time", *The Sacramento Bee*, August 12, 2012; Harrison Memorial Library website; The Church of the Wayfarer, Carmel, California website

Architectural history: Kent Seavey, *Images of America, Carmel: A History in Architecture*; Sally Woodbridge, *California Architecture*; David Gebhard, Robert Montgomery, Robert Winter, John Woodbridge, and Sally Woodbridge, *A Guide to Architecture in San Francisco & Northern California*; *Old Carmel* by Connie Wright, "M. J. Murphy—'The man who built Carmel'", *Carmel Residents Association Newsletter* online, September 2002; Rachel Carley, *The Visual Dictionary of American Domestic Architecture*; Marcia Reiss, *Architectural Details*; Leslie M. Freudenheim, *Building with Nature, Inspiration for the Arts & Crafts Home*; Robert Winter, Editor, *Towards a Simpler Way, The Arts & Crafts Architects of California*; Judy Hammond, "Door-to-door. Home Built Of Portals Saved From S.F. Quake Gets Reprieve", *Chicago Tribune*, July 30, 1995

Dictionaries and other reference guides: Edan Hughes, *Artists in California 1786-1940, Volume 2, L-Z*, 3rd Edition; *Who's Who in America, A Biographical Dictionary of Notable Living Men and Women in the United States*, Volume VI, 1910-1911 [Google Digitized Book]; *Webster's Biographical Dictionary*, First Edition; *Pacific Medical Journal*, Volume XLIX, Number 8, August 1906, p. 317, p. 409 [Google Digitized Book]

Biographies, autobiographies, and obituaries: Arnold Genthe, *As I Remember, The Sources of Modern Photography*; David Starr Jordan, *The Days of a Man, Being Memories of a Naturalist, Teacher, and Minor Prophet of Democracy, Illustrated, Volume One, 1851-1899*, 1922 [Google Digitized Book]; Edwin R. Bingham, *Charles F. Lummis, Editor of the Southwest*; Susan Goodman and Carl Dawson, *Mary Austin and the American West*; Esther Lanigan Stineman, *Mary Austin, Song of a Maverick*; "David Starr Jordan Dies at Age of 80", *New York Times* obituary, September 20, 1931; "Dr.

V. L. Kellogg, Scientist, was 69", *New York Times* obituary, August 9, 1937; New York Botanical Garden Library, *Daniel T. MacDougal Papers*, online; Mary Austin, *Earth Horizon*; *The Letters of Ambrose Bierce*, Edited by Bertha Clark Pope, 1922 [Internet Archive: www.archive.org]

Chapter 7
Carmel-by-the-Sea Artists and the Arts and Crafts Club

San Francisco Bay Area and General California history: Kevin Starr, *Americans and the California Dream 1850-1915*; Ed Herny, Shelley Rideout, Katie Wadell, *Berkeley Bohemia, Artists and Visionaries of the Early 20th Century*; Andrew Rolle, *California, A History, Fifth Edition*; James D. Hart, *A Companion to California, New Edition, Revised and Expanded*; Charles Warren Stoddard, "In Old Bohemia, Memories of San Francisco in the Sixties", *The Pacific Monthly*, December 1907, p. 639-650 [Google Digitized Book]; Philip L. Fradkin, *The Great Earthquake and Firestorms of 1906, How San Francisco Nearly Destroyed Itself*

Carmel and Monterey Peninsula history: J. D. Conway, City of Monterey, *Monterey Presidio, Pueblo, And Port, The Making Of America Series*; Harold and Ann Gilliam, *Creating Carmel*; George Wharton James, *The 1910 Trip of the H.M.M.B.A. to California and the Pacific Coast*, Chapter XII, p. 245-268 [Google Digitized Book]; Monica Hudson, *Images of America, Carmel-by-the-Sea*; Sydney Temple, *Carmel by-the-Sea*; Sharron Lee Hale, *A Tribute to Yesterday*; Harold and Ann Gilliam, *Creating Carmel*; Franklin Walker, *Seacoast of Bohemia*; Charles Warren Stoddard, *In the Footprints of the Padres*, New and Enlarged Edition, 1912 [Google Digitized Book]; Julie Cain, *Images of America, Monterey's Hotel Del Monte*; Connie Y. Chiang, Forward by William Cronon, *Shaping the Shoreline: Fisheries and Tourism on the Monterey Coast*; Michael Williams, "The Forest Theater at Carmel, A Dramatic Movement in the Shadow of Junipero Serra's Mission", *Sunset, The Pacific Monthly*, Volume XXIX, Number 3, September 1912, p. 319-325 [Google Digitized Book]; "Literary Monterey" by Henry Meade Bland, *Overland Monthly*, January 1909, Volume LIII, Number 1, p. 19-26 [Google Digitized Book]; Leonore Kothe, "In Old Monterey", *Overland Monthly*, Volume LVII, Second Series, Number 6, June 1911, p. 631-636 [Google Digitized Book]; Kathryne Wilson, "The Literary Colony at Carmel", *The Book News Monthly*, Volume 33, Number 7, April 1915, p. 364-367 [Google Digitized Book]

Artists: Anna Geil Andresen, *Historic Landmarks of Monterey, California. A Brief Sketch of the Landmarks of Monterey*, California Federation of Women's Clubs, Salinas, California 1917, p. 89-92 [Google Digitized Book]; Scott Shields, *Artists at Continent's End, The Monterey Peninsula Art Colony 1875-1907*; Helen Spangenberg, *Yesterday's Artists on the Monterey Peninsula*; Historic Context Statement Carmel-by-the-Sea, online, Adopted by the City Council September 9, 2008; Josephine Mildred Blanch, "The "Barbizon' of California, Some Interesting Studios of Old Monterey", *Overland Monthly*, Volume L, Second Series, Number 1, July 1907, p. 63-68 [Google Digitized Book]; Charles D. Robinson, "A Revival of Art Interest in California", *Overland Monthly*, Vol. XVII, Second Series, Number 102, June 1891, p. 649-652 [Google Digitized Book]; Carmel Art Association, *Six Early Women Artists: A Diversity of Style*, 1991; Beatric de Lack Krombach, "Art at Del Monte". *Out West Magazine*, Volume XLII, Number 2, February 1916, p. 67-70, p. 105 [Google Digitized Book]; Betty Hoag McGlynn, "The Carmel Art Association", Ruth Westphal, *Plein Air Artists of California, The North*; Eunice T. Gray, "The Chase School of Art at Carmel-by-the-Sea, California", *Art and Progress*, Volume VI, Number 4, February 1915, p. 118-120 [Google Digitized Book]; Ellen Dwyer Donovan, "California Artists and Their Work", *Overland Monthly*, Volume LI, Second Series, Number 1, January 1908, p. 25-33 [Google Digitized Book]; Nancy Boas, *Society of Six: California Colorists*; William H. Gerdts and Will South, *California Impressionism*

Architectural history: Leslie M. Freudenheim, *Building with Nature, Inspiration for the Arts & Crafts Home*, Chapter 3, "The Swedenborgian Church and the First Mission Style Chair"; Richard W. Longstreth, *On The Edge of the World: Four Architects in San Francisco at the Turn of the Century*; Kent Seavey, *Images of America, Carmel: A History in Architecture*

Dictionaries and other reference guides: Edan Hughes, *Artists in California 1786-1940, Volume 1, A-K, 3ʳᵈ Edition*; Edan Hughes, *Artists in California 1786-1940, Volume 2, L-Z, 3ʳᵈ Edition*; *The Oxford Dictionary of American Art and Artists*; *Who's Who in America, A Biographical Dictionary of Notable Living Men and Women in the United States*, Volume VI, 1910-1911 [Google Digitized Book]; *American Art Annual*, Florence N. Levy, Editor, Volume XIV, 1917 [Google Digitized Book]; *Who's Who in America, A Biographical Dictionary of Notable Living Men and Women in the United States*, Volume II, 1901-1902 [Google Digitized Book]; *University Chronicle, An Official Record*, The University of California Berkeley, Volume IV, Number 1, February 1901 [Google Digitized Book]

Biographies, autobiographies, and obituaries: Roy Nickerson, *Robert Louis Stevenson in California, A Remarkable Courtship*; Isobel Field, *This Life I've Loved, An Autobiography*; Mabel Urmy Seares, "William Keith and His Times", *California's*

Magazine, Edition De Luxe, Volume II, California's Magazine Company, San Francisco, California, 1916, p. 105-110 [Google Digitized Book]; Charles Moore, *Daniel H. Burnham, Architect, Planner of Cities, Volume I*, Houghton Mifflin Company, Boston and New York, 1921 [Google Digitized Book]; Charles Keeler, "The American Turner. William Keith and His Work." *Land of Sunshine*, Volume VIII, Number 6, May 1898, p. 253-259 [Google Digitized Book]; "William Keith Dead. Landscape Painter Was Famous for His California Scenes." *New York Times* obituary, April 14, 1911; Betty Hoag McGlynn, "Charles Rollo Peters", Ruth Westphal, *Plein Art Painters of California, The North*, p. 148-153; Arnold Genthe, *As I Remember, The Sources of Modern Photography*; F. W. Ramsdell, "Charles Rollo Peters", *Brush & Pencil, An Illustrated Magazine of the Arts & Crafts*, Volume IV, Number 4, July 1899, p. 205-212 [Google Digitized Book]; Janet B. Dominik, "Mary DeNeale Morgan", Ruth Westphal, *Plein Air Painters of California, The North*; *Old Carmel* by Connie Wright, "Frank and Jane Gallatin Powers", *Carmel Residents Association Newsletter* Online, February 2003; *Old Carmel* by Connie Wright, "Laura Maxwell, Pioneer", *Carmel Residents Association Newsletter* online, March 2004; *Old Carmel* by Connie Wright, "Mary DeNeale Morgan, 'horse and buggy artist'", *Carmel Residents Association Newsletter* online, January 2002; *Old Carmel* by Connie Wright, "Sydney Jones Yard, Tonalist Painter", *Carmel Residents Association Newsletter* online, March 2006; "Charles Chapel Judson", *New York Times* obituary, November 6, 1946; Sidney Lawrence, "The Ghirardelli Story", *California History*, Volume 81, Number 2, Spring-Fall, 2002, p. 81-90; George Wharton James, "Chris Jorgensen—A Versatile California Artist", *The National Magazine*, Volume XLII, July 1915, p. 609-616 [Google Digitized Book]; T. M. Pearce, Editor, *Literary America 1903-1934, The Mary Austin Letters*, Donald J. Hagerty, *The Life of Maynard Dixon*; Elsie Whitaker Martinez, *San Francisco Bay Area Writers and Artists* [Internet Archive: www.archive.org]

Chapter 8

The Coppa Crowd of Bohemians Comes to Carmel-by-the-Sea

San Francisco Bay Area and General California history: James D. Hart, *A Companion to California, New Edition, Revised and Expanded*; Kevin Starr, *Americans and the California Dream 1850-1915*; Lawrence Ferlinghetti and Nancy J. Peters, *Literary San Francisco, A Pictorial History from Its Beginnings to the Present Day*; Albert Parry, *Garrets and Pretenders, A History of Bohemianism in America*, originally published by Covici-Friede, Inc., New York, 1933; Franklin Walker, *San Francisco's Literary Frontier*; Helen Throop Purdy, *San Francisco As It Was, As It Is, and How to*

See It, 1912 [Google Digitized Book]; Will Irwin, *The City That Was, A Requiem of Old San Francisco*, 1908 [Google Digitized Book]; Andrew Rolle, *California A History, Fifth Edition*; "Constitution and By-Laws of The Bohemian Club of San Francisco", 1895 [Google Digitized Book]; Dr. Kevin Starr, "Sunset Magazine and the Phenomenon of the Far West", *Sunset Magazine: A Century of Western Living, 1898-1998, Historical Portraits and Bibliography*; Jean White, "A Landmark of San Francisco's Bohemia", *Overland Monthly*, Volume LXVII, Second Series, Number 3, March 1916, p. 186-188 [Internet Archive: www.archive.org]; Kevin Starr, *California: A History*; *Three Fearful Days, San Francisco Memoirs of the 1906 Earthquake & Fire*, Compiled and Introduced by Malcolm E. Barker; Office of Historic Preservation, *California Historical Landmarks*; *Historic Spots in California, Fourth Edition*, Revised by Douglas E. Kyle; Joseph Henry Jackson, "Everybody Knew the 'Block'," *New York Times*, May 27, 1951; Kevin Starr, *Inventing the Dream, California Through the Progressive Era*; *Taming the Elephant, Politics, Government, and Law in Pioneer California*, Edited by John F. Burns and Richard J. Orsi, 2003; Mabel Croft Deering, "San Francisco's Famous Bohemian Restaurant", *The Critic, An Illustrated Monthly Review of Literature, Art, and Life*, Volume XLVIII, June 1906, p. 523-528 [Google Digitized Book]; Ed Herny, Shelley Rideout, Katie Wadell, *Berkeley Bohemia, Artists and Visionaries of the Early 20th Century*; Jean White, "A Landmark of San Francisco's Bohemia", *Overland Monthly*, Volume LXVII, Second Series, Number 3, March 1916, p. 186-188 [Internet Archive: www.archive.org]; Frank Norris, *McTeague: A Story of San Francisco*, Introduction by Kevin Starr; William Deverell, *Railroad Crossing, Californians and the Railroad, 1850-1910*; Ella Sterling Cummins, *The Story of the Files, A Review of Californian Writers and Literature*, 1893 [Google Digitized Book]; Kevin Starr, *Inventing the Dream California Through the Progressive Era*; Elsie Whitaker Martinez, *San Francisco Bay Area Writers and Artists* [Internet Archive: www.archive.org]; Kevin Starr, *Golden Dreams, California in an Age of Abundance, 1950-1963*; George Wharton James, "The Influence of California Upon Literature, *The National Magazine*, Volume XXXVI, April 1912, p. 65-79 [Google Digitized Book]; Lawrence Clark Powell, *California Classics, The Creative Literature of the Golden State*; Kevin Starr, *Material Dreams, Southern California Through the 1920's*; Carey McWilliams, *Southern California: An Island on the Land*; *California, A Literary Chronicle*, Edited and Commentaries by W. Storrs Lee; Philip L. Fradkin, *The Great Earthquake and Firestorms of 1906, How San Francisco Nearly Destroyed Itself*; Nancy Boas, *Society of Six, California Colorists*; Philip L. Fradkin, *Magnitude 8, Earthquakes and Life Along the San Andreas Fault*

Carmel and Monterey Peninsula history: J. D. Conway, *Monterey Presidio, Pueblo, And Port, The Making Of America Series*; Agnes Foster Buchanan, "The Story of a Famous Fraternity of Writers and Artists" *The Pacific Monthly*, Volume XVII, January 1907, p. 65-83 [Google Digitized Book]; Michael Orth, "Ideality to Reality:

The Founding of Carmel", *The California Historical Society Quarterly*, Volume XLVIII, Number 3, September 1969; Scott Shields, *Artists at Continent's End, The Monterey Peninsula Art Colony 1875-1907;* Augusta Fink, *Monterey County, The Dramatic Story of Its Past;* Franklin Walker, *Seacoast of Bohemia;* Harold and Ann Gilliam, *Creating Carmel;* Sharron Lee Hale, *A Tribute to Yesterday;* Sidney Temple, *Carmel-by-the-Sea*

Architectural history: Sally Woodbridge, *California Architecture;* Peter Booth Wiley, *National Trust Guide–San Francisco: America's Guide for Architecture and History Travelers;* Agnes Foster Buchanan, "Some Early Business Buildings of San Francisco", *The Architectural Record,* Volume XX, July 1906, p. 15-32 [Google Digitized Book]; David Gebhard, Robert Montgomery, Robert Winter, John Woodbridge, and Sally Woodbridge, *A Guide to Architecture in San Francisco & Northern California;* Kent Seavey, *Images of America, Carmel: A History in Architecture*

Dictionaries and other reference guides: Dana Gioia, *California Poetry: From the Gold Rush, to the Present;* Webster's Biographical Dictionary, First Edition; Edan Hughes, *Artists in California 1786-1940,* Volume 1, A-K, 3rd Edition; Edan Hughes, *Artists in California 1786-1940,* Volume 2, L-Z; Who's Who in America, *A Biographical Dictionary of Notable Living Men and Women in the United States,* Volume VII, 1912-1913 [Google Digitized Book]; Webster's Biographical Dictionary, First Edition; Who's Who in America, *A Biographical Dictionary of Notable Living Men and Women in the United States,* Volume VI, 1910-1911 [Google Digitized Book]; *Press Reference Library (Western Edition), Notables of the West,* Volume II, 1915 [Google Digitized Book]; *The Oxford Dictionary of American Art and Artists;* "The Bohemian Club of San Francisco Certificate of Incorporation, Constitution, By-Laws and Rules, Officers, Committees and Members", 1904 [Google Digitized Book]; Who's Who in America, *A Biographical Dictionary of Notable Living Men and Women in the United States,* Volume V, 1908-1909 [Google Digitized Book]; *Atlantic Brief Lives,* Louis Kronenberger, Editor

Biographies, autobiographies, and obituaries: Helen MacKnight Doyle, *Mary Austin, Woman of Genius;* Susan Goodman and Carl Dawson, *Mary Austin and the American West;* Idwal Jones, "King of Bohemia", *Overland Monthly,* Volume LXXXV, Number 11, November 1927, p. 332-333 [Internet Archive: www.archive.org]; Mary Austin, "George Sterling at Carmel", *American Mercury,* Volume XI, Number 41, p. 65-72; "1869-1926", Edward F. O'Day, *Overland Monthly,* Volume LXXXV, Number 12, December 1927, p. 357-358 [Internet Archive: www.archive.org]; T. M. Pearce, Editor, *Literary America 1903-1924, The Mary Austin Letters;* Augusta Fink, *I-Mary, A Biography of Mary Austin;* Donald J. Hagerty, Forward by John Dixon, *Desert Dreams: The Art and Life of Maynard Dixon;* Donald J. Hagerty, *The Life of Maynard Dixon;* Arnold Genthe, *As I Remember, The Sources of Modern Photography;* Janet B. Dominik,

"Xavier Martinez", Ruth Westphal, *Plein Air Painters of California, The North*, p. 98-102; Russ Kingman, *A Pictorial Life of Jack London*; "Perry Newberry, 68, California Author. Writer of Boys' Books, Editor and Reformer, is Dead", *New York Times* obituary, December 8, 1938; *Old Carmel* by Connie Wright, "Perry Newberry: Our One-Man Band", *Carmel Residents Association Newsletter* online, November 2002 and March 2007; *Old Carmel* by Connie Wright, "Bertha 'Buttsky' Newberry", *Carmel Residents Association Newsletter* online, February 2007; "John Cosgrave, 83, Journalist, Dead. Chief of Sunday Supplement of The World for 15 Years was Co-Founder of *The Wave*", *New York Times* obituary, September 20, 1947; Edwin R. Bingham, *Charles F. Lummis, Editor of the Southwest*; George Sterling, "A Memoir of Ambrose Bierce", *The Letters of Ambrose Bierce*, Edited by Bertha Clark Pope [Internet Archive: www.archive.org]; Mary Austin, *Earth Horizon*; Henry Meade Bland, "Sterling, the Poet of Seas and Stars", *Overland Monthly*, Volume LXVI, Second Series, Number 6, December 1915, p. 475-478 [Google Digitized Book]; Charmian Kittredge London, "George Sterling—As I Knew Him", *Overland Monthly*, Volume LXXXV, Number 3, March 1927, p. 69-70, p. 76, p. 80, p. 83, p. 87, p. 90-91 [Internet Archive: www.archive.org]; George Sterling tribute issue of *San Francisco Water*, Volume VII, Number 3, July 1928; Esther Lanigan Steinman, *Mary Austin Song of a Maverick*; "Books and Writers", *Sunset*, p. 557-558 [Google Digitized Book]; *The Publishers' Weekly, The American Book Trade Journal*, Volume LXVII, Number 13, April 22, 1905 (Whole Number 1734), page 1159 [Google Digitized Book]; Donald Gray "Sterling in Type", *Overland Monthly*, Volume LXXXV, Number 11, November 1927, p. 328, p. 350-351 [Internet Archive: www.archive.org]; "Dr. Genthe is Dead; Photographer, 73...", *New York Times* obituary, August 11, 1942; "J. M. Hopper, Author of Short Stories, 80", *New York Times* obituary, August 30, 1956; *Old Carmel* by Connie Wright, "Jimmy Hopper—one of the Carmel Gang", *Carmel Residents Association Newsletter* online, September 2008; *The Editor*, Volume 44, Number 14, December 30, 1916, p. 625 [Google Digitized Book]; *Old Carmel* by Connie Wright, "Frederick Bechdolt: One of the Carmel Bunch", *Carmel Residents Association Newsletter* online, February 2004; "F. R. Bechdolt, 75, Western Novelist, Author of Many Stories and Books of Pioneering Days is Dead in California", *New York Times* obituary, April 14, 1950; Ninetta Eames, "Jack London", *Overland Monthly*, Volume XXXV, Second Series, Number 209, May 1900, p. 417-425 [Google Digitized Book]; *The Social Writings of Jack London*, Philip S. Foner, Editor; George Wharton James, "California's Literary Giants, Herman Whitaker", *The National Magazine*, Volume XXXVIII, June 1913, pages 451-462 [Google Digitized Book]; *Old Carmel* by Connie Wright, "Xavier Martinez, 'the mad Aztec'", *Carmel Residents Association Newsletter* online, October 2006; *Old Carmel* by Connie Wright, "Nora May French, 'A Stormy Petrel'", *Carmel Residents Association Newsletter* online, February 2006; John R. Dunbar, "Letters of George Sterling to Carey McWilliams", *The California Historical Society Quarterly*, Volume XLVI, Number 3, September 1967, p. 235-252; "Poetess

Kills Herself. Nora May French Took Cyanide of Potassium at a Friend's Bungalow.",
New York Times obituary, November 16, 1907

Literary works: Nora May French, *Poems*, 1910 [Google Digitized Book]; Jack
London, *The Valley of the Moon*, 1917 [Google Digitized Book]; George Sterling, *A*
Wine of Wizardry and Other Poems, 1909 [Google Digitized Book]; George Sterling,
The House of Orchids: and other Poems, 1911 [Google Digitized Book]; Charmian
London, *The Book of Jack London, Volume II*, 1921 [Google Digitized Book]; Jack
London's *Tales of Adventure*, Irving Shepard, Editor; Jack London, *The Son of the Wolf*,
Tales of the Far North, 1902 [Google Digitized Book]; Nora May French, "Ave Atque
Vale", *Sunset*, Volume XX, Number 2, December 1907, p. 386 [Google Digitized
Book]

Chapter 9

The Muckrakers and the Helicon Home Colony Arrivals in Carmel, 1908 and 1909

San Francisco Bay Area and General California history: Kevin Starr,
Americans and the California Dream 1850-1915; Lawrence Ferlinghetti and Nancy J.
Peters, *Literary San Francisco, A Pictorial History from Its Beginnings to the Present Day*;
Albert Parry, *Garrets and Pretenders, A History of Bohemianism in America*, originally
published by Covici-Friede, Inc., 1933; James D. Hart, *A Companion to California*,
New Edition, Revised and Expanded; Philip L. Fradkin, *The Great Earthquake and*
Firestorms of 1906, How San Francisco Nearly Destroyed Itself; Lawrence Clark Powell,
California Classics, The Creative Literature of the Golden State; Kevin Starr, *The Dream*
Endures, California Enters the 1940's; Kevin Starr, *Endangered Dreams, The Great*
Depression in California; *California, A Literary Chronicle*, Edited and Commentaries
by W. Storrs Lee; Kevin Starr, *Golden Dreams, California in an Age of Abundance*,
1950-1963; Ethel Duffy Turner, *Writers and Revolutionists: Oral History Transcript*,
1966-1967 [Internet Archive: www.archive.org]

Carmel and Monterey Peninsula history: Franklin Walker, *Seacoast of*
Bohemia; Harold and Ann Gilliam, *Creating Carmel*; Sharron Lee Hale, *A Tribute to*
Yesterday; Augusta Fink, *Monterey County, The Dramatic Story of Its Past*; Kathryne
Wilson, "The Literary Colony at Carmel", *The Book News Monthly*, Volume 33,
Number 7, March 1915, p. 364-367 [Google Digitized Book]; Daisy Bostick and
Dorothea Castelhun, *Carmel at Work and Play*; Michael Orth, "Ideality to Reality:

The Founding of Carmel", *The California Historical Society Quarterly*, Volume XLVIII, No. 3, September 1969; Sydney Temple, *Carmel-by-the-Sea*

General history: Stuart Eliot Morison, Henry Steele Commager, William E. Leuchtenburg, *A Concise History of the American Republic*

Architectural history: Sally Woodbridge, *California Architecture*; Kent Seavey, *Images of America, Carmel: A History in Architecture*

Dictionaries and other reference guides: Webster's *Biographical Dictionary*, First Edition; *Who's Who in America, A Biographical Dictionary of Notable Living Men and Women in the United States*, Volume VII, 1912-1913 [Google Digitized Book]; Fred B. Millett, *Contemporary American Authors, A Critical Survey and 219 Bio-Bibliographies*

Biographies, autobiographies and obituaries: T. M. Pearce, Editor, *Literary America 1903-1924, The Mary Austin Letters*; "Lincoln Steffens, Author, Dies at 70, 'Muckraker' Exposed Graft in the Nation—Wrote of It in 'The Shame of the Cities'", *New York Times* obituary, August 10, 1936; Alden Whitman, "Rebel With a Cause, Upton Sinclair, Author and Crusader for Social Justice, is Dead", *New York Times* obituary, November 26, 1968; Mary Austin, *Earth Horizon*; Augusta Fink, *I-Mary, A Biography of Mary Austin*; Justin Kaplan, *Lincoln Steffens, A Biography*; Esther Lanigan Stineman, *Mary Austin, Song of a Maverick*; Helen MacKnight Doyle, *Mary Austin, Woman of Genius*; "Perry Newberry, 68, California Author, Writer of Boys' Books, Editor and Reformer, Is Dead", *New York Times* obituary, December 8, 1938; *Old Carmel* by Connie Wright, "Perry Newberry: Our One-Man Band", *Carmel Residents Association Newsletter* online, November 2002 and March 2007; *Old Carmel* by Connie Wright, "Bertha 'Buttsky' Newberry", *Carmel Residents Association Newsletter* online, February 2007; Arnold Genthe, *As I Remember, The Sources of Modern Photography*; "American Writer in Prison. John K. Turner, Author of "Barbarous Mexico," Arrested by Diaz's Order", *New York Times*, February 20, 1913; "Turner Reported Free. Richard Harding Davis Writes Strong Appeal for Brother Author,"; *New York Times*, February 25, 1913; "Mexico to Expel Turner.", *New York Times*, February 28, 1913; Michael Williams, *The Book of the High Romance, A Spiritual Autobiography*, Chapter VI, "Helicon Hall", 1918, p. 130-158 [Google Digitized Book]; Charis Wilson and Wendy Madar, *Through Another Lens-My Years With Edward Weston*; Anthony Arthur, *Radical Innocent: Upton Sinclair*; "Sinclair Explains His Home Colony, 300 at His Meeting to Applaud Anti-Worry Syndicating. 100 Families are Ready, Doesn't was All Socialists—Meeting Favors Co-operation in Child Raising.", *New York Times*, July 18, 1906; "For a Co-Operative Home. The Plan for a Colony to be Discussed Here To-morrow Evening.", *New York Times*, July 16, 1906; "The Sinclair Colony." *New York Times*, June 24, 1906; Richard L. Lingeman, *Sinclair*

Lewis: *Rebel from Main Street*; Kay Baker Gaston, "The MacGowan Girls", *California History*, Summer 1980; "Fire Wipes Out Helicon Hall, And Upton Sinclair Hints that the Steel Trust's Hand May Be in It. Life Lost; Several Hurt, Woman Makes a Lifeline of Her Flannel Nightgown and Slides to Safety. Colony Future in Doubt, Founder Ready to Continue, but Says the Rest Must Decide—They Have Lost All.", *New York Times*, March 17, 1907; *Old Carmel* by Connie Wright, "Those MacGowan Sisters and the Carmel Bunch", *Carmel Residents Association Newsletter* online, May 2002; "Michael Williams, Editor, 73, is Dead, Founder of The Commonweal was Leader in Fight Against Persecution of Religions", *New York Times* obituary, October 13, 1950; "Carmel and Sinclair Lewis, an Uneasy Bond", *Old Carmel* by Richard Flower, *Carmel Residents Association Newsletter* online, November-December 2011, p. 5; Elizabeth Fry Page, "Feathers From an Eagle's Nest", *The Olympian, A Monthly Magazine Devoted to Literature, Education, and Amateur Sport*, Volume II, Number 1, July 1903, p. 27-31 [Google Digitized Book]; "Novelist Dies. Sinclair Lewis, 65, Dies In Rome Clinic, First American to Win Nobel Prize for Literature Wrote 'Babbitt' and 'Main Street', *New York Times* obituary, January 11, 1951; "William Benet, 64, Noted Poet, is Dead, Brother of Stephen Vincent, He Won Pulitzer Prize in 1942 for 'Dust Which is God', Also Wrote Many Novels, Was Well-Known Anthologist and Literary Columnist—An Editor for 31 Years", *New York Times* obituary, May 5, 1950; "J. H. Kellogg Dies; Health Expert, 91, *New York Times* obituary December 16, 1943; Scott Bruce and Bill Crawford, *Cerealizing America, The Unsweetened Story of American Breakfast Cereal*

Literary works: John Kenneth Turner, *Barbarous Mexico*, 1911 [Google Digitized Book]; Grace MacGowan Cooke, *The Grapple, A Story of the Illinois Coal Region*, 1905 [Google Digitized Book]; Upton Sinclair, *The Moneychangers*, 1908 [Google Digitized Book]; Upton Sinclair, Lauren Coodley, *The Land of Orange Groves and Jails: Upton Sinclair's California*; Sinclair Lewis, "A San Francisco Pleasure Cure Bring Echoes of the New City's Laughter", *Sunset*, Volume XXIV, Number 4, April 1910, p. 433-439 [Google Digitized Book]; Russ Kingman, *A Pictorial Life of Jack London*; Charmian London, *The Book of Jack London, Volume II*, 1921 [Google Digitized Book]; *From Baltimore to Bohemia, The Letters of H. L. Mencken and George Sterling*, Edited by S. T. Joshi

Chapter 10

The Simplicity of Life and a Typical Day in Carmel-by-the-Sea

San Francisco Bay Area and General California history: Kevin Starr, *Americans and the California Dream 1850-1915*; Kevin Starr, *Golden Dreams, California*

in an *Age of Abundance, 1950-1963*; James D. Hart, *A Companion to California, New Edition, Revised and Expanded*; Lawrence Ferlinghetti and Nancy J. Peters, *Literary San Francisco, A Pictorial History from Its Beginnings to the Present Day*; Jean White, "A Landmark of San Francisco's Bohemia", *Overland Monthly*, Volume LXVII, Second Series, Number 3, March 1916, p. 186-188 [Internet Archive: www.archive.org]; Mrs. Fremont Older, *California Missions and Their Romances*, original Coward-McCann, Inc., 1938, Kessinger Publishing, 2005; Ethel Duffy Turner, *Writers and Revolutionists: Oral History Transcript, 1966-1967* [Internet Archive: www.archive.org]; Lawrence Clark Powell, *California Classics, The Creative Literature of the Golden State*

Carmel and Monterey Peninsula history: Mary E. Delport, "The Spell of the Carmel Coast", *Overland Monthly*, Volume LXXIII, Second Series, February 1919, p. 106-115 [Google Digitized Book]; Henry Dumont, "The Pageant at Carmel", the *National Magazine*, Volume XXXV, October 1911, p. 151-157 [Google Digitized Book]; Daisy Bostick and Dorothea Castelhun, *Carmel at Work and Play*; Scott Shields, *Artists at Continent's End, The Monterey Peninsula Art Colony 1875-1907*; Franklin Walker, *Seacoast of Bohemia*; Kathryne Wilson, "The Literary Colony at Carmel", *The Book News Monthly*, Volume 33, Number 7, March 1915, p. 364-367 [Google Digitized Book]; Harold and Ann Gilliam, *Creating Carmel*; Michael Orth, "Ideality to Reality: The Founding of Carmel", *The California Historical Society Quarterly*, Volume XLVIII, Number 3, September 1969; Sharron Lee Hale, *A Tribute to Yesterday*; Michael Williams, "The Forest Theatre at Carmel, A Dramatic Movement in the Shadow of Junipero Serra's Mission", *Sunset, The Pacific Monthly*, Volume XXIX, Number 3, September 1912, p. 319-325 [Google Digitized Book]

General history: Stuart Eliot Morison, Henry Steele Commager, William E. Leuchtenburg, *A Concise History of the American Republic*

Architectural history: Sally Woodbridge, *California Architecture*; Kent Seavey, *Images of America, Carmel: A History in Architecture*

Dictionaries and other reference guides: *Webster's Biographical Dictionary*, First Edition; *The Oxford Dictionary of American Art and Artists*; "John Fleming Wilson '00", *The Princeton Alumni Weekly*, Volume XXII, Number 24, March 29, 1922, p. 550 [Google Digitized Book]; Geoffrey D. Smith, *American Fiction, 1901-1925: A Bibliography*; *Publisher's Weekly*, Volume LXXXIII, January through June 1913, p. 672 [Google Digitized Book]; *Who's Who in America, A Biographical Dictionary of Notable Living Men and Women in the United States*, Volume IV, 1906-1907 [Google Digitized Book]; *Who's Who in America, A Biographical Dictionary of Notable Living Men and Women in the United States*, Volume VII, 1912-1913 [Google Digitized Book]; Thomas Lansing Masson, *Our American Humorists*, Chapter XXXI, "Harry Leon Wilson",

1922, p. 303-304 [Google Digitized Book]; *Atlantic Brief Lives*, Louis Kronenberger, Editor; *Who's Who in America, A Biographical Dictionary of Notable Living Men and Women in the United States*, Volume V, 1908-1909 [Google Digitized Book]; *Who's Who in America, A Biographical Dictionary of Notable Living Men and Women in the United States*, Volume VI, 1910-1911 [Google Digitized Book]

Biographies, autobiographies, and obituaries: Augusta Fink, *I-Mary, A Biography of Mary Austin*; Esther Lanigan Stineman, *Mary Austin, Song of a Maverick*; Helen MacKnight Doyle, *Mary Austin, Woman of Genius*; T. M. Pearce, Editor, *Literary America 1903-1924, The Mary Austin Letters*; Arnold Genthe, *As I Remember, The Sources of Modern Photography*; Mary Austin, "George Sterling at Carmel", *American Mercury*, Volume XI, Number 41, p. 65-72; Richard L. Lingeman, *Sinclair Lewis: Rebel from Main Street*; Mary Austin, *Earth Horizon*; Anthony Arthur, *Radical Innocent: Upton Sinclair; From Baltimore to Bohemia, The Letters of H. L. Mencken and George Sterling*, Edited by S. T. Joshi; George Sterling, "A Memoir of Ambrose Bierce", *The Letters of Ambrose Bierce*, Edited by Bertha Clark Pope [Internet Archive: www. archive.org]; George Sterling, "The Shadow Maker", *The American Mercury*, Volume VI, Number 21, September 1925, p. 10-19; "Dr. Genthe is Dead; Photographer, 73...", *New York Times* obituary, August 11, 1942; "In the Realm of Bookland", *Overland Monthly*, Volume LIX, Second Series, Number 3, March 1912, p. 289 [Google Digitized Book]; *Sunset, The Pacific Monthly*, Volume XXIX, Number 3, September 1912, p. 511 [Google Digitized Book]; "Grant Wallace, Newsman, Was 87. Coast Artist and Writer Dies—Covered Russo-Japanese War, Worked on Films", *New York Times* obituary, August 14, 1954; Hartley Davis, "Reporters of To-day (sic), Stories of Our Foremost Newspaper Men and 'Beats' They Have Scored," *Everybody's Magazine*, Volume XIV, February 1906, Number 2, 1906, p. 200-209 [Google Digitized Book]; *Old Carmel* by Connie Wright, "Harry Leon Wilson–One of the Carmel Gang", *Carmel Residents Association Newsletter* online, April 2005; Charis Wilson and Wendy Madar, *Through Another Lens-My Years With Edward Weston*; "Guide to the Harry Leon Wilson Papers, ca. 1879-1939", Scope and Content, Online Archive of California, University of California at Berkeley, Bancroft Library [www.oac.cdlib.org]; "Harry L. Wilson, Author, 72, Dead", *New York Times* obituary, June 30, 1939; "Booth Tarkington, Novelist, 76, Dead, Creator of Penrod and Other Beloved Characters Twice Won Pulitzer Prizes, Also was a Playwright, Author of 'The Gentleman From Indiana'–Working on a New Book, Though Nearly Blind", *New York Times* obituary, May 20, 1946; Bruce Weber, "Charis Wilson, Model and Muse, Dies at 95", *New York Times* obituary, November 24, 2009

Literary works: Jack London, *The Valley of the Moon*; John Fleming Wilson, "Ghost Island Light", *Lighthouse Horrors: Tales of Adventure, Suspense, and the Supernatural*, Edited by Charles G. Waugh, Martin Harry Greenberg, and Jenny-Lynn Azarian

Chapter 11

The Forest Theatre

San Francisco Bay Area and General California history: Porter Garnett, *The Bohemian Jinks, A Treatise*, Bohemian Club of San Francisco, 1908 [Google Digitized Book]; Sheldon Cheney, *The Open-Air Theatre*, 1918 [Google Digitized Book]; Kevin Starr, *Americans and the California Dream 1850-1915*; James D. Hart, *A Companion to California, New Edition, Revised and Expanded*; Kevin Starr, *Embattled Dreams California in War and Peace, 1940-1950*; Dr. Kevin Starr, "Sunset Magazine and the Phenomenon of the Far West", *Sunset Magazine: A Century of Western Living, 1898-1998, Historical Portraits and Bibliography*; Albert Parry, *Garrets and Pretenders, A History of Bohemianism in America*, originally published by Covici-Friede, Inc., 1933; Helen Throop Purdy, *San Francisco As It Was, As It Is, and How to See It*, 1912 [Google Digitized Book]; Ernest Peixotto, *Romantic California*, 1914 [Google Digitized Book]; *San Francisco, The Financial, Commercial, & Industrial Metropolis of the Pacific Coast, Official Records, Statistics, and Encyclopedia*, 1915 [Google Digitized Book]; Will Irwin, *The City That Was, A Requiem of Old San Francisco*, 1908 [Google Digitized Book]; Kevin Starr, *Inventing the Dream, California Through the Progressive Era*; Gray Brechin, *Imperial San Francisco, Urban Power, Earthly Ruin*; Ed Herny, Shelley Rideout, Katie Wadell, *Berkeley Bohemia, Artists and Visionaries of the Early 20th Century*; Lawrence Ferlinghetti and Nancy J. Peters, *Literary San Francisco, A Pictorial History from Its Beginnings to the Present Day*

Carmel and Monterey Peninsula history: Sharron Lee Hale, *A Tribute to Yesterday*; Scott Shields, *Artists at Continent's End, The Monterey Peninsula Art Colony 1875-1907*; Augusta Fink, *Monterey County, The Dramatic Story of Its Past*; Harold and Ann Gilliam, *Creating Carmel*; Agnes Foster Buchanan, "The Story of a Famous Fraternity of Writers and Artists", *The Pacific Monthly*, Volume XVII, January 1907, p. 65-83 [Google Digitized Book]; Franklin Walker, *Seacoast of Bohemia*; Harold and Ann Gilliam, *Creating Carmel*; *History of Monterey, Santa Cruz, and San Benito Counties, California, Cradle of California's History and Romance*, Volume II, 1925; Kathryne Wilson, "The Literary Colony at Carmel", *The Book News Monthly*, Volume 33, Number 7, March 1915, p. 364-367 [Google Digitized Book]; Daisy Bostick and Dorothea Castelhun, *Carmel at Work and Play*; Sidney Temple, *Carmel-by-the-Sea*; Daisy Bostick, *Carmel–Today and Yesterday*

The Forest Theatre: Michael Williams, "The Forest Theatre at Carmel, A Dramatic Movement in the Shadow of Junípero Serra's Mission", *Sunset, The Pacific Monthly*, Volume XXIX, Number 3, September 1912, p. 319-325 [Google Digitized Book]; Wendell Cole, "Myth Makers and the Early Years of the Carmel Forest

Theatre", Edited by Dunbar H. Ogden, with Douglas McDermott and Robert Károly Sarlós, *Theatre West: Image and Impact*, p. 43-52; *Old Carmel* by Connie Wright, "Herbert Heron", *Carmel Residents Association Newsletter* online, November 2007; Connie Wright, "A Carmel Original–The Seven Arts Building", *Carmel Residents Association Newsletter* online, July 2001; Grace MacFarland, "Annual Plays at Carmel's Forest Theatre", *Overland Monthly*, Volume LXVIII, Second Series, Number 3, September 1916, p. 239-243 [Google Digitized Book]; Henry Dumont, "The Pageant at Carmel", the *National Magazine*, Volume XXXV, October 1911, p. 151-157 [Google Digitized Book]; "The Month's Rodeo", *Sunset*, Volume XXXI, Number 4, October 1913, p. 776 [Google Digitized Book]

Dictionaries and other reference guides: Dana Gioia, *California Poetry: From the Gold Rush, to the Present; Directory of Graduates of the University of California, 1864-1916* [Google Digitized Book]; *The American Literary Yearbook*, Volume 1, 1919 [Google Digitized Book]; Steve Shipp, *American Art Colonies, 1850-1930: A Historical Guide to America's Original Art Colonies and Their Artists; The University of California Chronicle*, Volume 9, 1907 [Google Digitized Book]

Biographies, autobiographies and obituaries: T. M. Pearce, Editor, *Literary America 1903-1924, The Mary Austin Letters*; Arnold Genthe, *As I Remember, The Sources of Modern Photography*; Jean Barman, *Constance Lindsay Skinner: Writing on the Frontier*; Stanley Wertheim, *A Stephen Crane Encyclopedia*; Kay Baker Gaston, "The MacGowan Girls", *California History*, Summer 1980, p. 116-125; Augusta Fink, *I-Mary, A Biography of Mary Austin*; *Old Carmel* by Connie Wright, "Harry Leon Wilson–One of the Carmel Gang", *Carmel Residents Association Newsletter* online, April 2005; Charis Wilson and Wendy Madar, *Through Another Lens*; Esther Lanigan Stineman, *Mary Austin, Song of a Maverick*; Susan Goodman and Carl Dawson, *Mary Austin and the American West*; Mary Austin, *Earth Horizon*; Van Wyck Brooks, *Scenes and Portraits: Memories of Childhood and Youth*

Literary works: "A Vase" by Herbert Heron, *Overland Monthly and Out West*, Volume LVII, Number 4, April 1911, p. 412 [Google Digitized Book]; Grace Sartwell Mason, John Northern Hilliard, *The Golden Hope*, 1916 [Google Digitized Book]; T. Nelson Downs, Edited by John Northern Hilliard, With a New Introduction by Charles R. Reynolds, *The Art of Magic*

Chapter 12

Epilogue

San Francisco Bay Area and General California history: Lawrence Ferlinghetti and Nancy J. Peters, *Literary San Francisco, A Pictorial History from Its Beginnings to the Present Day*; Kevin Starr, *Americans and the California Dream 1850-1915*; Lawrence Clark Powell, *California Classics, The Creative Literature of the Golden State*; Ethel Duffy Turner, *Writers and Revolutionists: Oral History Transcript, 1966-1967* [Internet Archive: www.archive.org]; Kevin Starr, *Golden Dreams, California in an Age of Abundance, 1950-1963*; James D. Hart, *A Companion to California, New Edition, Revised and Expanded*; George Wharton James, *Exposition Memories: Panama-California Exposition, San Diego, 1916*, The Radiant Life Press, Pasadena, California, 1917 [Google Digitized Book]; Albert Parry, *Garrets and Pretenders, A History of Bohemianism in America*; Kevin Starr, *California, A History*; Kevin Starr, *Material Dreams, Southern California Through the 1920's*; Office of Historic Preservation, *California Historical Landmarks*; *Historic Spots in California, Fourth Edition*, Revised by Douglas E. Kyle; Nancy Boas, *Society of Six, California Colorists*; Philip L. Fradkin, *The Great Earthquake and Firestorms of 1906, How San Francisco Nearly Destroyed Itself*; Carey McWilliams, *Southern California, An Island on the Land*; Kevin Starr, *Inventing the Dream California Through the Progressive Era*; *California, A Literary Chronicle*, Edited and Commentaries by W. Storrs Lee; Kevin Starr, *Endangered Dreams, The Great Depression In California*; Ed Herny, Shelley Rideout, Katie Wadell, *Berkeley Bohemia, Artists and Visionaries of the Early 20th Century*; Elsie Whitaker Martinez, *San Francisco Bay Area Writers and Artists* [Internet Archive: www.archive.org]; *Three Fearful Days, San Francisco Memoirs of the 1906 Earthquake & Fire*, Compiled and Introduced by Malcolm E. Barker

Carmel and Monterey Peninsula history: Michael Orth, "Ideality to Reality: The Founding of Carmel", *The California Historical Society Quarterly*, Volume XLVIII, Number 3, September 1969; Harold and Ann Gilliam, *Creating Carmel*; Franklin Walker, *Seacoast of Bohemia*; Agnes Foster Buchanan, "The Story of a Famous Fraternity of Writers and Artists" *The Pacific Monthly*, Volume XVII, January 1907, p. 65-83 [Google Digitized Book]; Scott Shields, *Artists at Continent's End, The Monterey Peninsula Art Colony 1875-1907*; Daisy Bostick and Dorothea Castelhun, *Carmel at Work and Play*; Grace MacFarland, *Monterey, Cradle of California's Romance: The Story of A Lost Port That was Found Again and A Dream That Came True*, 1914 [Google Digitized Book]; Sydney Temple, *Carmel-by-the-Sea*; Monica Hudson, *Images of America, Carmel-by-the-Sea*; Burl Wiles, *The Monterey Peninsula: A Postcard Journey*; Ray A. March, *River in Ruin: The Story of the Carmel River*; Sharron Lee Hale, *A Tribute to Yesterday*; Carmel Planning Commission, August 8, 2012 meeting notes,

p. 46; *History of Monterey, Santa Cruz, and San Benito Counties, California, Cradle of California's History and Romance*, Volume II, 1925; Helen Spangenberg, *Yesterday's Artists on the Monterey Peninsula*; Augusta Fink, *Monterey County, The Dramatic Story of Its Past*; Historic Context Statement Carmel-by-the-Sea, online, Adopted by the City Council September 9, 2008, p. 52-54; Writers' Program of Work Projects Administration in Northern California, *The WPA Guide to the Monterey Peninsula*; Wendell Cole, "Myth Makers and the Early Years of the Carmel Forest Theatre", Edited by Dunbar H. Ogden, with Douglas McDermott and Robert Károly Sarlós, *Theatre West: Image and Impact*, p. 43-52; Henry Dumont, "The Pageant at Carmel", the *National Magazine*, Volume XXXV, October 1911, p. 151-157 [Google Digitized Book]; Kathryne Wilson, "The Literary Colony at Carmel", *The Book News Monthly*, Volume 33, Number 7, March 1915, p. 364-367 [Google Digitized Book]; Michael Williams, "The Forest Theater at Carmel, A Dramatic Movement in the Shadow of Junípero Serra's Mission", *Sunset, The Pacific Monthly*, Volume XXIX, Number 3, September 1912, p. 319-325 [Google Digitized Book]; Grace MacFarland, "Annual Plays at Carmel's Forest Theatre", *Overland Monthly*, Volume LXVIII, Second Series, Number 3, September 1916, p. 239-243 [Google Digitized Book]

Architectural history: David Gebhard, Robert Montgomery, Robert Winter, John Woodbridge, and Sally Woodbridge, *A Guide to Architecture in San Francisco & Northern California*; Dave Weinstein, *Signature Architects of the San Francisco Bay Area*; Susan Dinkelspiel Cerny, *An Architectural Guidebook to San Francisco and the Bay Area*; Robert Winter, Editor, *Towards a Simpler Way, The Arts & Crafts Architects of California*, Chapter 4, Robert Judson Clark, "Louis Christian Mullgardt", p. 41-50; "Louis Christian Mullgardt: An Architect with a Capital 'A'", *Heritage News, For Members of the San Francisco Architectural Heritage*, Volume XXIX, Number 5, September/October 2001, p. 5-8, online; Kent Seavey, *Images of America, Carmel: A History in Architecture*

Dictionaries and other reference guides: Dana Gioia, *California Poetry: From the Gold Rush, to the Present*; Steve Shipp, *American Art Colonies, 1850-1930: A Historical Guide to America's Original Art Colonies and Their Artists*; *Atlantic Brief Lives*, Louis Kronenberger, Editor; Fred B. Millett, *Contemporary American Authors, A Critical Survey and 219 Bio-Bibliographies*; Edan Hughes, *Artists in California 1786-1940*, Volume 2, L-Z, 3rd Edition; "John Fleming Wilson '00", *The Princeton Alumni Weekly*, Volume XXII, Number 24, March 29, 1922, p. 550 [Google Digitized Book]; Geoffrey D. Smith, *American Fiction, 1901-1925: A Bibliography*; *American Art Annual*, Florence N. Levy, Editor, Volume 9, 1911 [Google Digitized Book]; Frank Morton Todd, *The Chamber of Commerce Handbook for San Francisco, Historical and Descriptive, A Guide for Visitors*, 1913 [Google Digitized Book]; *Webster's Biographical Dictionary*, First Edition; *The American Literary Yearbook*, Hamilton Traub, Editor, Volume 1,

1919 [Google Digitized Book] Edan Hughes, *Artists in California 1786-1940, Volume 1, A-K, 3rd Edition*; *Who's Who in America, A Biographical Dictionary of Notable Living Men and Women in the United States*, Volume VII, 1912-1913 [Google Digitized Book]; *The Oxford Dictionary of American Art and Artists*; *Who's Who in America, A Biographical Dictionary of Notable Living Men and Women in the United States*, Volume IV, 1906-1907 [Google Digitized Book]; *Commonweal Magazine* website

Biographies, autobiographies, and obituaries: T. M. Pearce, Editor, *Literary America 1903-1924, The Mary Austin Letters*; Esther Lanigan Stineman, *Mary Austin, Song of a Maverick*; Augusta Fink, *I-Mary, A Biography of Mary Austin*; Albert Bender, "George Sterling: The Man", "1869-1926", *Overland Monthly*, Volume LXXXV, Number 12, December 1927, p. 363 [Internet Archive: www.archive.org]; George Sterling tribute issue of *San Francisco Water*, Volume VII, Number 3, July 1928, p. 12-13; "George Sterling is Found Dead." *Special to the New York Times*, November 18, 1926; James Hoopes, *Van Wyck Brooks, In Search of American Culture*; "Van Wyck Brooks, Author, 77, Dead, Biographer, Literary Critic and Historian Received Pulitzer Prize in '37, Wrote Pictorial Prose, Stressed American 'Memory' and Sense of Belonging to Continuing Tradition", *New York Times* obituary, May 3, 1963; Justin Kaplan, *Lincoln Steffens: A Biography*; Mary Austin, "George Sterling at Carmel", *American Mercury*, Volume XI, Number 41, p. 65-72; Mary Austin, *Earth Horizon*; Charmian Kittredge London, "George Sterling—As I Knew Him", *Overland Monthly*, Volume LXXXV, Number 3, March 1927, p. 69-70, p. 76, p. 80, p. 83, p. 87, p. 90-91 [Internet Archive: www.archive.org]; *Old Carmel* by Connie Wright, "Sydney Jones Yard, Tonalist Painter", *Carmel Residents Association Newsletter* online, March 2006; *Old Carmel* by Connie Wright, "Mary DeNeale Morgan, 'horse and buggy artist'", *Carmel Residents Association Newsletter* online, January 2002; Janet B. Dominik, "Mary DeNeale Morgan", Ruth Westphal, *Plein Air Painters of California, The North*; Helen Spangenberg, *Yesterday's Artists on the Monterey Peninsula*; Russ Kingman, *A Pictorial Life of Jack London*; *Jack London's Tales of Adventure*, Irving Shepard, Editor; Charmian London, *The Book of Jack London, Volume II* [Google Digitized Book]; George Wharton James, "Jack London, Cub of the Slums, Hero of Adventure, Literary Master, and Social Philosopher", *National Magazine*, Volume XXXVII, January 1913, p. 682-696 [Google Digitized Book]; "Jack London's New Home Burns.", *New York Times*, August 24, 1913; "Mrs. Jack London, 84, Widow of Novelist", *Special to the_New York Times*, January 15, 1955; "Jack London Dies Suddenly on Ranch, Novelist is Found Unconscious from Uremia, and Expires After Eleven Hours." *New York Times* obituary, November 23, 1916; "London to be Cremated. Author's Funeral to be Held in Oakland Today—His Mother Very Ill." *New York Times*, November 24, 1916; *Old Carmel* by Connie Wright, "Frank and Jane Gallatin Powers", *Carmel Residents Association Newsletter* online, February 2003; Donald Gray "Sterling in Type", *Overland Monthly*, Volume LXXXV, Number 11,

San Francisco, California, November 1927, p. 328, p. 350-351 [Internet Archive: www.archive.org]; "1869-1926", Edward F. O'Day, *Overland Monthly*, Volume LXXXV, Number 12, December 1927, p. 357-358 [Internet Archive: www.archive. org]; James D. Phelan, "George Sterling", *Overland Monthly*, Volume LXXXV, Number 11, San Francisco, California, November 1927, p. 343 [Internet Archive: www.archive.org]; John R. Dunbar, "Letters of George Sterling to Carey McWilliams", *The California Historical Society Quarterly*, Volume XLVI, Number 3, September 1967, p. 235-252; James Rorty, "Living Inseparables", *Overland Monthly*, Volume LXXXV, Number 12, December 1927, p. 367 [Internet Archive: www. archive.org]; *Overland Monthly*, Volume LXXXIV, Number 1, San Francisco, California, January 1926, [Internet Archive: www.archive.org]; Henry Louis Mencken, George Sterling, *From Baltimore to Bohemia: The Letters of H. L. Mencken and George Sterling*, Edited by S. T. Joshi; Vernon Kellogg, "George Sterling", *Overland Monthly*, Volume LXXXV, Number 12, December 1927, p. 369 [Internet Archive: www.archive.org]; George Sterling, "The Shadow Maker", *The American Mercury*, Volume VI, Number 21, September 1925, p. 10-19; "Carmel and Sinclair Lewis, an Uneasy Bond", *Old Carmel* by Richard Flower, Carmel Residents Association Newsletter online, November-December 2011, p. 5; "Idwal Jones, "Sterling: A Tribute", in the George Sterling tribute issue of *San Francisco Water*, Volume VII, Number 3, July 1928; Susan Goodman and Carl Dawson, *Mary Austin and the American West*; "Mary Austin Dead; Noted Writer, 65. Author of More Than Score of Books Succumbs in Sleep to Heart Attack. Authority on Indians. Determined Feminist Also Was Playwright—Taught School First in Southwest." *New York Times* obituary, August 14, 1934; Helen MacKnight Doyle, *Mary Austin, Woman of Genius*; "Mrs. Mabel Dodge Luhan Dies; Patron of Arts and Letters, 83. Author's Soirees Here Drew Intellectuals—She Aided Post-Impressionism", *New York Times* obituary, August 14, 1962; Justin Kaplan, *Lincoln Steffens, A Biography*; Stanley Wertheim, *A Stephen Crane Encyclopedia*; Sidney Lawrence, "The Ghirardelli Story", *California History*, Volume 81, Number 2, Spring-Fall, 2002; George Wharton James, "Chris Jorgensen—A Versatile California Artist", *The National Magazine*, Volume XLII, July 1915, p. 609-616 [Google Digitized Book]; "Yosemite Man", *Time*, Volume XXVIII, Number 26, December 28, 1936; Early Artists in Yosemite, "Indians and Other Sketches," (1936) by Mrs. H. J. Taylor, online; "Lincoln Steffens, Author, Dies at 70, 'Muckraker' Exposed Graft in the Nation—Wrote of It in 'The Shame of the Cities'", *New York Times* obituary, August 10, 1936; Joan Cook, "Ella Winter Stewart, Journalist and Widow of Donald O. Stewart", *New York Times* obituary, August 5, 1980; *Old Carmel* by Connie Wright, "Perry Newberry: Our One-Man Band", *Carmel Residents Association Newsletter* online, November 2002 and March 2007; *Old Carmel* by Connie Wright, "Bertha 'Buttsky' Newberry", *Carmel Residents Association Newsletter* online, February 2007; "Perry Newberry, 68, California Author, Writer of Boys' Books, Editor and Reformer, Is Dead", *New York Times* obituary, December

8, 1938; Charis Wilson and Wendy Madar, *Through Another Lens-My Years With Edward Weston*; "Harry L. Wilson, Author, 72, Dead, He Was Creator of Ruggles of Red Gap, Bunker Bean and Merton of the Movies, Began as Stenographer, Wrote Plays With Tarkington—Many Stories Were Made Features in the Films", *New York Times* obituary, June 30, 1939; "Guide to the Harry Leon Wilson Papers, ca. 1879-1939", Scope and Content, Online Archive of California, University of California at Berkeley, Bancroft Library [www.oac.cdlib.org]; "Harry Leon Wilson Sued For Divorce, His Wife, Formerly Helen Cook (sic), Accuses Author of Desertion and Failure to Provide. Hiding of Assets Charged. Recent Settlement Is Attacked and Half of Property Is Asked In California Action", *New York Times*, February 9, 1927; *Old Carmel* by Connie Wright, "Harry Leon Wilson—One of the Carmel Gang", *Carmel Residents Association Newsletter* Online, April 2005; "Author and Artist in Duel With Fists, Harry Leon Wilson and Theodore Criley Fight Five Knockdown Rounds in California.", *New York Times*, March 31, 1922; Bruce Weber, "Charis Wilson, Model and Muse, Dies at 95", *New York Times* obituary, November 24, 2009; "Dr. Genthe is Dead; Photographer, 73...", *New York Times* obituary, August 11, 1942; Janet B. Dominik essay on Xavier Martinez, in Ruth Westphal, *Plein Air Painters of California, The North*; *Old Carmel* by Connie Wright, "Xavier Martinez, 'the mad Aztec'", *Carmel Residents Association Newsletter* online, October 2006; "Mrs. Elsie Martinez Dies at 93", *Monterey Peninsula Herald* obituary, February 3, 1984, p. 4; Kay Baker Gaston, "The MacGowan Girls", *California History, The Magazine of the California Historical Society*, Summer 1980, p. 116-125; *Old Carmel* by Connie Wright. "Those MacGowan Sisters and the Carmel Bunch", *Carmel Residents Association Newsletter* online, May 2002; "Charles Chapel Judson", *New York Times* obituary, November 6, 1946; *Old Carmel* by Connie Wright, "Mary DeNeale Morgan, 'horse and buggy artist'", *Carmel Residents Association Newsletter* online, January 2002; Janet B. Dominik, "Mary DeNeale Morgan", Ruth Westphal, *Plein Air Painters of California, The North*; Carmel Art Association, *Six Early Women Artists: A Diversity of Style*; "F. R. Bechdolt, 75, Western Novelist, Author of Many Stories and Books of Pioneering Days is Dead in California", *New York Times* obituary, April 14, 1950; *Old Carmel* by Connie Wright, "Frederick Bechdolt: One of the Carmel Bunch", *Carmel Residents Association Newsletter* online, February 2004; *The Editor*, Volume 44, Number 14, December 30, 1916, p. 625 [Google Digitized Book]; "William Benet, 64, Noted Poet, is Dead, Brother of Stephen Vincent, He Won Pulitzer Prize in 1942 for 'Dust Which is God', Also Wrote Many Novels, Was Well-Known Anthologist and Literary Columnist—An Editor for 31 Years", *New York Times* obituary, May 5, 1950; "Michael Williams, Editor, 73, is Dead, Founder of The Commonweal was Leader in Fight Against Persecution of Religions", *New York Times* obituary, October 13, 1950; "Spanish Split", *Time*, Monday July 4, 1938; "Sinclair Lewis Dies in Italy, His biting, realistic novels were bombshells in the '20's, but in the end even Main Street was happy.", *Life*, Volume 30, Number 4, January

22, 1951, p. 69-72; "Novelist Dies. Sinclair Lewis, 65, Dies In Rome Clinic, First American to Win Nobel Prize for Literature Wrote 'Babbitt' and 'Main Street', *New York Times* obituary January 11, 1951; Richard L. Lingeman, *Sinclair Lewis: Rebel from Main Street*; Arnold Genthe, *As I Remember, The Sources of Modern Photography*; "Michael Lewis, The Actor, Sinclair's Son, Dies at 44", *New York Times* obituary, March 7, 1975; "Grant Wallace, Newsman, was 87. Coast Artist and Writer Dies—Covered Russo-Japanese War, Worked on Films", *New York Times* obituary, August 14, 1954; "J. M. Hopper, Author of Short Stories, 80", *New York Times* obituary, August 30, 1956; *Old Carmel* by Connie Wright, "Jimmy Hopper—one of the Carmel Gang", *Carmel Residents Association Newsletter* online, September 2008; *Old Carmel* by Connie Wright, "M. J. Murphy—'The man who built Carmel'", *Carmel Residents Association Newsletter* online, September 2002; "Van Wyck Brooks, Author, 77, Dead, Biographer, Literary Critic and Historian Received Pulitzer Prize in '37, Wrote Pictorial Prose, Stressed American 'Memory' and Sense of Belonging to Continuing Tradition", *New York Times* obituary, May 3, 1963; James Hoopes, *Van Wyck Brooks, In Search of American Culture*; *Old Carmel* by Connie Wright, "Laura Maxwell, Pioneer", *Carmel Residents Association Newsletter* online, March 2004; *Old Carmel* by Connie Wright, "Herbert Heron", *Carmel Residents Association Newsletter* online, November 2007; "A Carmel Original-The Seven Arts Building", Connie Wright, *Carmel Residents Association Newsletter* online, July 2001; Alden Whitman, "Rebel With a Cause, Upton Sinclair, Author and Crusader for Social Justice, is Dead", *New York Times* obituary, November 26, 1968; Anthony Arthur, "Upton Sinclair, Times Topics", *New York Times*

Literary works: Clark Ashton Smith, *Odes and Sonnets*, 1918 [Google Digitized Book]; Jack London, *The Valley of the Moon*; John Fleming Wilson, "Ghost Island Light", *Lighthouse Horrors: Tales of Adventure, Suspense, and the Supernatural*, Edited by Charles G. Waugh, Martin Harry Greenberg, and Jenny-Lynn Azarian; George Sterling, *Beyond the Breakers and Other Poems*, 1914 [Google Digitized Book]; George Sterling, *The Caged Eagle: and Other Poems*, 1916 [Google Digitized Book]; George Sterling, *Rosamund: a Dramatic Poem*, 1920 [Google Digitized Book]; George Sterling, *Lilith: A Dramatic Poem*, 1920 [Google Digitized Book]; George Sterling, *Sails and Mirage and Other Poems*, 1921 [Google Digitized Book]; John Kenneth Turner, *Challenge to Karl Marx*, 1941; James Hopper, *What Happened in the Night and Other Stories*, 1913 [Google Digitized Book]; James Hopper, *Coming Back With the Spitball: A Pitcher's Romance*, 1914 [Google Digitized Book]; T. Nelson Downs, Edited by John Northern Hilliard, With a New Introduction by Charles R. Reynolds

BIBLIOGRAPHY

Websites:

Edward Henry Weston, 1886 – 1958, A Detailed Chronology, Compiled and Edited by Dick Rinehart, Edward Weston Chronology, Kim & Gina Weston Photography, http://www.kimweston.com/edward-weston/ edward-weston-biography/edward-weston-chronology/

All Saints' Episcopal Church, Carmel, California, http://www.allsaintscarmel.org/mission-and-vision/

New York Botanical Garden Library, Daniel T. MacDougal Papers, http://library.nybg.org/finding_guide/archv/macdougal_ppb.html

Mission Ranch Carmel, http://missionranchcarmel.com/ and http://missionranchcarmel.com/about.html

Carmel Planning Commission, August 8, 2012 meeting notes, p. 46, http://ci.carmel.ca.us/carmel/index.cfm/linkservid/ E9253A4D-3048-7B3D-C53C14A09720CD28/showMeta/0/

"Carmel House Names", Google Maps, http://maps.google.com/maps/ ms?hl=en&ie=UTF8&t=h&vps=2&jsv=336c&oe=UTF8&msa=0&msi d=213616720187771726786.0004a200f030f7318b959

Historic Context Statement, Carmel-by-the-Sea, Adopted by the City
Council September 9, 2008, http://ci.carmel.ca.us/carmel/index.cfm/
linkservid/A836D277-3048-7B3D-C52E40C677DF9680/showMeta/0/

National Register of Historic Places, California, Monterey County, http://
www.nationalregisterofhistoricplaces.com/ca/Monterey/state.html

National Historic Landmarks Program, The Big Four House, Sacramento
California, http://tps.cr.nps.gov/nhl/detail.cfm?ResourceId=1604&Reso
urceType=Building

"Guide to the Harry Leon Wilson Papers, ca. 1879-1939", Scope and
Content, Online Archive of California, University of California at
Berkeley, Bancroft Library,
http://www.oac.cdlib.org/findaid/ark:/13030/tf796nb2hn/entire_text/

Ethel Duffy Turner scrapbook at University of California at Berkeley,
http://www.oac.cdlib.org/search?style=oac4;titlesAZ=e;idT=
UCb110205200

Commonweal Magazine, "A Brief History of Commonweal",
http://commonwealmagazine.org/brief-history-commonweal

Historic Context Statement Carmel-by-the-Sea, online, Adopted
by the City Council September 9, 2008, http://ci.carmel.
ca.us/carmel/index.cfm?LinkServID=A836D277-3048-7B3D-
C52E40C677DF9680&showMeta=0

"History of the Pine Inn", Pine Inn Hotel, Carmel-by-the-Sea, California,
http://www.pineinn.com/history/

The Church of the Wayfarer, Carmel, California,
http://www.churchofthewayfarer.com/church/ and http://www.
churchofthewayfarer.com/church/historical-milestones/index.htm

The Sunset Center, Carmel, California, history,
http://www.sunsetcenter.org/history.html

Harrison Memorial Library website,
http://hm-lib.org/about/index.html

Daniel P. Faigin, webmaster@cahighways.org, California Highways: Trails
and Roads: El Camino Real, www.cahighways.org/elcamino.html, ©
1996-2006

Early Artists in Yosemite, "Indians and Other Sketches," (1936)
by Mrs. H. J. Taylor, http://www.yosemite.ca.us/library/ and
yosemite_indians_and_other_sketches/early_artists.html

Online Newsletters:

"A Carmel Original-The Seven Arts Building", Connie Wright, *Carmel
Residents Association Newsletter* online, July 2001,
http://www.carmelresidents.org/News0107.html

Old Carmel by Connie Wright, "Mary DeNeale Morgan, 'horse and buggy
artist'", *Carmel Residents Association Newsletter* online, January 2002,
ttp://www.carmelresidents.org/News0201.html

Old Carmel by Connie Wright, "Those MacGowan Sisters and the
Carmel Bunch", *Carmel Residents Association Newsletter* online, May 2002,
http://www.carmelresidents.org/News0205.html

Old Carmel by Connie Wright, "M. J. Murphy—'The man who built
Carmel'", *Carmel Residents Association Newsletter* online, September 2002,
http://www.carmelresidents.org/News0209.html

Old Carmel by Connie Wright, "Frank and Jane Gallatin Powers",
Carmel Residents Association Newsletter online, February 2003,
http://www.carmelresidents.org/News0302.html

Old Carmel by Connie Wright, "Frederick Bechdolt: One of the Carmel Bunch", *Carmel Residents Association Newsletter* online, February 2004, www.carmelresidents.org/News0402.html

Old Carmel by Connie Wright, "Laura Maxwell, Pioneer", *Carmel Residents Association Newsletter* online, March 2004, http://www.carmelresidents.org/News0403.html

Old Carmel by Connie Wright, "Harry Leon Wilson–One of the Carmel Gang", *Carmel Residents Association Online* newsletter, April 2005, http://www.carmelresidents.org/News0504.html

Old Carmel by Connie Wright, "Nora May French, 'A Stormy Petrel'", *Carmel Residents Association Newsletter* online, February 2006, http://www.carmelresidents.org/News0602.html

Old Carmel by Connie Wright, "Sydney Jones Yard, Tonalist Painter", *Carmel Residents Association Newsletter* online, March 2006, http://www.carmelresidents.org/News0603.html

Old Carmel by Connie Wright, "Xavier Martinez, 'the mad Aztec'", *Carmel Residents Association Newsletter* online, October 2006, http://www.carmelresidents.org/News0610.html

Old Carmel by Connie Wright, "Perry Newberry: Our One-Man Band", *Carmel Residents Association Newsletter* online, November 2002, http://www.carmelresidents.org/News0211.html and March 2007, http://www.carmelresidents.org/News0703.html

Old Carmel by Connie Wright, "Bertha 'Buttsky' Newberry", *Carmel Residents Association Newsletter* online, February 2007, http://www.carmelresidents.org/News0702.html

Old Carmel by Connie Wright, "Herbert Heron", *Carmel Residents Association Newsletter* online, November 2007, http://www.carmelresidents.org/News0711.html#OldCarmel

Old Carmel by Connie Wright, "Jimmy Hopper—one of the Carmel Gang", *Carmel Residents Association Newsletter* online, September 2008, www.carmelresidents.org/News0809.html

Old Carmel by Richard Flower, "Carmel and Sinclair Lewis, an Uneasy Bond", *Carmel Residents Association Newsletter* online, November-December 2011, p. 5, http://www.carmelresidents.org/News/CRANews2011_11_12.pdf

"Louis Christian Mullgardt: An Architect with a Capital 'A'", *Heritage News, For Members of the San Francisco Architectural Heritage*, Volume XXIX, No. 5, September/October 2001, p. 5-8 online: http://www.sfheritage.org/bw_old/newsletters/VOL29NO5.pdf

California Historical Society Quarterly

John R. Dunbar, "Letters of George Sterling to Carey McWilliams", *The California Historical Society Quarterly*, Volume XLVI, Number 3, California Historical Society, San Francisco, California, September 1967, p. 235-252

Kay Baker Gaston, "The MacGowan Girls", *California History, The Magazine of the California Historical Society*, San Francisco, California, Summer 1980, p. 116-125

Sidney Lawrence, "The Ghirardelli Story", *California History*, Volume 81, No. 2, California Historical Society, San Francisco, California, Spring-Fall, 2002, p. 81-90

Michael Orth, "Ideality to Reality: The Founding of Carmel", *The California Historical Society Quarterly*, Volume XLVIII, No. 3, San Francisco, California, September 1969, p. 195-210

Newspaper Articles:

Bettina Boxall, "$84-million removal of a dam on Carmel River set to begin Dismantling of the silt-filled San Clemente, to start next month, is being called California's largest-ever dam removal.", *Los Angeles Times*, June 23, 2013, online:
http://www.latimes.com/news/local/la-me-dam-removal-20130624,0,4731164.story

Judy Hammond, "Door-to-Door. Home Built Of Portals Saved From S.F. Quake Gets Reprieve", *Chicago Tribune*, July 30, 1995, online:
http://articles.chicagotribune.com/1995-07-30/business/9507300115_1_carmel-history-doors-affordable

Kevin Howe, "San Carlos Cathedral statue coming home with face-lift. Statue to be on display inside church before return to niche", *Monterey Herald*, October 9, 2009

"Mrs. Elsie Martinez Dies at 93", *Monterey Peninsula Herald*, February 3, 1984, p. 4

Allen Pierleoni, "Travel Spotlight: 102-year-old Carmel Drug Store Holds Its Place in Time", *The Sacramento Bee*, August 12, 2012

Laura Poole, "Seismic retrofit under way at Carmel Mission Basilica, Carmel Basilica retrofit project expected to be finished by next fall", *Monterey Herald*, October 3, 2012

New York Times Articles:

"Mr. Simmons Acquitted", *New York Times*, June 26, 1887

"The True Romance." Book Review of *Isidro*, *New York Times*, April 29, 1905

"The Sinclair Colony." *New York Times*, June 24, 1906

"For a Co-Operative Home. The Plan for a Colony to be Discussed Here To-morrow Evening.", *New York Times*, July 16, 1906

"Sinclair Explains His Home Colony, 300 at His Meeting to Applaud Anti-Worry Syndicating. 100 Families are Ready, Doesn't was All Socialists—Meeting Favors Co-operation in Child Raising.", *New York Times*, July 18, 1906

"Fire Wipes Out Helicon Hall, And Upton Sinclair Hints that the Steel Trust's Hand May Be in It. Life Lost; Several Hurt, Woman Makes a Lifeline of Her Flannel Nightgown and Slides to Safety. Colony Future in Doubt, Founder Ready to Continue, but Says the Rest Must Decide—They Have Lost All.", *New York Times*, March 17, 1907

"Poetess Kills Herself. Nora May French Took Cyanide of Potassium at a Friend's Bungalow.", *New York Times* obituary, November 16, 1907

"'The Arrow Maker' A Pictorial Play, Tribal Customs and Dances Interwoven in Old Love Story at the New Theatre. Splendid Scenic Display", *New York Times*, February 28, 1911

"William Keith Dead. Landscape Painter Was Famous for His California Scenes." *New York Times* obituary, April 14, 1911

"American Writer in Prison. John K. Turner, Author of "Barbarous Mexico," Arrested by Diaz's Order", *New York Times*, February 20, 1913

"Turner Reported Free. Richard Harding Davis Writes Strong Appeal for Brother Author,", *New York Times*, February 25, 1913

"Mexico to Expel Turner.", *New York Times*, February 28, 1913

"Jack London's New Home Burns.", *New York Times*, August 24, 1913

"Famous Times Writer Dies In California, Major Ben C. Truman Served New York Times as Correspondent in Civil War and Was President Johnson's Secretary." *New York Times* obituary, July 30, 1916

"Jack London Dies Suddenly on Ranch, Novelist is Found Unconscious from Uremia, and Expires After Eleven Hours." *New York Times* obituary, November 23, 1916

"London to be Cremated. Author's Funeral to be Held in Oakland Today—His Mother Very Ill." *New York Times*, November 24, 1916

"Author and Artist in Duel With Fists, Harry Leon Wilson and Theodore Criley Fight Five Knockdown Rounds in California.", *New York Times*, March 31, 1922

"George Sterling is Found Dead." *Special to the New York Times*, November 18, 1926

"Harry Leon Wilson Sued For Divorce, His Wife, Formerly Helen Cook (sic), Accuses Author of Desertion and Failure to Provide. Hiding of Assets Charged. Recent Settlement Is Attacked and Half of Property Is Asked In California Action", *New York Times*, February 9, 1927

"David Starr Jordan Dies at Age of 80", *New York Times* obituary, September 20, 1931

"Harry Leon Wilson Hurt. Novelist and Young Woman Are in Auto Crash in California", *New York Times*, June 11, 1932

"Mary Austin Dead; Noted Writer, 65. Author of More Than Score of Books Succumbs in Sleep to Heart Attack. Authority on Indians. Determined Feminist Also Was Playwright—Taught School First in Southwest." *New York Times* obituary, August 14, 1934

"Lincoln Steffens, Author, Dies at 70, 'Muckraker' Exposed Graft in the Nation—Wrote of It in 'The Shame of the Cities', Long a Reporter here,

In Famous Autobiography He Told of Quest for Truth in America and Abroad.", *New York Times* obituary, August 10, 1936

"Dr. V. L. Kellogg, Scientist, was 69", *New York Times* obituary, August 9, 1937

"Perry Newberry, 68, California Author, Writer of Boys' Books, Editor and Reformer, Is Dead", *New York Times* obituary, December 8, 1938

"Harry L. Wilson, Author, 72, Dead, He Was Creator of Ruggles of Red Gap, Bunker Bean and Merton of the Movies, Began as Stenographer, Wrote Plays With Tarkington—Many Stories Were Made Features in the Films", *New York Times* obituary, June 30, 1939

"Dr. Genthe is Dead; Photographer, 73. His Portraits of Presidents and Leading Figures of Stage Brought World Fame, Started in San Francisco, Took Notable Pictures of Fire and Earthquake in 1906—Art Patron and Writer", *New York Times* obituary, August 11, 1942

"J. H. Kellogg Dies; Health Expert, 91, *New York Times* obituary, December 16, 1943

"Booth Tarkington, Novelist, 76, Dead, Creator of Penrod and Other Beloved Characters Twice Won Pulitzer Prizes, Also was a Playwright, Author of 'The Gentleman From Indiana'—Working on a New Book, Though Nearly Blind", *New York Times* obituary, May 20, 1946

"Charles Chapel Judson", *New York Times* obituary, November 6, 1946

"John Cosgrave, 83, Journalist, Dead. Chief of Sunday Supplement of The World for 15 Years was Co-Founder of The Wave", *New York Times* obituary, September 20, 1947

"F. R. Bechdolt, 75, Western Novelist, Author of Many Stories and Books of Pioneering Days is Dead in California", *New York Times* obituary, April 14, 1950

"William Benet, 64, Noted Poet, is Dead, Brother of Stephen Vincent, He Won Pulitzer Prize in 1942 for 'Dust Which is God', Also Wrote Many Novels, Was Well-Known Anthologist and Literary Columnist—An Editor for 31 Years", *New York Times* obituary, May 5, 1950

"Michael Williams, Editor, 73, is Dead, Founder of The Commonweal was Leader in Fight Against Persecution of Religions", *New York Times* obituary, October 13, 1950

"Novelist Dies. Sinclair Lewis, 65, Dies In Rome Clinic, First American to Win Nobel Prize for Literature Wrote 'Babbitt' and 'Main Street', *New York Times* obituary, January 11, 1951

Joseph Henry Jackson, "Everybody Knew the 'Block'," *New York Times*, May 27, 1951

"Grant Wallace, Newsman, Was 87. Coast Artist and Writer Dies— Covered Russo-Japanese War, Worked on Films", *New York Times* obituary, August 14, 1954

"Mrs. Jack London, 84, Widow of Novelist", *Special to the New York Times*, January 15, 1955

"J. M. Hopper, Author of Short Stories, 80", *New York Times* obituary, August 30, 1956

"Mrs. Mabel Dodge Luhan Dies; Patron of Arts and Letters, 83. Author's Soirees Here Drew Intellectuals—She Aided Post-Impressionism", *New York Times* obituary, August 14, 1962

"Van Wyck Brooks, Author, 77, Dead, Biographer, Literary Critic and Historian Received Pulitzer Prize in '37, Wrote Pictorial Prose, Stressed American 'Memory' and Sense of Belonging to Continuing Tradition", *New York Times* obituary, May 3, 1963

Alden Whitman, "Rebel With a Cause, Upton Sinclair, Author and Crusader for Social Justice, is Dead", *New York Times* obituary, November 26, 1968

Anthony Arthur, "Upton Sinclair, Times Topics", *New York Times*, http://www.nytimes.com/ref/timestopics/topics_uptonsinclair.html

"Michael Lewis, The Actor, Sinclair's Son, Dies at 44", *New York Times* obituary, March 7, 1975

Joan Cook, "Ella Winter Stewart, Journalist and Widow of Donald O. Stewart", *New York Times* obituary, August 5, 1980

Bruce Weber, "Charis Wilson, Model and Muse, Dies at 95", *New York Times* obituary, November 24, 2009

Magazine articles, 1930's onwards:

"Sinclair Lewis Dies in Italy, His biting, realistic novels were bombshells in the '20's, but in the end even Main Street was happy.", *Life*, Volume 30, Number 4, Time Inc., New York, January 22, 1951, p. 69-72

Religion: "Spanish Split", *Time*, Monday July 4, 1938 issue, www.time.com/time/magazine/article/0,9171,759948,00.html

"Yosemite Man", *Time Magazine*, Volume XXVIII, No. 26, December 28, 1936, http://205.188.238.109/time/printout/0,8816,771908,00.html

Magazine articles, 1927 and earlier:

Albert Bender, "George Sterling: The Man", *Overland Monthly*, Volume LXXXV, Number 12, San Francisco, California, December 1927, p. 363 [Internet Archive: www.archive.org]

Josephine Mildred Blanch, "The 'Barbizon' of California, Some Interesting Studios of Old Monterey", *Overland Monthly*, Volume L, Second Series, Number 1, Overland Monthly Publishing Co., San Francisco, California, July 1907, p. 63-68 [Google Digitized Book]

Henry Meade Bland, "Literary Monterey", *Overland Monthly*, Volume LIII, Number 1, Overland Monthly Publishing Co., San Francisco, California, January 1909, p. 19-26 [Google Digitized Book]

Henry Meade Bland, "Sterling, the Poet of Seas and Stars", *Overland Monthly*, Volume LXVI–Second Series, Number 6, Overland Monthly Publishing Co., San Francisco, California, December 1915, p. 475-478 [Google Digitized Book]

Agnes Foster Buchanan, "Some Early Business Buildings of San Francisco", *The Architectural Record*, Volume XX, The Architectural Record Co., New York, July 1906, p. 15-32 [Google Digitized Book]

Agnes Foster Buchanan, "The Story of a Famous Fraternity of Writers and Artists" *The Pacific Monthly*, Volume XVII, The Pacific Monthly Publishing Company, Portland, Oregon, January 1907, p. 65-83 [Google Digitized Book]

Hartley Davis, "Reporters of To-day (sic), Stories of Our Foremost Newspaper Men and 'Beats' They Have Scored," *Everybody's Magazine*, Volume XIV, Number 2, The Ridgway-Thayer Company, Publishers, New York, February 1906, p. 200-209 [Google Digitized Book]

Mabel Croft Deering, "San Francisco's Famous Bohemian Restaurant", *The Critic, An Illustrated Monthly Review of Literature, Art, and Life*, Volume XLVIII, The Critic Company by G. P. Putnam's Sons, New Rochelle, New York, June 1906, p. 523-528 [Google Digitized Book]

Mary E. Delport, "The Spell of the Carmel Coast", *Overland Monthly*, Volume LXXIII, Second Series, Overland Monthly Co. Publishers, San Francisco, California, February 1919, p. 106-115 [Google Digitized Book]

Ellen Dwyer Donovan, "California Artists and Their Work", *Overland Monthly*, Volume LI, Second Series, Number 1, Overland Monthly Publishing Co., San Francisco, California, January 1908, p. 25-33 [Google Digitized Book]

Henry Dumont, "The Pageant at Carmel", *National Magazine*, Volume XXXV, Chapple Publishing Company, Ltd., Boston, Massachusetts, October 1911, p. 151-157 [Google Digitized Book]

Ninetta Eames, "Jack London", *Overland Monthly*, Volume XXXV, Second Series, Number 209, Overland Monthly Publishing Company, San Francisco, California, May 1900, p. 417-425 [Google Digitized Book]

The Editor, The Journal of Information for Literary Workers, Volume 44, Number 14, The Editor Company, Ridgewood, New Jersey, December 30, 1916, p. 625 [Google Digitized Book]

Edwin Emerson, Jr. "When West Met East", *Sunset*, Volume XV, Number 6, Southern Pacific Company Publishers, San Francisco, California, October 1905, p. 515-530 [Google Digitized Book]

Nora May French, "Ave Atque Vale", *Sunset*, Volume XX, Number 2, Passenger Department, Southern Pacific Company Publishers, San Francisco, California, December 1907, p. 386 [Google Digitized Book]

Donald Gray "Sterling in Type", *Overland Monthly*, Volume LXXXV, Number 11, San Francisco, California, November 1927, p. 328, p. 350-351 [Internet Archive: www.archive.org]

Eunice T. Gray, "The Chase School of Art at Carmel-by-the-Sea, California", *Art and Progress*, Volume VI, Number 4, Published by the American Federation of the Arts, New York and Washington D.C., February 1915, p. 118-120 [Google Digitized Book]

Herbert Heron, "A Vase", *Overland Monthly*, Volume LVII, Second Series, Number 4, Overland Monthly Publishing Co., San Francisco, California, April 1911, p. 412 [Google Digitized Book]

History of the Bench and Bar of California, Edited by Joseph Clement Bates, Bench and Bar Publishing Co., San Francisco, California, 1912, p. 469 [Google Digitized Book]

James Hopper, "Locomotive Jones, A Football Fantasy" *Sunset*, Volume XIV, Number 1, Southern Pacific Company Publishers, San Francisco, California, November 1905, p. 3-8 [Google Digitized Book]

George Wharton James, "California's Literary Giants, Herman Whitaker", *The National Magazine*, Volume XXXVIII, Chapple Publishing Company, Ltd., Boston, Massachusetts, June 1913, pages 451-462 [Google Digitized Book]

George Wharton James, "Chris Jorgensen—A Versatile California Artist", *The National Magazine*, Volume XLII, Chapple Publishing Company, Ltd., Boston, Massachusetts, July 1915, p. 609-616 [Google Digitized Book]

George Wharton James, "Jack London, Cub of the Slums, Hero of Adventure, Literary Master, and Social Philosopher", *The National Magazine*, Chapple Publishing Company, Ltd., Boston, Massachusetts, Volume XXXVII, January 1913, p. 682-696 [Google Digitized Book]

George Wharton James, "The Influence of California Upon Literature, *The National Magazine*, Volume XXXVI, Chapple Publishing Company, Ltd., Boston, Massachusetts, April 1912, p. 65-79 [Google Digitized Book]

Idwal Jones, "King of Bohemia", *Overland Monthly*, Volume LXXXV, Number 11, November 1927, p. 332-333 [Internet Archive: www.archive.org]

"In the Realm of Bookland", *Overland Monthly*, Volume LIX–Second Series, No. 3, The Overland Monthly Publishing Co., San Francisco, California, March 1912, p. 289 [Google Digitized Book]

Charles Keeler, "The American Turner. William Keith and His Work." *Land of Sunshine*, Volume VIII, Number 6, Land of Sunshine Publishing Co., Los Angeles, California, May 1898, p. 253-259] [Google Digitized Book]

Leonore Kothe, "In Old Monterey", *Overland Monthly*, Volume LVII–Second Series, Number 6, Overland Monthly Publishing Co., San Francisco, California, June 1911, p. 631-636 [Google Digitized Book]

Leonore Kothe, "The Monterey Cypress", *Overland Monthly*, Volume LXVI, Second Series, Number 6, Overland Monthly Publishing Co., San Francisco, California, December 1915, p. 469-473 [Google Digitized Book]

Beatric de Lack Krombach, "Art at Del Monte". *Out West Magazine*, Volume XLII, Number 2, Published by Cruse Carriel, Whittier, California, February 1916, p. 67-70, p. 105 [Google Digitized Book]

Sinclair Lewis, "A San Francisco Pleasure Cure Bring Echoes of the New City's Laughter", *Sunset*, Volume XXIV, Number 4, Southern Pacific Company Publishers, San Francisco, California, April 1910, p. 433-439 [Google Digitized Book]

Charmian Kittredge London, "George Sterling–As I Knew Him", *Overland Monthly*, Volume LXXXV, Number 3, San Francisco, California, March 1927, p. 69-70, p. 76, p. 80, p. 83, p. 87, p. 90-91 [Internet Archive: www.archive.org]

Grace MacFarland, "Annual Plays at Carmel's Forest Theatre", *Overland Monthly*, Volume LXVIII, Second Series, Number 3, Overland Monthly Co. Publishers, San Francisco, California, September 1916, p. 239-243 [Google Digitized Book]

Edward F. O'Day, "1869-1926", *Overland Monthly*, Volume LXXXV, Number 12, San Francisco, California, December 1927, p. 357-358 [Internet Archive: www.archive.org]

Pacific Medical Journal, Volume XLIX, Number 8, San Francisco, California, August 1906, p. 317, p. 409 [Google Digitized Book]

Elizabeth Fry Page, "Feathers From an Eagle's Nest", *The Olympian, A Monthly Magazine Devoted to Literature, Education, and Amateur Sport*, Volume II, Number 1, The Olympian Publishing Company, Nashville, Tennessee, July 1903, p. 27-31 [Google Digitized Book]

James D. Phelan, "George Sterling", *Overland Monthly*, Volume LXXXV, Number 11, San Francisco, California, November 1927, p. 343 [Internet Archive: www.archive.org]

The Publishers' Weekly, The American Book Trade Journal, Volume LXVII, Number 13, Office of the Publishers' Weekly, New York, April 22, 1905 (Whole Number 1734), page 1159 [Google Digitized Book]

The Publisher's Weekly, The American Book Trade Journal, Volume LXXXIII, Office of the Publishers' Weekly, New York, January through June 1913, p. 672 [Google Digitized Book]

Henry Clay Quinby, "The Chapel at Del Monte", *Sunset*, Volume XVI, Number 3, Passenger Department, Southern Pacific Company Publishers, San Francisco, California, January 1906, p. 298 [Google Digitized Book]

F. W. Ramsdell, "Charles Rollo Peters", *Brush & Pencil, An Illustrated Magazine of the Arts & Crafts*, The Arts & Crafts Publishing Co., Chicago, Illinois, Volume IV, Number 4, July 1899, p. 205-212 [Google Digitized Book]

James Rorty, "Living Inseparables", *Overland Monthly*, Volume LXXXV, Number 12, San Francisco, California, December 1927, p. 367 [Internet Archive: www.archive.org]

Mabel Urmy Seares, "William Keith and His Times", *California's Magazine, Edition De Luxe, Volume II*, California's Magazine Company, San Francisco, California, 1916, p. 105-110 [Google Digitized Book]

George R. Stewart, Jr., Introduction to "San Carlos Day, An Article in a California Newspaper by Robert Louis Stevenson," *Scribner's Magazine*, Volume LXVIII, Charles Scribner's Sons, New York, August 1920, p. 209-211 [Google Digitized Book]

Charles Warren Stoddard, "In Old Bohemia, Memories of San Francisco in the Sixties", *The Pacific Monthly*, Pacific Monthly Publishing Company, Portland, Oregon, December 1907, p. 639-650 [Google Digitized Book]

Jean White, "A Landmark of San Francisco's Bohemia", *Overland Monthly*, Vol. LXVII, Second Series, Number 3, Overland Monthly Publishing Company, San Francisco, California, March 1916, p. 186-188 [Internet Archive: www.archive.org]

Michael Williams, "The Forest Theater at Carmel, A Dramatic Movement in the Shadow of Junípero Serra's Mission", *Sunset, The Pacific Monthly*, Volume XXIX, Number 3, San Francisco, California, September 1912, p. 319-325 [Google Digitized Book]

Kathryne Wilson, "The Literary Colony at Carmel", *The Book News Monthly*, Volume 33, Number 7, John Wanamaker, Philadelphia, Pennsylvania, April 1915, p. 364-367 [Google Digitized Book]

"John Fleming Wilson '00", *The Princeton Alumni Weekly*, Volume XXII, Number 24, Princeton, New Jersey, March 29, 1922, p. 550 [Google Digitized Book]

George Sterling tribute issue of *San Francisco Water*, Volume VII, Number 3, Spring Valley Water Company Publication, San Francisco, California, July 1928, p. 12-13

Books, prior to 1922:

Anna Geil Andresen, *Historic Landmarks of Monterey, California. A Brief Sketch of the Landmarks of Monterey*, California Federation of Women's Clubs, Salinas, California 1917 [Google Digitized Book]

The American Literary Yearbook, Hamilton Traub, Editor, Volume 1, Paul Traub, Publisher, Henning, Minnesota, 1919 [Google Digitized Book]

Mary Austin, *Isidro*, Houghton Mifflin & Co., Boston and New York, 1905 [Google Digitized Book]

"The Bohemian Club of San Francisco Certificate of Incorporation, Constitution, By-Laws and Rules, Officers, Committees and Members" San Francisco Bohemian Club, Press of H. S. Crocker Co., San Francisco, California, 1904 [Google Digitized Book]

The Catholic Encyclopedia, Knights of Columbus, Volume One, The Encyclopedia Press, Inc., New York, 1913 [Google Digitized Book]

Sheldon Cheney, *The Open-Air Theatre*, Mitchell Kennerley, New York, 1918 [Google Digitized Book]

Grace MacGowan Cooke, *The Grapple, A Story of the Illinois Coal Region*, L. C. Page & Company, Boston, Massachusetts, 1905 [Google Digitized Book]

Ella Sterling Cummins, *The Story of the Files, A Review of Californian Writers and Literature*, Issued under the Auspices of the World's Fair Commission of California, Columbian Exposition, 1893, San Francisco, California, 1893 [Google Digitized Book]

Directory of Graduates of the University of California, 1864-1916, Published by the California Alumni Association, University of California, Berkeley, 1916 [Google Digitized Book]

Nora May French, *Poems*, Edited by Henry Anderson Lafler, The Strange Company, San Francisco, California, 1910 [Google Digitized Book]

Porter Garnett, *The Bohemian Jinks, A Treatise*, Bohemian Club of San Francisco, 1908 [Google Digitized Book]

James Hopper and Fred. R. Bechdolt, *9009*, The Musson Book Company, Toronto, 1908 copyright [Google Digitized Book]

Will Irwin, *The City That Was, A Requiem of Old San Francisco*, B.W. Huebsch, New York, 1908 [Google Digitized Book]

Helen Hunt Jackson, *A Century of Dishonor, A Sketch of the United States Government's Dealings With Some of the Indian Tribes, New Edition Enlarged by the Addition of the Report of the Needs of the Mission Indians of California*, Little, Brown and Company, Boston, Massachusetts, 1917 [Google Digitized Book]

Helen Hunt Jackson, *Glimpses of California and the Missions*, With Illustrations by Henry Sandham, Little, Brown & Company, Boston, Massachusetts, 1914 [Google Digitized Book]

George Wharton James, *The 1910 Trip of the H.M.M.B.A. to California and the Pacific Coast*, Chapter XII, Bolte & Braden Company, San Francisco, 1911, p. 245-268 [Google Digitized Book]

George Wharton James, *Exposition Memories: Panama-California Exposition, San Diego, 1916*, The Radiant Life Press, Pasadena, California, 1917 [Google Digitized Book]

David Starr Jordan, *The Days of a Man, Being Memories of a Naturalist, Teacher, and Minor Prophet of Democracy*, Illustrated, Volume One, 1851-1899, World Book Company, Yonkers-on-Hudson, New York, 1922 [Google Digitized Book]

William Reno Kane, Editor, *The Editor, The Journal of Information for Literary Workers*, Volume 44, Number 14, The Editor Company, Ridgewood, New Jersey, December 30, 1916, p. 625 [Google Digitized Book]

Florence N. Levy, Editor, *American Art Annual*, Volume IX, The American Federation of Arts, New York, New York, 1911 [Google Digitized Book]

Florence N. Levy, Editor, *American Art Annual*, Volume XIV, The American Federation of Arts, Washington, D.C., 1917 [Google Digitized Book]

Charmian London, *The Book of Jack London, Volume I*, The Century Co., New York, 1921 [Google Digitized Book]

Charmian London, *The Book of Jack London, Volume II*, The Century Co., New York, 1921 [Google Digitized Book]

Jack London, *The Son of the Wolf, Tales of the Far North*, Isbister and Company, Limited, London, 1902 [Google Digitized Book]

Jack London, *The Valley of the Moon*, The Review of Reviews Company, New York, 1917 [Google Digitized Book]

Grace MacFarland, *Monterey, Cradle of California's Romance: The Story of A Lost Port That was Found Again and A Dream That Came True*, Weybret-Lee Co. Press, Monterey, 1914 [Google Digitized Book]

Edwin Markham, *California the Wonderful*, Hearst International Library Co., New York, 1914 [Google Digitized Book]

Grace Sartwell Mason, John Northern Hilliard, *The Golden Hope*, D. Appleton and Company, New York, 1916 [Google Digitized Book]

Thomas Lansing Masson, *Our American Humorists*, Chapter XXXI, "Harry Leon Wilson", Moffat, Yard, and Company, New York, 1922, p. 303-304 [Google Digitized Book]

Memorial and Biographical History of the Coast Counties of Central California, Illustrated, Henry D. Barrows, Editor of the Historical Department, Luther A. Ingersoll, Editor of the Biographical Department, The Lewis Publishing Co., Chicago, Illinois, 1893 [Google Digitized Book]

Charles Moore, *Daniel H. Burnham, Architect, Planner of Cities, Volume I*, Houghton Mifflin Company, Boston and New York, 1921 [Google Digitized Book]

Mrs. Fremont Older, *California Missions and Their Romances*, original Coward-McCann, Inc., 1938, Kessinger Publishing, 2005

Ernest Peixotto, *Romantic California*, Charles Scribner's Sons, New York, 1914 [Google Digitized Book]

Press Reference Library (Western Edition), Notables of the West, Volume II, International News Service, New York, 1915 [Google Digitized Book]

Helen Throop Purdy, *San Francisco As It Was, As It Is, and How to See It*, Paul Elder and Company Publishers, San Francisco, 1912 [Google Digitized Book]

Nellie Van De Grift Sanchez, *Spanish and Indian Place Names of California, Their Meaning and Their Romance*, A. M. Robertson, San Francisco, California, 1914 [Google Digitized Book]

"Constitution and By-Laws of The Bohemian Club of San Francisco", The San Francisco Bohemian Club, 1895 [Google Digitized Book]

San Francisco, The Financial, Commercial, & Industrial Metropolis of the Pacific Coast, Official Records, Statistics, and Encyclopedia, Compiled Under the Direction of the San Francisco Chamber of Commerce, Information and Statistical Department, H. S. Crocker Co., San Francisco, 1915 [Google Digitized Book]

Santa Cruz County California, Wallace W. Elliott & Co., San Francisco, California 1879 [Google Digitized Book]

University Chronicle, An Official Record, The University of California Berkeley, Berkeley, California, Volume IV, Number 1, February 1901 [Google Digitized Book]

Upton Sinclair, *The Moneychangers*, B. W. Dodge & Company, New York, 1908 [Google Digitized Book]

Louis Stanislas Slevin and M. E. Slevin, *Guide Book to the Mission of San Carlos at Carmel and Monterey, California*, Carmel, California, 1912 [Google Digitized Book]

Clark Ashton Smith, *Odes and Sonnets*, The Book Club of California, San Francisco, California, 1918 [Google Digitized Book]

Frances Norris Rand Smith, *The Architectural History of Mission San Carlos Borromeo Carmelo, California*, California Historical Survey Commission, Berkeley, California, 1921 [Google Digitized Book]

George Sterling, *A Wine of Wizardry and Other Poems*, A. M. Robertson, San Francisco, California, 1909 [Google Digitized Book]

George Sterling, "A Memoir of Ambrose Bierce", *The Letters of Ambrose Bierce*, Edited by Bertha Clark Pope, The Book Club of California, San Francisco, California, 1922 [Internet Archive: www.archive.org]

George Sterling, *Lilith: A Dramatic Poem*, The Book Club of California, San Francisco, California, 1920 [Google Digitized Book]

George Sterling, *Rosamund: A Dramatic Poem*, The Book Club of California, San Francisco, California, 1920 [Google Digitized Book]

George Sterling, *Sails and Mirage and Other Poems*, A. M. Robertson, San Francisco, California, 1921 [Google Digitized Book]

George Sterling, *The House of Orchids: and Other Poems*, A. M. Robertson, San Francisco, California 1911 [Google Digitized Book]

George Sterling, *The Testimony of the Suns and Other Poems*, First Edition November 1903, Second Edition November 1904, A. M. Robertson, San Francisco, 1904 [Google Digitized Book]

Robert Louis Stevenson, "The Old Pacific Capital", *Across the Plains, with other Memories and Essays*, Chatto & Windus, Piccadilly, London, 1892 [Google Digitized Book]

Charles Warren Stoddard, *In the Footprints of the Padres*, New and Enlarged Edition, Introduction by Charles Phillips, Copyright 1901, 1911 A. M. Robertson, Published by Taylor, Nash, & Taylor, San Francisco, 1912 [Google Digitized Book]

Frank Morton Todd, *The Chamber of Commerce Handbook for San Francisco, Historical and Descriptive, A Guide for Visitors*, San Francisco Chamber of Commerce Publicity Committee, San Francisco, 1913 [Google Digitized Book]

Major Ben C. Truman, *Tourists' Illustrated Guide to the Celebrated Summer and Winter Resorts of California Adjacent to and Upon the Lines of the Central and Southern Pacific Railroads*, H. S. Crocker & Co., Printers and Publishers, San Francisco, California 1883 [Google Digitized Book]

John Kenneth Turner, *Barbarous Mexico*, Charles H. Kerr & Company, Chicago, Illinois, 1911 [Google Digitized Book]

U.S. Congressional Serial Set, 61st Congress, 2nd Session, 1909-1910, Senate Documents, U. S. Congress, Volume 56, Government Printing Office, Washington, D. C., 1913 [Google Digitized Book]

Who's Who in America, A Biographical Dictionary of Notable Living Men and Women in the United States, John W. Leonard, Editor, Volume II,

1901-1902, A. N. Marquis & Company, Publishers, Chicago, Illinois, 1901 [Google Digitized Book]

Who's Who in America, A Biographical Dictionary of Notable Living Men and Women in the United States, Albert Nelson Marquis, Editor, Volume IV, 1906-1907, A. N. Marquis & Company, Publishers, Chicago, Illinois, 1906 [Google Digitized Book]

Who's Who in America, A Biographical Dictionary of Notable Living Men and Women in the United States, Volume V, 1908-1909, A. N. Marquis & Company, Publishers, Chicago, Illinois, 1908 [Google Digitized Book]

Who's Who in America, A Biographical Dictionary of Notable Living Men and Women in the United States, Albert Nelson Marquis, Editor, Volume VI, 1910-1911, A. N. Marquis & Company, Publishers, Chicago, Illinois, 1910 [Google Digitized Book]

Who's Who in America, A Biographical Dictionary of Notable Living Men and Women in the United States, Albert Nelson Marquis, Editor, Volume VII, 1912-1913, A. N. Marquis & Company, Publishers, Chicago, Illinois, 1912 [Google Digitized Book]

Michael Williams, *The Book of the High Romance, A Spiritual Autobiography*, The MacMillan Company, New York, 1918 [Google Digitized Book]

Benjamin C. Wright, *San Francisco's Ocean Trade, Past and Future. A Story of the Deep Water Service of San Francisco, 1848 to 1911. Effect the Panama Canal Will Have Upon It*, A. Carlisle & Co., San Francisco, 1911 [Google Digitized Book]

Books:

Stephen E. Ambrose, *Nothing Like It In The World, The Men Who Built the Transcontinental Railroad 1863-1869*, Simon & Schuster, New York, 2000

Anthony Arthur, *Radical Innocent: Upton Sinclair*, Random House, New York, 2006

Mary Austin, *Earth Horizon*, Houghton, Mifflin & Company, Boston, Massachusetts, 1932

Mary Austin, "George Sterling at Carmel", *American Mercury*, Volume XI, Number 41, The American Mercury, Inc. Publishers, Camden, New Jersey, May 1927, p. 65-72, in *American Mercury Magazine, May to August 1927*, Kessinger Publishing, LLC, LaVergne, TN, 2003

Compiled and Introduced by Malcolm E. Barker, *Three Fearful Days, San Francisco Memoirs of the 1906 Earthquake & Fire*, Londonborn Publications, San Francisco, 2006

Jean Barman, *Constance Lindsay Skinner: Writing on the Frontier*, University of Toronto Press, Scholarly Publishing Division, Toronto, Ontario, Canada, 2002

Elizabeth Barratt and the Carmel Valley Historical Society, *Images of America Carmel Valley*, Arcadia Publishing, Charleston, South Carolina, 2010

Edwin R. Bingham, *Charles F. Lummis, Editor of the Southwest*, Henry E. Huntington Library and Art Gallery, San Marino, California, Copyright 1955, Second Printing 2006

Nancy Boas, *Society of Six, California Colorists*, originally: Bedford Arts Publishers, San Francisco, California, 1988; reprint: University of California Press, Berkeley, Los Angeles, 1997

Daisy Bostick and Dorothea Castelhun, *Carmel–At Work and Play*, Cypress Press, Monterey, California, 1925

Daisy Bostick and Dorothea Castelhun, *Carmel–Today and Yesterday*, Herald Printers, Monterey, California, 1945

Gray Brechin, *Imperial San Francisco, Urban Power, Earthly Ruin*, University of California Press, Berkeley and Los Angeles, California, 1999

William H. Brewer, *Up and Down California in 1860-1864, The Journal of William H. Brewer, 4th Edition with Maps*, University of California Press, Berkeley and Los Angeles, California, 2003

Van Wyck Brooks, *Scenes and Portraits: Memories of Childhood and Youth*, E. P. Dutton and Company, New York, New York, 1954

Scott Bruce and Bill Crawford, *Cerealizing America, The Unsweetened Story of American Breakfast Cereal*, Faber and Faber, Boston, Massachusetts, 1995

Taming the Elephant, Politics, Government, and Law in Pioneer California, Edited by John F. Burns and Richard J. Orsi, California Historical Society, University of California Press, Berkeley and Los Angeles, California, 2003

Julie Cain, *Images of America, Monterey's Hotel Del Monte*, Arcadia Publishing, Charleston, South Carolina, 2005

Rachel Carley, *The Visual Dictionary of American Domestic Architecture*, Henry Holt and Company, Inc., New York, 1994

Carmel Art Association, *Six Early Women Artists: A Diversity of Style*, Carmel Art Association, Carmel, California, 1991

Susan Dinkelspiel Cerny, *An Architectural Guidebook to San Francisco and the Bay Area*, Gibbs Smith, Publisher, Salt Lake City, Utah, 2007

Connie Y. Chiang, Forward by William Cronon, *Shaping the Shoreline: Fisheries and Tourism on the Monterey Coast*, University of Washington Press, Seattle, Washington, 2008

Wendell Cole, "Myth Makers and the Early Years of the Carmel Forest Theatre", Edited by Dunbar H. Ogden, with Douglas McDermott and

Robert Károly Sarlós, *Theatre West: Image and Impact*, University of California, Berkeley, California, 1990, p. 43-52

J. D. Conway, City of Monterey, *Monterey Presidio, Pueblo, And Port, The Making Of America Series*, Arcadia Publishing, Charleston, South Carolina, First Published in 2003, Reprinted in 2006

Kim Coventry, *Monterey Peninsula, The Golden Age*, Arcadia Publishing, Charleston, South Carolina, 2002

Richard Henry Dana, Jr. *Two Years Before the Mast, A Personal Narrative*, (1840), 3rd Edition, New American Library, New York, 1985

Don DeNevi and Noel Francis Moholy, *Junípero Serra, The Illustrated Story of the Franciscan Founder of California's Missions*, Harper & Row Publishers, San Francisco, California, 1985

William Deverell, *Railroad Crossing, Californians and the Railroad, 1850-1910*, University of California Press, Berkeley and Los Angeles, California, 1994

T. Nelson Downs, Edited by John Northern Hilliard, With a New Introduction by Charles R. Reynolds, *The Art of Magic*, Dover Publications, Inc., Mineola, New York, 1980

Helen MacKnight Doyle, *Mary Austin, Woman of Genius*, Gotham Press, New York, 1939

Ferol Egan, *Last Bonanza Kings, The Bourns of San Francisco*, University of Nevada Press, Las Vegas and Reno, Nevada, 1998

Lawrence Ferlinghetti and Nancy J. Peters, *Literary San Francisco, A Pictorial History from Its Beginnings to the Present Day*, City Lights Books and Harper & Row Publishers, San Francisco and New York, 1980

Isobel Field, *This Life I've Loved, An Autobiography*, Longmans, Green and Co., New York, copyright 1937, Great West Books, Lafayette, California, 2005 edition

Adobes in the Sun, Portraits of a Tranquil Era, Text by Augusta Fink with Amelie Elkinton, Photographs by Morley Baer, Chronicle Books, San Francisco, California, 1972

Augusta Fink, *I-Mary, A Biography of Mary Austin*, The University of Arizona Press, Tucson, Arizona, 1983

Augusta Fink, *Monterey County, The Dramatic Story of Its Past*, Western Tanager Press, Santa Cruz, California, 1972

Philip S. Foner, Editor, *The Social Writings of Jack London*, Citadel Press, Secaucus, New Jersey, 1964

Philip L. Fradkin, *Magnitude 8, Earthquakes and Life Along the San Andreas Fault*, University of California Press, Berkeley, California, 1999

Philip L. Fradkin, *The Great Earthquake and Firestorms of 1906, How San Francisco Nearly Destroyed Itself*, University of California Press, Berkeley and Los Angeles, California, 2005

Leslie M. Freudenheim, *Building with Nature, Inspiration for the Arts & Crafts Home*, Gibbs Smith Publisher, Salt Lake City, Utah, 2005

David Gebhard, Robert Montgomery, Robert Winter, John Woodbridge, Sally Woodbridge, *A Guide to Architecture in San Francisco & Northern California*, Peregrine Smith, Inc., Santa Barbara, California and Salt Lake City, Utah, 1973

Arnold Genthe, *As I Remember, The Sources of Modern Photography*, John Day, in Association with Reynal & Hitchcock, New York, 1936, Reprint Arno Press Inc., 1979

William H. Gerdts and Will South, *California Impressionism*, Abbeville Publishers, New York, 1998

Harold and Ann Gilliam, *Creating Carmel, The Enduring Vision*, Gibbs Smith, Publisher, Layton, Utah, 1992

Dana Gioia, Chryss Yost, and Jack Hicks, Editors, *California Poetry: From the Gold Rush to the Present*, A California Legacy Book, Heyday Books, Berkeley, California, 2004

Susan Goodman and Carl Dawson, *Mary Austin and the American West*, University of California Press, Berkeley and Los Angeles, California, 2009

John Steele Gordon, *An Empire of Wealth, The Epic History of American Economic Power*, Harper Collins Publishers, New York, New York, 2004

Donald J. Hagerty, Forward by John Dixon, *Desert Dreams: The Art and Life of Maynard Dixon*, Revised Edition, Gibbs Smith, Publisher, Layton, Utah, 1998

Donald J. Hagerty, *The Life of Maynard Dixon*, Gibbs Smith, Publisher, Layton, Utah, 2010

Sharron Lee Hale, *A Tribute to Yesterday*, Valley Publishers, Santa Cruz, California, 1980

James D. Hart, *A Companion to California, New Edition, Revised and Expanded*, University of California Press, Berkeley, California, 1987

Ed Herny, Shelley Rideout, Katie Wadell, *Berkeley Bohemia, Artists and Visionaries of the Early 20th Century*, Gibbs Smith, Publisher, Layton, Utah, 2008

History of Monterey, Santa Cruz, and San Benito Counties, California, Cradle of California's History and Romance, Volume II, Illustrated, The S. J. Clarke Publishing Co., 1925

James Hoopes, *Van Wyck Brooks, In Search of American Culture*, University of Massachusetts Press, 1977

Monica Hudson, *Carmel-by-the-Sea*, Arcadia Publishing, Charleston, South Carolina, 2006

Edan Hughes, *Artists in California 1786-1940*, Volume 1, A-K, 3rd Edition, Sheridan Books, Inc., Ann Arbor, Michigan, 2002

Edan Hughes, *Artists in California 1786-1940*, Volume 2, L-Z, 3rd Edition, Sheridan Books, Inc., Ann Arbor, Michigan, 2002

Illustrated History of Monterey County, California, Elliott & Moore Publishers, San Francisco, 1881; 1979 Edition by Valley Publishers, Fresno, California, 1979

Tomas Jaehn, "The Southern Pacific Launches a New Vehicle to Develop Its Market", *Sunset Magazine: A Century of Western Living, 1898-1998, Historical Portraits and Bibliography*, Stanford University Libraries, Stanford, California, 1998

Richard Janick, Laurie Boone, and Kent Seavey, *Architecture of the Monterey Peninsula*, Monterey Peninsula Museum of Art, Monterey, California, 1976

From Baltimore to Bohemia, The Letters of H. L. Mencken and George Sterling, Edited by S. T. Joshi, Fairleigh Dickinson University Press, New Jersey, 2001

Justin Kaplan, *Lincoln Steffens: A Biography*, Simon and Schuster, New York, paperback edition 2004, original edition 1974

Russ Kingman, *A Pictorial Life of Jack London*, Crown Publishers, New York, 1979

The California Missions, A Complete Pictorial History and Visitor's Guide, Dorothy Krell, Editor, A Sunset Pictorial Book, Soft Cover Edition, Sunset Books, Menlo Park, California, 1979

Alfred L. Kroeber, *Handbook of the Indians of California*, California Book Co., Ltd., Berkeley, California 1953 (photolithograph of 1925 book)

Atlantic Brief Lives, A Biographical Companion to the Arts, Louis Kronenberger, Editor, Little, Brown, and Company, Boston, Massachusetts, 1971

Historic Spots in California, 4th *Edition*, Revised by Douglas E. Kyle, Authors: Mildred Brooke Hoover, Hero Eugene Rensch, Ethel Grace Rensch, and William N. Abeloe, Stanford University Press, Stanford, California, 1990

California, A Literary Chronicle, Edited and Commentaries by W. Storrs Lee, Funk & Wagnalls, New York, 1968

Richard L. Lingeman, *Sinclair Lewis: Rebel from Main Street*, Random House, Inc., New York, 2002 (Hardcover) [Borealis Books, Minnesota Historical Society, St. Paul, Minnesota, 2005 paperback]

Jack London, *The Valley of the Moon*, University of California Press, Berkeley and Los Angeles, California, 1998

Richard W. Longstreth, *On The Edge of the World: Four Architects in San Francisco at the Turn of the Century*, University of California Press, Berkeley and Los Angeles, California, 1998

Ray A. March, *River in Ruin, The Story of the Carmel River*, University of Nebraska Press, Lincoln, Nebraska, 2012

Monterey in 1786, Life in a California Mission. The Journals of Jean Francois de La Perouse, Introduction and Commentary by Malcolm Margolin,

Santa Clara University, Santa Clara, California, Heyday Books, Berkeley, California, 1989

Elsie Whitaker Martinez, *San Francisco Bay Area Writers and Artists*, Interviewed by Franklin D. Walker and Willa Klug Baum, University of California, Bancroft Library, Regional Oral History Office, Berkeley, California, 1969 [Internet Archive: www.archive.org]

Carey McWilliams, *Southern California: An Island on the Land*, Gibbs Smith Publisher, Layton, Utah, 1973

Fred B. Millett, *Contemporary American Authors, A Critical Survey and 219 Bio-Bibliographies*, Harcourt, Brace, and Company, New York, 1944

The Oxford History of the American West, Edited by Clyde A. Milner II, Carol A. O'Connor, Martha A. Sandweiss, Oxford University Press, New York, New York, 1994

Ann Lee Morgan, *The Oxford Dictionary of American Art and Artists*, Oxford University Press, New York, New York, 2007

Stuart Eliot Morison, Henry Steele Commager, William E. Leuchtenburg, *A Concise History of the American Republic*, Oxford University Press, New York, New York, 1977

Roy Nickerson, *Robert Louis Stevenson in California, A Remarkable Courtship*, Chronicle Books, San Francisco, California, 1982

Frank Norris, *McTeague: A Story of San Francisco*, Introduction by Kevin Starr, Penguin Classics, Viking Penguin, Inc., New York, New York, 1982

Office of Historic Preservation, California State Parks, *California Historical Landmarks*, State of California, The Resources Agency, Sacramento, California, 1996

Richard J. Orsi, *Sunset Limited, The Southern Pacific Railroad and The Development of The American West, 1850-1930,* University of California Press, Berkeley and Los Angeles, California, 2005

Francisco Palou, George Wharton James, *Francisco Palou's Life and Apostolic Labors of the Venerable Father Junipero Serra, Founder of the Franciscan Missions of California (1913),* Pasadena, CA, 1913, Kessinger Publishing, 2009

Albert Parry, *Garrets and Pretenders, A History of Bohemianism in America,* originally published by Covici-Friede, Inc., New York, 1933, Cosimo, Inc., 2005

T. M. Pearce, Editor, *Literary America 1903-1934, The Mary Austin Letters,* Greenwood Press, Inc., Westport, Connecticut, 1979

Leonard Pitt, *The Decline of the Californios, A Social History of the Spanish-Speaking Californians, 1846-1890,* Updated with a new Foreword by Ramon A. Gutierrez, University of California Press, Berkeley and Los Angeles, California, 1998

Lawrence Clark Powell, *California Classics, The Creative Literature of the Golden State,* Capra Press, Santa Barbara, California, 1971

Laura Bride Powers, *Old Monterey, California's Adobe Capital,* San Carlos Press, San Francisco, California, 1934

Marcia Reiss, *Architectural Details,* Thunder Bay Press, San Diego, California, 2004

W. W. Robinson, *Land in California, The Story of Mission Lands, Ranchos, Squatters, Mining Claims, Railroad Grants, Land Scrip, Homesteads,* University of California Press, Berkeley and Los Angeles, Copyright 1948, 1st Paperback printing, 1979

Andrew Rolle, *California, A History, Fifth Edition,* Harlan Davidson, Inc., Wheeling, Illinois, 1998

Kent Seavey, *Images of America, Carmel A History in Architecture*, Arcadia Publishing, Charleston, South Carolina, 2007

Kent Seavey and the Heritage Society of Pacific Grove, *Images of America Pacific Grove*, Arcadia Publishing, Charleston, South Carolina, 2005

Jack London's Tales of Adventure, Illustrated, Edited by Irving Shepard, Doubleday and Co., Inc., Garden City, New York, 1956

Scott Shields, *Artists at Continent's End, The Monterey Peninsula Art Colony 1875-1907*, University of California Press, Berkeley and Los Angeles, California, 2006

Steve Shipp, *American Art Colonies, 1850-1930: A Historical Guide to America's Original Art Colonies and Their Artists*, Greenwood Press, Westport, Connecticut, 1996

Upton Sinclair, Lauren Coodley, *The Land of Orange Groves and Jails: Upton Sinclair's California*, Heydey Books, Santa Clara, California, 2004

August Derleth, Donald Wandrei, "Clark Ashton Smith: Master of Fantasy", Clark Ashton Smith, *Out of Space and Time*, Arkham House Publishers, Inc., 1971, Bison Books, Board of Regents of the University of Nebraska, Lincoln, Nebraska, 2006

Geoffrey D. Smith, *American Fiction, 1901-1925: A Bibliography*, Cambridge University Press, Cambridge, England, 1997

G. E. Kidder Smith, *Sourcebook of American Architecture, 500 Notable Buildings from the 10th Century to the Present*, Princeton Architectural Press, New York, New York, 1996

Helen Spangenberg, *Yesterday's Artists on the Monterey Peninsula*, Monterey Peninsula Museum of Art, Monterey, California, 1976

Dr. Kevin Starr, "Sunset Magazine and the Phenomenon of the Far West", *Sunset Magazine: A Century of Western Living, 1898-1998, Historical Portraits and Bibliography*, Stanford University Libraries, Stanford, California, 1998

Kevin Starr, *Americans and the California Dream, 1850-1915*, Oxford University Press, New York, New York, 1973

Kevin Starr, *California: A History*, A Modern Library Chronicles Book, New York, 2005

Kevin Starr, *Endangered Dreams, The Great Depression In California*, Oxford University Press, New York, New York, 1996

Kevin Starr, *Golden Dreams, California in an Age of Abundance, 1950-1963*, Oxford University Press, New York, New York, 2009

Kevin Starr, *Inventing the Dream California Through the Progressive Era*, Oxford University Press, New York, New York, 1985

Kevin Starr, *Material Dreams, Southern California Through the 1920's*, Oxford University Press, New York, New York, 1990

Kevin Starr, *The Dream Endures, California Enters the 1940's*, Oxford University Press, New York, New York, 1997

Lincoln Steffens, *The Shame of the Cities*, "Contents", Farrar, Straus, and Giroux, New York, 1904

George Sterling, "The Shadow Maker", *The American Mercury*, Volume VI, Number 21, Alfred A. Knopf Publisher, New York, September 1925, p. 10-19, Kessinger Publishing reprint, 2003

Esther Lanigan Stineman, *Mary Austin, Song of a Maverick*, Yale University Press, New Haven, Connecticut, 1989

Sydney Temple, *Carmel By-The-Sea, from Aborigines to Coastal Commission*, Angel Press, Monterey, California, 1987

Jeffrey T. Tilman, *Arthur Brown Jr.: Progressive Classicist (Classical America Series in Art and Architecture)*, W. W. Norton & Co., New York, New York, 2005

Ethel Duffy Turner, *Writers and Revolutionists: Oral History Transcript, 1966-1967*, Interview Conducted by Ruth Teiser, University of California Berkeley, Bancroft Library, Regional Oral History Office, Berkeley, California, 1967 [Internet Archive: www.archive.org]

John Kenneth Turner, *Challenge to Karl Marx*, Reynal and Hitchcock, New York, 1941

Dale L. Walker, *Bear Flag Rising, The Conquest of California, 1846*, A Forge Book, Tom Doherty Associates, New York, New York, 1999

Franklin D. Walker, *San Francisco's Literary Frontier*, Alfred A. Knopf, New York, 1939

Franklin D. Walker, *Seacoast of Bohemia*, Peregrine Smith, Santa Barbara, California, 1973

John Walton, *Storied Land, Community and Memory in Monterey*, University of California Press, Berkeley and Los Angeles, California, 2003

Webster's Biographical Dictionary, First Edition, G. and C. Merriam Company Publishers, Springfield, Massachusetts, 1943

Webster's New Collegiate Dictionary, G. and C. Merriam Company Publishers, Springfield, Massachusetts, 1940 Edition

Dave Weinstein, *Signature Architects of the San Francisco Bay Area*, Gibbs Smith Publisher, Layton, Utah, 2006

Ruth Westphal, *Plein Art Painters of California, The North*, Westphal Publishing, Irvine, California, second printing 1993

Stanley Wertheim, *A Stephen Crane Encyclopedia*, Greenwood Press, Westport, Connecticut, 1997

Burl Willes, *The Monterey Peninsula, A Postcard Journey*, Gibbs Smith, Salt Lake City, Utah, 2005

Peter Booth Wiley, *National Trust Guide-San Francisco: America's Guide for Architecture and History Travelers*, John Wiley & Sons, Inc., New York, New York, 2000

Towards a Simpler Way, The Arts & Crafts Architects of California, Robert Winter, Editor, University of California Press, Berkeley, California, 1997

Writers' Program of Work Projects Administration in Northern California, *The WPA Guide to the Monterey Peninsula*, University of Arizona Press, Tucson, Arizona, 1941

Sally B. Woodbridge, *California Architecture, Historic American Buildings Survey*, Chronicle Books, San Francisco, California, 1988

Charis Wilson and Wendy Madar, *Through Another Lens-My Years With Edward Weston*, North Point Press, Farrar, Straus and Giroux, New York, 1998

John Fleming Wilson, "Ghost Island Light", *Lighthouse Horrors: Tales of Adventure, Suspense, and the Supernatural*, Edited by Charles G. Waugh, Martin Harry Greenberg, and Jenny-Lynn Azarian, Down East Books, Camden, Maine, 1993

PHOTO CREDITS

California Views

Photographs and permission for use from Pat Hathaway, California Views Historical Photograph Collection, Monterey, California.

California Views Photo Archives
469 Pacific Street
Monterey, California 93940-2702
Phone (831) 373-3811
http://www.caviews.com/

Harrison Memorial Library

Photographs and permission for use from Henry Meade Williams Local History Department at the Harrison Memorial Library, Carmel, California.

Local History
Mission Street & Sixth Avenue
Carmel, CA 93921
Phone (831) 624-1615
http://www.hm-lib.org/history/

Library of Congress

-Historic American Buildings Survey/Historic American Engineering
Record/Historic American Landscapes Survey
-Arnold Genthe Collection
-George Grantham Bain Collection
-Harris & Ewing Collection

Library of Congress Prints and Photographs Division Washington, D.C.
20540 USA http://hdl.loc.gov/loc.pnp/pp.print

INDEX

Havens, Frank 137, 145, 205
Havens, Lila 185, 205
Helicon Hall 152, 153, 156, 157, 245, 246, 263
Helicon Home Colony 149, 153, 154, 155, 156, 158, 159, 160, 244
Heron, Herbert 178, 179, 180, 181, 182, 183, 200, 209, 223, 250, 256, 260, 270
Heron, Opal 180, 183
hide and tallow trade 27, 28, 33
Highlands Inn 208, 221
Hiley, Alan 137, 146, 147
Hilliard, John Northern 179, 209, 250, 256, 276, 283
Himmelsbach, Dr. William 102
Holme, Garnet 181, 182, 183, 215
Hopkins, Mark 52
Hopper, James 138, 140, 142, 143, 144, 145, 146, 147, 148, 154, 158, 165, 168, 180, 183, 194, 196, 199, 220, 221, 256, 270, 275
"Hopper's Rock" 143
Hotel Carmelo 94, 95, 102, 103, 112, 113
Hotel Del Monte 52, 57, 58, 59, 60, 61, 62, 63, 64, 79, 80, 87, 88, 91, 95, 100, 132, 133, 146, 217, 231, 232, 233, 238, 282
Hotel Del Monte Art Gallery 132, 133
Hunter, Abbie Jane 93, 94, 95
Huntington, Collis Potter 52, 78
Huntington & Hopkins Hardware Store 52, 78

I

Ide, William B. 38
Irwin, Will 149, 193, 241, 249, 275

J

Jacks, David 43, 46, 47, 48, 49, 50, 51, 56, 57, 63, 74, 87, 230
Jackson, Helen Hunt 89, 90, 235, 275
James, George Wharton 89, 228, 229, 233, 238, 240, 241, 243, 251, 253, 254, 270, 275, 289
Jeffers, Robinson 206
Jesuit 5, 6
John Begg and Company 27, 28
Johns, Cloudsley 178
Jones, Thomas ap Catesby 35
Jordan, David Starr 101, 237, 264, 275
Jorgensen, Chris 89, 128, 129, 131, 132, 139, 188, 209, 240, 254, 270
Josselyn, Lewis 109, 189
Judah, Theodore 52
Judson, Charles Chapel 127, 132, 215, 240, 255, 265
Juniper Street 93, 112, 140, 221

K

Keith, William 89, 124, 125, 126, 132, 135, 239, 240, 263, 271, 273
Kellogg, Charlotte 180, 183
Kellogg, John Harvey 158
Kellogg, Vernon 180, 183, 254
King Charles III 6, 7

L

Lafler, Henry 137, 138, 144, 146, 147, 159
Laguna del Rey 58
Land Act of 1851 43
Land Commission 43
land grant 25, 28, 32, 36, 43, 46, 53, 54
lantern 106
La Pérouse, Jean François Galaup Comte de 18
La Playa Hotel 128, 188, 209, 221